THE SILENT REVOLUTION: MEDIA, DEMOCRACY, AND THE FREE TRADE DEBATE

THE SILENT REVOLUTION: MEDIA, DEMOCRACY, AND THE FREE TRADE DEBATE

Edited by James P. Winter

ACTEXPRESS

A publishing service offered by

University of Ottawa Press
Ottawa • London • Paris

Canadian Cataloguing in Publication Data

Main entry under title:
The Silent revolution:
media, democracy, and the free trade debate

ISBN 0-7766-0296-9

1. Mass media--Canada--Political aspects.
2. Canada. Parliament--Elections, 1988.
3. Free trade--Canada.
4. Mass media and business--Political aspects.
I. Winter, James P. (James Patrick), 1952-

P92.C3S44 1990 324.7'33'0971 C90-090241-8

These proceedings are published
as received from the authors;
the normal editorial intervention
has been omitted in the interest
of rapid dissemination.

Production and design:
Jean-Paul Morisset

Cover design:
Communication graphique Gagnon-Bélanger

Cover illustration:
Courtesy of Terry "Aislin" Mosher
The Montreal Gazette, and
The Council of Canadians

Printed and bound in Canada
Second printing, 1990

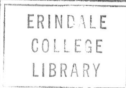

CONTENTS

To Joseph S. Tully, who nurtured a young man's interest in politics, and cultivated a sense of national pride.

CONTRIBUTORS

Ron Adams is host of the CBC radio programme Media File, in Toronto.

Doug Baer is professor of sociology at the University of Western Ontario, in London.

Brian Bannon is a business reporter for *The Windsor Star*.

Maude Barlow is chairperson of the Council of Canadians, in Ottawa.

David Crane is business editor for *The Toronto Star*.

Satya Das is an editorial columnist with *The Edmonton Journal*.

Peter Desbarats is dean of the graduate school of journalism, at the University of Western Ontario, London.

Hattie Dyck is Truro bureau chief for *The Halifax Chronicle-Herald and Mail Star,* Truro, Nova Scotia.

Fred Fletcher is professor of political science, York University, Toronto.

Alan Frizzell is professor of journalism, Carleton University, Ottawa.

Martin Goldfarb is a pollster with Goldfarb Consultants, Toronto.

Patrick Gossage is a communication consultant for the Liberal Party, and former press secretary to Pierre Trudeau.

Herb Gray is a Windsor MP and acting opposition leader in the House of Commons.

John Harvard is a Liberal MP and communication critic, and former CBC journalist.

Lesley Hughes is the host for CBC's Information Radio, Winnipeg.

Steven Langdon is a Windsor MP and was a 1989 NDP leadership candidate.

Jennifer Lewington is Washington correspondent for *The Globe and Mail.*

Terry "Aislin" Mosher is editorial cartoonist for the Montreal *Gazette.*

Howard McCurdy is a Windsor MP and was a 1989 NDP leadership candidate.

Peggy Nash is with the CAW in Toronto.

Frances Russell is a political columnist for *The Free Press,* in Winnipeg.

Rick Salutin is a Toronto author, playwright, and is on the editorial board of *This Magazine.*

Robin Sears is Principal Secretary to Ontario NDP leader Bob Rae.

Lorne Slotnick is a former labour reporter for *The Globe and Mail,* now with the Southern Ontario Newspaper Guild.

Doug Smith is a Winnipeg-based editor of *This Magazine*.

Susan Spratt is on the editorial collective of *Canadian Dimension*, and is active in the Winnipeg labour movement.

Geoffrey Stevens writes for *The Toronto Star*, and was formerly managing editor of *The Globe and Mail*.

Ian Waddell is an NDP MP and communication critic, and 1989 leadership candidate.

Anthony Westell is director of the school of journalism at Carleton University in Ottawa, and a columnist with *The Toronto Star*.

James Winter is professor of communication studies at the University of Windsor.

INTRODUCTION

"The testimony of the orators could probably be used to show that by the middle of the fourth century (B.C.) the silent revolution had been accomplished, and the cultivated Greek public had become a community of readers."[1]

This book is the result of an unusual gathering held at the University of Windsor in the summer of 1989. For two days, more than 30 politicians, journalists, and academics debated the role played by the media in the 1988 Federal, "free trade" election. These panelists were heard and challenged by audience/participants ranging from members of the Windsor media and academic community, to interested observers from other cities and provinces.

Highlights of the conference included a thoughtful and provocative keynote address by journalism dean and long-time journalist, Peter Desbarats, contained in Chapter One. Professor Desbarats argues that increasing concentration and monopolization of the newspaper industry has led to homogeneous content. He says commercial influences, marketing experts and the era of professional business managers have

---

[1] E.A. Havelock, *Preface To Plato,* Grosset & Dunlap, N.Y., 1963, p.41.

has led to homogeneous content. He says commercial influences, marketing experts and the era of professional business managers have led to a "Eunuch-like, make-no-waves, make-no-enemies style of journalism," which is a shirking of journalistic responsibility. Although he opposes some aspects of its coverage, Desbarats argues for a return to *The Toronto Star's* style of "crusading journalism."

In Chapter Two, journalist Brian Bannon and journalist-turned academic Anthony Westell come to the media's defense. Bannon says, "I've yet to see any evidence linking corporate concentration and ownership of the media, to bias in reporting." Westell argues that content analyses conducted since the election indicate that the media were balanced, rather than supporting free trade. Hence, he says, there is no evidence that the corporate elite which owns the media use them to advance their own values. Others take issue with this.

Journalist and playwright Rick Salutin tells us in Chapter Three that the Conservative Government had an explicitly anti-democratic communication strategy for the Free Trade Agreement (FTA). Its goal was to "rely less on educating the general public than on getting across the message that the trade initiative is a good idea, in other words, a selling job," with which the media cooperated.

We learn in Chapter Four of a threatened strike, if the FTA was defeated. Journalist Doug Smith's insightful view is that business leaders effectively threatened to strike by withholding capital and investments, if the Conservatives lost. No media mention was made of this: yet, if Bob White, the CAW and the labour movement had taken similar strike-threat actions *against* the FTA, they would have been roundly denounced in the media.

Chapter Five is chock-full of condemnations of the media's cozy relationship with the "corporate-Conservative alliance." One commentator is NDP communication critic and leadership candidate, Ian Waddell; but the other three are working journalists. Perhaps most eloquent amongst this articulate group is Winnipeg *Free Press* columnist Frances Russell, who says: "...we journalists are defiling our principles and debasing our calling."

Globe and Mail Washington correspondent Jennifer Lewington explains American attitudes toward the FTA, and Canadians, in Chapter Six. She says there was so little coverage of the FTA in the U.S. because Americans increasingly see their world in terms of external militaristic or economic threats to "national security." In these terms, Canadians are no threat at all: just "warm, fuzzy folks to the North."

In Chapter Seven, pollster Martin Goldfarb dons his anthropologist's hat, to argue that the media are the last bastion of Canadian identity, and he fears losing that identity through media concentration and cost efficiencies. He says the media trusts should be broken up. Pollsters, according to Mr. Goldfarb, interpret the issues for journalists and the public, occupying the crucial middle ground between politicians, media and public.

In Chapter Eight, I draw on the academic literature to argue that the media are big business, and hence supported the pro- free trade side in the election. This chapter was a background paper for the conference, eliciting considerable comments, both favourable and unfavourable, from participants. To answer some of the criticism, I've added an analysis of *Globe and Mail* coverage of the election.

The last chapter contains my own conclusions to the debate on these pages. I argue that newspapers pander to their advertisers rather than the public which they ostensively serve; that Canadian society and history are rife with monopolies and yet our language, media and culture are void of such terms; that public enterprise is an anathema to Conservatives, for it restricts the access and profits of their corporate cronies; and that the media are the accommodating delivery system for the corporate-Conservative agenda, including but by no means limited to, the FTA.

I have attempted to be prescriptive, by providing suggested alternatives to the current "neo-conservative" course, to use CBC journalist Lesley Hughes' term. These suggestions are wide-ranging rather than mere bandaid measures, for the problems with which we are coming to grips are endemic to our socio-political-economic system. Addressing them will mean shaking up and improving upon that system. While their pervasiveness is at first daunting, there are important signs of change and hope. The most important of these is, of course, people like those on these pages, who continue to struggle to be aware and unmanipulated, despite the best efforts of a powerful elite and their delivery system. In addition there are the so-called popular movements or coalitions such as the Council of Canadians and the Pro-Canada Network. Despite unprecedented spending by the other side, efforts by these groups *almost* prevailed. As Rick Salutin notes, this represents at least a partial victory for democracy.

There is also reason for hope in the progress we've made in the past 25 years or so. When we focus on the so-called conservative social movement, and see Thatcherism and Reaganism and Mulroneyism all around, we tend to ignore the anti-free trade coalition which in the last election consisted of everyone but business. We ignore the victory inherent in the 54% who voted for one or the other of the Parties opposed to the FTA. And as Noam Chomsky pointed out in *Necessary Illusions*, his 1989 CBC Massey Lectures, we forget that when president John Kennedy sent the U.S. Air Force to attack rural Vietnam, no one objected. Yet, twenty years later, "...the Reagan administration was driven underground..." in Contragate, forced to resort to clandestine terror in Central America.

Just as Americans learned a lesson in Vietnam, Canadians learned from the free trade election. That's why, as I write this, a Gallup Poll indicates that 70% of adult Canadians feel free trade will not benefit them personally; about half of those polled say the FTA is making us too much like Americans; an almost equal number say the FTA puts our cultural sovereignty at risk. Only 23% said the FTA will increase employment, compared to 38% at the time of the election.

So there is cause for optimism, although to return to the above example of American support for the Contras, one would not want to ignore recent events in Panama, or the Grenadian invasion of a couple of years ago!

I've briefly suggested in the concluding chapter that we: democratize our political system with proportional representation in parliament, and that we set about democratizing the media. We also must return to our public ownership traditions, before privatization and "natural" concentration mean K.C. Irving, the Reichmann brothers, and Ken Thomson own the whole country. In so-doing, I've attempted to answer those who maintain that Canada must adapt to the so-called "world economy," a euphemism for further rationalization and concentration, in the interest of big business.

To help bring about these developments, we will require a programme of public education, in which I hope these pages can play some small part.

Many people contributed to this book, but as the editor I must claim responsibility for any errors or omissions, which are unintentional. I am particularly indebted to Catherine Morrison, Executive Director of the Council of Canadians, for her heroic efforts co-ordinating the conference. Maude Barlow deserves thanks from all of us for her tireless, cheerful and creative efforts on our behalf. You're on everybody's top ten list, Maude, not just Peter Gzowski's! Thanks too of course to that persistent and unparalleled patriot, Mel Hurtig.

Ann Gallant, Sheila La Belle and Lina Beaudry provided their usual cheerful secretarial support. Janet Morris transcribed the conference proceedings. Daniel Belair, Dwayne Winseck and Ed Corrigan were a great help at the conference. Thanks to Marion Brown for providing her audio tapes. Rick Loebach and Sean Moriarty gave generously of their computing expertise. I would like to thank Toivo Roht, Director of the University of Ottawa Press, and his staff, especially Jean-Paul Morisset. Thanks to all those who attended the conference, and especially those contributing to these pages. The University of Windsor, the Council of Canadians, Torstar Corporation and Joseph Caba provided funding for the conference, and for this book. Special thanks are owed to Zbigniew Fallenbuchl, Dean of Social Sciences at the University of Windsor.

Thanks to my family, friends and colleagues for your ongoing support, advice and encouragement. Finally, and most importantly, thank you Paula for your constant love, help, and tolerance.

James Winter,
Wheatley, Ontario
November, 1989

CHAPTER ONE

JOURNALISTIC CRUSADES

Introduction:

Peter Desbarats, Dean of the Graduate School of Journalism at the University of Western Ontario, sets the stage in this first chapter for the discussions which follow. Dean Desbarats has had a lengthy career in the media, both broadcasting and print, and has published several books. Prior to his address, we have introductory comments by Maude Barlow, Chairperson of the Council of Canadians, and former advisor on Women's Issues to Prime Minister Pierre Trudeau. In her truly inimitable style, Ms. Barlow identifies the crux of the matter. Following Dean Desbarat's remarks, we have a response by Professor James Winter, and David Crane, economic columnist with *The Toronto Star*. This is followed by comments from local Windsor MPs Steven Langdon, Herb Gray, and Howard McCurdy.

sector, and the harmonization of our social and economic system. She says we are witnessing the privatization of essential public services, in the "Thatcherization" of Canada. There's been a net job loss of 57,000 since January 1989. Food prices are increasing. We've lost control of our resources. She says if the other side had been proven as right as the anti-free trade forces have, to date, there would have been media coverage and editorials and the Council of Canadians members would have had their noses rubbed in it. To the media, she addresses the question: "who was right?"

Peter Desbarats calls the fall 1988 federal election the "most remarkable in our recent history." He tackles the thorny issue of *The Toronto Star's* coverage of free trade and the case against *The Star* brought before the Ontario Press Council, also a topic addressed by David Crane of *The Star*. Desbarats argues that increasing concentration and monopolization of the newspaper industry has led to homogeneous content. Commercial influences, marketing experts and the era of professional business managers have led to a "Eunuch-like, make-no-waves, make-no-enemies style of journalism," which is a shirking of journalistic responsibility. Although he opposes some aspects of its coverage, Desbarats argues for a return to *The Toronto Star's* style of "crusading journalism."

David Crane says the explanation of the Toronto *Star*'s case before the Ontario Press Council, is very simple. *The Star* was brought before the Council by an irate reader, over its free trade coverage. He says *The Star* is a crusading newspaper, with a clear and identifiable point of view on issues. Mr. Crane has facts and figures with which to defend the paper's coverage. But the reader who complained to the Press Council about *Star* coverage discussed his strategy with the Conservative Party. They tried to have the complaint heard in the middle of the election campaign, to discredit the paper and to influence the campaign.

Steve Langdon says the so-called "crisis of the left," identified by Dean Desbarats, doesn't exist in our society. Social democratic approaches are receiving more support now than ever before, he says. In our new society, the anachronisms and dinosaurs may turn out to be the huge media conglomerates which are threatened by diverse sources. In the next election, people are not going to be voting on abstractions or probabilities, but on the facts, such as the thousands of jobs which have been lost thanks to the FTA. Faced with these realities, voters will reject both the Conservatives and the FTA in 1992.

Herb Gray points out that while there are some very distinguished journalists at this conference, there aren't any publishers. That may make our efforts here interesting but not totally realistic. The increasingly heavy hand of publishers is evident in what happened to the *Montreal Gazette* in the closing days of the election, with the publisher's front-page editorial favouring the FTA. We also have to look at what's happening at the *Globe and Mail*, with the firing of people such as Geoffrey Stevens, who is here at this conference. Gray says we can only hope that *The Toronto Star* will continue to increase its circulation beyond the confines of Metropolitan Toronto, and that it will offer an alternative voice.

Howard McCurdy asks what it is that compels us in the direction of dependency, as a nation? For too long he says, this country has been dependent on its resources, because it was so easy to enrich ourselves and to ensure our short-term security. Now we have to come to grips with the fact that our competitors are totally committed to creativity and innovation and the use of technology to build rather than to exploit. But none of that was said in the election. We talked about the attack on our social programs, *et cetera*, but we didn't say anything about how one really builds an economy which can compete in the worlds of both economic and social justice. And in this, the debate failed us all.

Maude Barlow:

It's my firm belief, and I speak on behalf of the Council of Canadians, that our country's going through nothing short of a revolution. I happen to think it's not very good for our country; I know there are other people who see it as good and necessary, and perhaps some people in this room feel that. I think that's part of what the dialogue can be about this weekend.

We're seeing the growing influence of the corporate sector and corporate values in this country, and we're seeing those values very deeply influence the goals and the decision making of our legislators. We're watching the harmonization of our social and economic systems into a system which is foreign to ours. We're watching and witnessing the privatization of essential public services. Services in fact, have been one of the ways we've kept this country together; kept a national perspective, East, West and North, and resisted the financial temptation to see our direction going North and South. Essentially I think we are witnessing the "Thatcherization" of Canada. Or to quote Molson's Mickey Cohen, "This is not pleasant stuff. You've got to say to Northern Canada, You're on your own, to Atlantic Canada, we're sorry; you're on your own."

This weekend serves as an opportunity for us to explore the role of the media in this revolution, from the beginning of the Free Trade debate, and right through the election. More importantly we'll explore our future together, because as far as the Council is concerned, this issue is an on-going one. We don't believe it was finally and forever decided in the last election; it is something we're working towards getting information on, we're gathering information and planning to put a case to the Canadian people in the next election. How we do that, and how we interact with the media, is a subject for us at this conference.

Questions which are important, essential, to those of us concerned with Canadian sovereignty, are as follows.

When public opinion shifted in this country from 70% in favour of free trade to the last major poll taken before the election which told us that only 39% were for this agreement and 51% were against, how is it that only two daily newspapers out of 110 in this country had an editorial position reflecting the concerns of the majority of Canadians? I think it's important for us to ask the question: Is it possible that corporate concentration in the media pre-determines their general position on free trade and related issues? Does the corporate concentration in the media mean the people who make the final decisions reflect a pro-business bias?

How can organizations like the Council of Canadians (COC) and other members of the Pro-Canada network, participate equally in the formation of public opinion on this issue and others, when we do not have and are never likely to have the kind of access to resources that the Business Council on National Issues (BCNI) had? Indeed, you may be aware that the COC is now waging quite a strong war against the government's apparent decision to allow those companies which gave an enormous amount of money to the pro-free trade side to write off millions of dollars of tax deductions for business purposes. This is the strategy they're taking and it's being accepted. They're saying they needed free trade for business so the fact that they put many untold millions into this lobby was a justified business expense. However, people in companies who gave to the Council of Canadians apparently are not going to be allowed to write off their contribution because they were trying to change public opinion and so they were being political.

In fact, it appears that some companies have been writing off their political lobbying for several years. And a real, pressing question for us in terms of asking questions about the media is this: has no one been asking about the blatant use of tax deductions for pro-business lobbyists who have been lobbying the government? Why have there not been more questions?

Finally, I would like to be permitted to be a little cynical. This was an election unlike any other I've ever seen. It was very much an "either / or" kind of thing. Either free trade was wonderful and was what we needed to salvage the country, or it was going to be the end. It strikes me that there must be an awful lot of Canadians who are curious about who's winning this; who was right. I don't see nearly enough information or analysis in the mainstream media asking that question. They've got to put out the statements made by the two sides, and to analyze after the fact who was right.

Well, let me remind you that according to the Conference Board of Canada, there was a net job loss of 57,000 from January to June, 1989. In fact, the Canadian Labour Congress estimates that at least half of those jobs can be related to free trade. Food prices are going up and free trade isn't going to be able to stop that. It might even be part of the cause.

Energy prices are going up; in fact Canada just placed a sales tax on energy. But of course that's not going to apply to exported energy. So we're going to be in the wonderful position of having American consumers of our energy paying less money than we do. We have lost control of our energy in that the National Energy Board no longer has the right or the authority to stop any export application by any North American company. And the government broke its promise not to destroy our social infrastructure. Whether you believe it should do this or not, one would have to agree that before the election they promised, "We will not touch social programs. Give us free trade, and it will help us to enhance our social programs." And of course, using the deficit as a smoke screen, they've done the opposite. My cynical statement is that if the other side had been proven as right as we are being proven, I think there would have been more about it in the media. I think we would have seen a lot of editorials, we might have had our noses rubbed in it. I direct this as a challenge to the media in this country. I think it's a fair question to ask: "Who was right?"

I also want to remind you that the government never talks about free trade benefits. The Alliance for Trade and Job Opportunities which was going to match us report card for report card: we're working on our fourth and they have not put one out yet. They don't mention free trade either. They got what they wanted and it is in their self interest to drop it now. Well, it's not in the interest of all Canadians. Again, whatever side we were on before the election, it was something that rocked our country and I think it's incumbent upon us all to watch its progress, monitor it and tell that story and that's what this is about this weekend.

Peter Desbarats:

I'm going to talk about the media's role in the election. Most of what I have to say will deal with the media but I'm going to start out by talking a bit about the election in an effort to set the stage for the discussions that will be held tomorrow. And some of this of course is familiar to many of you, more familiar to many of you than it is to me, but I thought it wouldn't hurt to review what we saw in 1988.

The Federal election of 1988 was the most remarkable of our recent history. I think journalists are always saying that elections are *not* "most remarkable" but I think this one really was. Support for the two major parties, according to the polls, showed fluctuations during the campaign that were unusually rapid and extreme. The election terminated the political careers of two national party leaders. Of more significance in the long term, the election was dominated by a single issue, and that alone made it unusual in an age of personality politics.

The debate about free trade, intellectually complex and emotionally powerful as it was, was nothing less than a debate about the meaning of our history, the challenge of our times to traditional concepts of nationality in this part of North America, and the shape of our future. In this debate the news media played a major, controversial role. This conference is going to discuss this role and its implications for the future of media objectivity, political journalism, and the role of news media generally in our democracy. In these introductory remarks, my focus also will be on the media rather than on the questions of national identity and survival, raised by the election results.

In retrospect the 1988 election illuminates and may help us to better understand a number of critical developments in contemporary news media, in particular the awesome power of television, the decline of objectivity as a useful journalistic concept, the growing influence of marketing on the practice of journalism, and the changing role of newspapers as transmitters and interpreters of political information.

I don't want to spend much time on the first and most obvious of these: the power of television. John Turner's success in the nationally televised debate and his subsequent leap upward in the polls was simply the most recent illustration of this well established and often-cited phenomenon. Turner's tantalizing glimpse of victory had nothing to do with the effectiveness of his arguments against free trade. It was the image of John Turner that moved us emotionally. Like a figure of Greek tragedy, battered, bleeding and inevitably doomed, Turner showed a desperate personal courage on television that compelled admiration. The Prime Minister, no more glib than usual, was simply blasted off the screen and almost out of the race by Turner's genuinely heroic performance, amplified by the polls, and the subsequent re-evaluation of Turner's chances by the news media.

As usual, the selection of photographs of party leaders used by newspapers most quickly and graphically reveals their changing preferences. Turner's performance on T.V. transformed the campaign overnight from a one-sided route into a genuine contest, at least for a few weeks. Unfortunately for the Liberal leader, it also revealed, by the time Canadians voted, how quickly the television image fades. Turner's personal fight for survival, at least on television, affected many Canadians who were unmoved emotionally and intellectually by his claim to be waging a battle for the survival of Canada. Part of the problem in this respect lay in Turner himself, in his lingering reputation as a big business lawyer of conservative economic and political views. And in his inability to make the nationalist position in the campaign intellectually coherent. But even if Turner had been able to reproduce the kind of conviction and intellectual originality that Pierre Trudeau and Rene Levesque had, it would have made little difference. Ed Broadbent with a more consistent political record, greater personal credibility, and a more thoughtful cast of mind, found it just as impossible to mount an effective nationalist challenge to the Conservative's continental vision.

This revealed the bankrupt state of what I might call the traditional nationalist position in Canada: the Walter Gordon school of economic and cultural nationalism, that had attracted myself and many others in the 1960's. In that decade, so strongly did I feel about this issue that I enroled in the Committee for an Independent Canada, the first and only political lobby that I allowed myself to join as a working journalist. With this background, it was not surprising that my instinctive reaction to Prime Minister Mulroney's initial proposal for free trade was negative. Despite this, I found myself during the campaign (and I'm sure my own reaction was typical of a fairly large number of Canadians) becoming more and more critical of the Liberal and NDP opposition to the trade agreement. It wasn't only Turner's strategic conversion to nationalism that I had trouble accepting. A bigger problem was the inability of both opposition parties to escape from the old formulas of Walter Gordon, and to evolve alternative visions of Canada that responded to current economic, social and political circumstances.

There were many aspects of Mulroney's conservativism that alarmed me but at least it was identifiable, and at least it was a product of the times. Of course it was derived from Thatcherism and Reaganism but it fit Mulroney more comfortably than nationalism suited Turner, and it did represent a specific response to a new set of international conditions. It certainly was not just a continuation, obviously, of Diefenbaker's nationalism and of Diefenbaker's, at times, anti-American brand of conservativism. Turner's 1988 campaign speeches on the other hand sounded as if they had been taken from the files of the old Committee for an Independent Canada.

Both Turner and Broadbent also suffered from what has been called the identity crisis of the left: the inability of the left in Western countries to move beyond an analysis of capitalism rooted in the 19th century and to respond positively to the renewed energy of conservativism in the 1980's. The same conditions have contributed to confusion among Quebec nationalists whose vision of an independent Quebec, originally formulated back in the 1950's, required a major economic role for the state. The apparent triumph of what is usually called "economic nationalism" in Quebec after the defeat of the referendum, has left Quebec separatists drifting as aimlessly toward the future as are their nationalist compatriots in English-speaking Canada, after the 1988 election. Although this historic coincidence may contain the seeds of some future collaboration, there are no signs at all of significant new directions these days among Canada's aging leftists and nationalists. And none may emerge for some time unless a sharp change in economic or political conditions, a global recession for instance, triggered or complicated by environmental conditions, causes a rejection of today's orthodoxy and a search for radical solutions again.

The problems of the left today are not as they might at first appear to be, simply a digression from my main media theme. They are closely related to the difficulties modern media are encountering in their efforts to report and interpret current political events such as the free trade debate. It is not simply coincidence that these difficulties were exemplified in 1988 in *The Toronto Star*.

The Star is an unusual newspaper in a number of respects. With an average daily circulation of 562,232 in 1988, it is by far, the largest of our newspapers, more than two hundred thousand copies larger than its closest rivals, *Le Journal de Montreal*, *The Globe and Mail* and *The Toronto Sun*. It is the only one of our major big city daily newspapers to remain independent of chain ownership, although that independence was modified in 1985 by the exchange of shares with the Southam Group that gave each partner in the deal a minority share of the other. *The Star* also has retained to an unusual degree something of the ideology that once enabled its Tory opponents to label it "The Red Star of Toronto" and the "The King Street Pravda". In the early 1970's, as someone who identified himself as, quote "progressive" in the style of the 1960's, and as an economic nationalist, I slipped easily into the role of *The Star's* national affairs columnist in Ottawa. In fact, I was somewhat taken aback during my initial interview with publisher Beland Honderich, to realize that the premise of our discussion was that *The Star* was a radical, even a revolutionary newspaper and that Honderich appeared to be asking whether I was sufficiently committed to revolutionary economics and social reform.

This vision of *The Star* as a crusading, independent newspaper was transmitted to Honderich through an unbroken chain of ownership from the 1920's, when Joseph Atkinson moved the newspaper to the left of its traditionally Liberal position. Atkinson's support of labour unions, and welfare legislation at that time, brought *The Star* in conflict with its third largest shareholder, Sir John Eaton, who protested against what he called *The Star's* Bolshevistic trend. "I don't tell you how to run your store", Atkinson is quoted as saying to Sir John. In reply Eaton's withdrew its department store advertising from *The Star* for a full year. Until Sir John Eaton's death ended the dispute, *The Star* was without its largest advertiser. When Eaton's returned, it was on *The Star's* terms.

Atkinson is described by his biographer Ross Harkness as a publisher who ran a newspaper with a mission and who regarded advertising as a "necessary evil." Atkinson was a man of pronounced views on many social and political questions and he assumed that his newspaper would promulgate them. In this, he was like William Randolf Hearst, Joseph Pulitzer, E. W. Scripps and other North American press barons of that time. *The Star* resembled the crusading newspapers of Hearst, Pulitzer and Scripps, with their frequent front page campaigns and arbitrary news coverage.

In the 1980's *The Star* has retained enough of its character to become an anachronism on the Canadian newspaper scene. In North America today, large daily newspapers are usually owned by conglomerates with holdings in newspaper groups, magazines, radio and television and quite often, non-media enterprises. Thomas Griffith, who retired last year after forty years as an editor and media columnist at *Life* and *Time*, recently commented on the passing of the press lords, the old press lords whom he said gave strength and vitality to the age of personal journalism, and their replacement by media barons whose interests as he said are primarily managerial and financial, and, as he said, "who care less about the craft of journalism than they do about their investments."

In an age of multimedia giants and interlocking ownerships which meld media with other types of businesses, *The Star* is an oddity devoted primarily to publishing and still capable of arousing passions in its journalists and readers. So it was predictable that the free trade debate and the election campaign of 1988 would act like a whiff of gun powder in the nostrils of the old war horse. Free trade, sponsored by a Conservative government supported by its old rival, *The Globe and Mail*, touched all *The Star*'s sensitive nerve endings. Free trade was continentalist. It was the product of, and an incentive to, a decline in public ownership and a resurgence of capitalist enterprise in both Canada and the U.S., and it appeared to threaten the social welfare philosophy *The Star* has consistently upheld.

Although *The Star* was acting true to form in its campaign against free trade, the public reaction to this indicated how singular this type of media behaviour had become. A few decades ago, readers might have violently disagreed with what *The Star* was saying. In 1988 some of them challenged *The Star*'s right to say it. *The Star* acknowledged the gravity of this reaction by devoting a full page after the election to an analysis and rationale of its coverage, under the byline of its editor John Honderich. "Without doubt" he wrote, "the free trade debate has been one of the most intense and the manner in which it was conducted, one of the most controversial in this nation's history". As controversial sometimes (he admitted), had been *The Star*'s role in that debate. Critics such as trade deal negotiator Simon Reisman and economist John Crispo have accused *The Star* of being a rag and a non-stop propaganda agency. Others, including some readers, said the paper's coverage was one-sided. Honderich's response to this raised more questions than it answered; at least I thought so. At the outset he based his discussion on a definition of a good newspaper taken from American playwright Arthur Miller; a definition that was really too vague to be useful. "A good newspaper, I suppose," Miller had written, "is a nation talking to itself". No one could dispute Miller's observation or facility of phrase, but as a starting point for a discussion of a newspaper's role in 1988, it didn't lead anywhere. Honderich then presented his own criteria:

> A responsible newspaper must be accurate and fair. It must present all sides of the debate. But *The Star* went one step further. Having identified free trade to be a matter of such concern on its editorial pages, the paper's editors made a conscious effort to highlight and give prominence to all stories and all interpretations of the agreement; this was deliberate. We didn't hide our editorial point of view, nor did we hide our concern.

Now in the context of that article, Honderich's statement about not hiding *The Star*'s editorial point of view, was ambiguous. It could have referred, given its placement in the article, to the paper's whole editorial content. In fact, I did take it to refer to the paper's whole editorial content, not just the editorial pages.

"How one can be fair in news coverage while openly employing an editorial point of view?" was the question Honderich chose not to confront. The editor's commentary was accompanied by *The Star*'s own analysis of its published commentary on free trade during the campaign. Its letters to the editor ran three to one against free trade, because the ratio of letters received, according to *The Star*, rose to as high as 9 to 1 against. Articles in its special free trade forum section on its opinion page ran 28 to 21 against the government's proposal. But this was balanced, according to *The Star*, by an eleven to two ratio in favour of the agreement, in the Monday forum of its Business Today section. Its decision to publish a front page editorial before the election was, as Honderich said, "part of the newspapering tradition," although by *The Star*'s own account, only five of Canada's one hundred and eleven daily newspapers did so in the 1988 campaign.

One of *The Star*'s critical readers felt so strongly about what he termed "a steady barrage of negative, one-sided information in the newspaper", that he brought the issue before the Ontario Press Council. His own content analysis from October 1987 to April 1988 showed that news stories in *The Star* ran 236 to 93 against free trade, during that time. *The Star* disputed the accuracy of his statistics and rejected the charge that it was deliberately and systematically biased. However, it also declared that "it prides itself on being a crusading newspaper," and "its purpose was to provoke discussion so that in the end truth would emerge". I should note a few contradictions in *The Star*'s performance before the Press Council, which may or may not have been related to the essence of its case. The reader supplied the Council and *The Star* with details of his complaint, including a fairly elaborate content analysis, eight months before the Ontario Press Council hearing. Although the Council's usual procedure is to have written summaries of evidence and argument available to both parties before a hearing, and it officially suggests both parties follow this procedure, *The Star* provided a detailed written response only at the actual hearing.

The Council stated in its adjudication that it "regretted this". *The Star* also vetoed an open hearing which the reader requested, since, as it said, no third party was involved. Somewhat strange conduct for a newspaper that had been one of the initial members of the Press Council, and one of its earliest supporters. Strange conduct for editors who profess to believe in the virtues of full disclosure and open discussion.

However, the central question in all this is not whether *The Star* was biased in its coverage and commentary on free trade -- most of us probably would acknowledge that it was to some degree -- but whether it should have been. The most important contention was that *The Star* had an obligation; or to use the words of the reader's submission to the Press Council, "a public trust that required impartiality". These are not only his words, they are taken directly from the Statement of Principles for Canadian daily newspapers, adopted in 1977 by the Canadian Daily Newspaper Publishers Association (CDNPA). The statement says, "The operation of a newspaper is, in effect, a public trust." The statement goes on to say, "The newspaper keeps faith with its readers by presenting the news comprehensively, accurately and fairly, and by acknowledging mistakes promptly." In all fairness, it should also be mentioned that this statement of principles the CDNPA adopted has its own, what you might call, "notwithstanding clause", recognizing the right of all newspapers to have their own codes of ethics and "to maintain standards of conduct in conformity with their own goals."

The Ontario Press Council adjudication did not indicate how *The Star* dealt with the apparent conflict between the balanced presentation of the CDNPA statement, evidence of at least some imbalance in its own presentation of the free trade debate, and its own statement that "we didn't hide our editorial point of view". In *The Star*'s case, these questions were less urgent than they might have been, not only because it is something of an anachronism, as I've already said, but because the entire Toronto newspaper scene is an anomaly in North America. At a time when daily newspapers were disappearing in Canada and the U.S. and the chain-owned monopoly newspaper was becoming the norm, Toronto increased its number of newspapers from two, for a few days between the death of the Telegram and the launch of The Toronto *Sun*, or a few hours perhaps, to four.

In 1988, Toronto newspaper readers could choose among a range of opinions on the free trade issue. In fact because the three other newspapers supported the Free Trade Agreement and the Mulroney government in varying degrees, there was truth in *The Star*'s claim that it contributed an alternative point of view to a newspaper debate that might have been imbalanced without it.

The survival of *The Star* as an independent newspaper may not extend much further into the future than the current standstill agreement with Southam, which expires in June 1990. Southam is desperately preparing its defenses now against take-over, by paring costs in an effort to increase profitability. But many analysts doubt the success of this tactic. A possible scenario is that *The Star* will buy Southam. In any event, there is every likelihood that the process of newspaper consolidation will continue in Canada, as it has in the U.S.

Because our newspaper industry is patterned after the American one, and strongly influenced by it, we can sometimes foresee trends in Canada by looking at what is happening to the south. One of the most recent studies has reversed the findings of the early 1980's: that chain ownership in the U.S. had reached a plateau at that time. It now appears that the 1980's has been a decade of further consolidation in the U.S., with competitive newspapers continuing to disappear and more recently, national chains buying out smaller chains. Less than 2% of U.S. cities now have competitive dailies.

Between 1961 and 1986 the number of chain-owned newspapers in the U.S. increased from 560 to over 1,100, and the average number of dailies owned by each chain increased from 5.1 to 9.1. This might indicate that the process of consolidation in our own newspaper industry will continue, although already the Canadian industry is more highly concentrated than in the U.S., and most other developed countries. Competition itself, of course, is no guarantee of excellence or diversity in journalism these days. John Bustema, an assistant professor of journalism at the University of Minnesota, explained the disappearance of head-to-head daily newspaper competition as a result of, rather than the cause of, lessening competition. There is little product differentiation among daily newspapers in the U.S., he stated. The content of typical competing dailies is very similar, giving readers no reason to purchase more than one. This similarity is a product of the decline of the partisan press, the establishment of objectivity in presenting news, and balance in selecting editorial page features.

The lack of differing content typically creates homogeneous audiences for advertisers. As a result, advertisers flock disproportionately to the larger circulation dailies. We've seen that happen over and over again in the past few decades in Canada.

Journalism historians have traced the development of objectivity as a journalistic goal, at least in large part, to the growth of the mass circulation daily. As fewer newspapers embraced larger and larger circulations, news had to be written in a neutral or objective way to avoid offending segments of this large audience. In recent decades, this philosophy has been formalized by experts in the marketing of newspapers.

There's nothing new about the marketing of journalism and the conflict between commercial and journalistic values. They've been part of the industry, almost from the very beginning. They were there when I first entered a newsroom in the 1950's, and they're still there. In recent decades while this characteristic, this conflict, has remained constant, the balance of forces has altered significantly. On the commercial side, a more organized approach to marketing has rapidly developed, without a corresponding development of expertise on the professional or journalistic side. The result has been a capture of management by default, by the marketing experts on Canadian newspapers. In the process, almost incidentally, the nature of journalism in Canada has undergone a significant change. It's worth looking at this development for a moment, because it has been dominant in the U.S. for some time and is rapidly making headway in Canada.

The science of marketing newspapers developed in the U.S. in response to a serious decline of newspaper readership, after the advent of television. An article in the trade publication, *Press Time*, in February, 1988, referred to the four decades-long decline in readership in the U.S., as the most vexing problem for most U.S. daily newspapers.

Since 1970, total newspaper circulation in the U.S. has been almost static. In relation to population growth, it has been in sharp decline. There is also evidence that newspaper subscribers are reading less, remembering less of what they read, and relying more and more on television for news. A 1987 survey in the U.S. reported that 42% of Americans now feel that they are getting all the news they need from television. Forty-two percent! Alarmed by declining circulation penetration, or the number of newspapers sold in relation to the number of potential readers, American publishers of the past decade spent heavily to redesign the appearance of their newspapers, and change the content. Not surprisingly, this created a proliferation of newspaper consultants, all of whom offered recipes guaranteed -- well almost -- to restore failing circulations. Their combined efforts succeeded only in slowing the annual rate of decline of American newspapers from 2% in 1977 to 0.3% by 1987.

Newspaper readership in Canada has reflected the same trends, although less drastically. Per capita circulation hit a high in 1955, just about the time television came in, plummeted steadily until 1975 under the impact of television -- in per capita circulation, not total circulation -- and then started to rebound slightly. Since 1980, growth has been slow, with total newspaper circulation increasing by only 343,000 copies.

Total newspaper circulation in the U.S., however, increased by less than this in the same period, despite its far larger potential market.

The response to this in the U.S., and now increasingly in Canada, under the guidance of U.S. consultants, has been an attempt to apply standard marketing strategies to newspapers. The primary instrument has been the public opinion survey. The premise is that newspapers are in trouble because something is "wrong" in the newspaper-reader relationship, and that the problem can be identified by asking readers what is wrong with their newspapers. The questions are designed and the answers interpreted by the consultants. The two current examples of Canadian newspapers undergoing this process are *The Calgary Herald* and *The London Free Press*.

The prescriptions that this kind of diagnosis usually produces tend to be remarkably similar, regardless of variations in the history, location and internal characteristics of the client newspapers. Invariably, there is a finding that the newspaper has indeed become remote from its readership, otherwise the consultants wouldn't have any point in being there. The solution usually lies in a careful positioning of the newspaper in relation to its market and the introduction of a new design or look for the newspaper, influenced heavily in the 1980's by *U.S.A. Today*. More use of colour, graphics, boxes of type designed to make the newspaper look brighter, friendlier and easier to read. To accommodate the graphics and their underlying philosophy, stories are shorter and less complex, with an emphasis on people rather than systems and abstract ideas.

Although there's something disturbingly contradictory about Canada's relatively healthy newspaper industry seeking advice from a much more troubled American industry, no one could reasonably oppose the idea of taking a fresh look at newspapers. Many critics have been saying for some time that the industry is too production-oriented and inward looking. Years of high profits, relatively low editorial wages, lack of professional development, and constant loss of the best talent to other fields, have taken their toll. By the 1980's, the industry was ready for some new ideas, and it was unlikely they would be generated by editors already in place. Using outside consultants was a logical step. The problem with these consultants lies not in what they do, but why they do it. The process of forcing any news organization to open its objectives and methods to question, is healthy. It's also good to force journalists to consider the total objectives of their media organizations; to shake them out of the smug isolation of their newsroom, and to invite them to consider questions of circulation, advertising, promotion and profitability. Problems for the journalists arise when the motivation for this process is flawed, when it's driven primarily by commercial objectives. The use of readership or market surveys as the initial and primary instrument of change reveals the basic philosophy of most consultants: in essence that marketing news is the same as marketing any other product. An organization which adopts this philosophy is one short step away from accepting the idea that newspaper publishing is no different from any other business. This position contradicts the industry's own contention that the operation of a newspaper is, in effect, a public trust. The concept of marketing the news is based on the idea that newspapers and other news organizations provide a service to readers, viewers, and listeners, if we extend it to radio and television.

No one can argue with that, but the definition of service is crucial. Newspaper consultants tend to define it narrowly, as information that the customer or client appears to need or want, as revealed by surveys. In its pure form, this concept has no place for the professional expertise of journalists or the creativity of journalism: two elements that are essential to the success of any news organization. At both the *Calgary Herald* and the *London Free Press,* the response of journalists to the marketing concept as applied by American consultants has indicated the existence of a real problem. At *The Calgary Herald*, the managing editor, resenting the intrusion of U.S. consultants into an area of editorial content which she considered to be her own territory, created her own newsroom committee in an attempt to regain journalistic control of the process. In London the editor was fired and three senior editors resigned. Stress clinics for journalists continue to be held at the *London Free Press*, indicating a continuing problem.

At both papers, where the consultants' work coincided with a period of cost cutting in an effort to increase profits, the long term outcome of all this is uncertain. The adoption of marketing techniques by the newspaper industry has coincided, not coincidentally, with the growth of newspaper and multimedia groups. The individualistic publisher of a previous era has been replaced by a generation of professional managers with business rather than journalistic skills. The symbol of the current era in journalism is the anonymous MBA in the newsroom, rather than the Hearsts and Atkinsons of old. Parallel, relevant, contemporary developments include the recruiting of journalists from a relatively narrow segment of the middle class, the spread and hardening of conservative attitudes in North American and western societies, and the phenomenal growth of information bureaucracies in government and industry. In combination, these and other factors have produced, in a gradual process that is imperceptible to the consumers of news, a narrowing of focus and a homogenization of content in our major news media. Paradoxically, as news media become more pervasive and influential, they offer us more and more of less and less.

This has led some of the most distinguished critics of U.S. media to detect the beginnings of something akin to an official system of information in major American media. A system that behaves in the most important areas of public concern in ways that resemble, curiously, state-controlled systems of information in what used to be called the communist world. As if to illustrate this, the U.S. has displayed a rigidity recently in dealing with changes in the Soviet Union and the cold war, that contrasts strangely with the current vitality and excitement of the Soviet press and its contribution to positive changes in Soviet society. This is not to say the Soviet press is freer than the North American press, but simply to draw attention to the direction in which each appears to be heading. While the press of the Communist world becomes more liberated, diverse and relevant, our media show opposite tendencies.

All of us have also been struck, I'm sure, by the contrast between the current demonstrations in China for a free press, clearly identified by the Chinese as one of the basic elements of economic and political progress, and evidence in our own society of a lack of understanding of the news media's role, or hostility towards the news media. After the massive budget leak in Ottawa a few weeks ago, most writers of letters to the editor seemed more anxious to castigate Doug Small and Global Television rather than the official and dangerous sloppiness Global had exposed.

The process of marketing information that is of service to a defined segment of the public, continues apace in Canada. Our most important national newspaper, *The Globe and Mail*, has become increasingly a publisher of service oriented magazines devoted to travel, fashion, entertainment and features about prominent business personalities. The character of this hydraheaded newspaper/magazine enterprise contains more than enough inherent conflicts to explain the changes in senior personnel occurring there recently. Magazines such as *Toronto Life*, that are devoted primarily to service information, have been hugely successful, while those with a different agenda continue to struggle: *Saturday Night* is the most current example of this.

The Toronto Star, despite its unorthodox behaviour in the '88 election, is in the main, a service-oriented newspaper. If this trend continues as it seems destined to, it raises questions about the future character and role of major newspapers. Will they become almost exclusively carriers of advertisements and service information? Will they become less and less congenial for journalists of unorthodox and unpopular views? Overlooked and unmentioned in the marketing approach to journalism, perhaps because it's impossible to measure it, manufacture it, or control it, is the intimate relationship between the unorthodox, the radical and the creative.

Journalists often understand this instinctively. They understand there is no automatic correlation between talent and education; between diligence and brilliance; between method and quality. The best journalism often comes unexpectedly from the most surprising sources. Historically, the organizations in which journalism has flourished have been those which have married a minimum system of supervision, with a maximum of freedom, idealism and encouragement, and which have learned to accommodate these facts: that the best journalism is often the least popular. That there is no way to resolve all of the conflicts between the commercial and public trust aspects of news enterprises. That in fact, it would be a mistake to attempt to resolve them in favour of one side or the other.

Many journalists know these things but they have difficulty formulating them in effective terms, as pollster Martin Goldfarb notes in Chapter Seven. There is no journalistic equivalent, at least in Canada, to the science of opinion polling and marketing that enables the newspaper consultant to speak with such authority. To devise a sound and rational methodology for journalism is difficult, but not impossible, as it requires among journalists a much greater knowledge of: the history of journalism, its aims and ideals, its relationship to freedom and its role in a free society, its corporate structures, its ethical dilemmas and its distinctive challenges of management, all requirements that our journalism schools aim to impart but which have to be taught more effectively. Armed with this knowledge, journalists can perhaps meet the marketers on more equal terms and recreate the kind of constructive dialogue that existed years ago, between the best publishers and their advertising and circulation departments. Nobody wants to return to the arrogance, bullying and intolerance of the old press lords, as Thomas Griffith wrote recently, after forty years in American journalism, but the Eunuch-like, 'make no waves', 'make no enemies' journalism that is practised in many American newspapers today is a shirking of responsibility.

The American newspaper scene of today that Thomas Griffith describes, and perhaps its political concomitant, will be ours tomorrow unless we find some way to chart and follow a better course. And this finally is to come full circle in this discourse. This is what the free trade debate in the last election was all about, and why the role of the media in that debate revealed so much -- not only about our news media but about our country. While I've been critical of the *Toronto Star's* tactics before the Ontario Press Council, I certainly support the kind of journalism *The Star* practised during the 1988 election campaign. But instead of tying themselves in knots trying to reconcile objective and crusading journalism, the editors of *The Star* should have proudly defended an older tradition of committed journalism. A tradition uniquely embodied in the history of their own newspaper. Only try to imagine the free trade debate and the 1988 campaign without *The Toronto Star,* and without the CBC, I would have to add, and you have some idea of what the future could be like. It would not be the kind of journalism or the kind of country that most of us would find inspiring.

Jim Winter:

Thank you Peter for a very thoughtful discussion of some of the issues which faced us last fall and which are facing us as we go into this day or so of discussion. I was sitting there initially as Peter was unfolding his talk, thinking, "no Peter don't do it that way". Thinking, "Peter talk about the question of why it is that *The Toronto Star* was an anachronism," because I didn't understand at that point where he was going. But that's precisely, at least in my own reading, what it was he was doing. And when he talked about *The Toronto Star* and the way that it treated the campaign, I was sitting there thinking "What about *The Globe*? What about their treatment?" But in a much more sophisticated way of course, he's talked about what *The Globe's* coverage was like while hardly mentioning the name of *The Globe and Mail.*

So why is it that *The Toronto Star* is an anachronism? Why is it that the days of the Scripps and the Hearsts and the Pulitzers are gone; the good aspects of those yellow journalism publications that they had? Because essentially, newspapers are written for advertisers, which is a point Peter didn't really emphasize, but I would like to do so briefly. Of course, increasingly, he who pays the piper calls the tune. So aside from the pervasive influence of concentration, which Peter referred to and elaborated for us, there's also the pervasive influence of advertising which I discuss in Chapter Eight.

It was encouraging for me as a professor here at Windsor with a more "radical" reputation in a more radical department, to hear someone who comes from the University of Western Ontario say these things. Western has, as we know, a much more conservative reputation. It was also encouraging to hear these thoughts from Peter, who has one foot in academia and the other one in the media. But then, we have gathered here an unusually thoughtful group of excellent professional journalists, as well.

Peter has independently touched upon some of the same arguments I make in Chapter Eight, in talking about the commercial objectives of the press, receiving "more and more of less and less," to use Peter's words. I refer to the kind of content we get as "Pablum Canada," quoting someone who testified before the Kent Royal Commission on Newspapers in 1980. So the days of Joseph Atkinson are gone, whom Peter described as saying that advertising was a necessary evil. Or E.W. Scripps in the United States, who founded a newspaper without ads, and supported it for a while. He described advertisers as "the enemy," and himself as a socialist. Obviously these days are long gone. Now it is the public, and the proponents of the public interest, who are "the enemies" of newspaper publishers.

David Crane:

I'd like to talk about the Ontario Press Council case to which Peter referred, in which a complaint was filed against *The Toronto Star* as to the fairness of its coverage. Perhaps what I could do is just to take you through the defense that we made, which was in the end accepted by the Press Council.

Basically what we did when we went to the Council was first of all to explain the role of a crusading newspaper, and to show that the role *The Star* has played in Canadian public life for most of its history, has been that of a crusading newspaper, with a clear and identifiable point of view. There has never been any attempt in the paper to hide its point of view, or to mislead the readers as to where it stands on issues. We have over the years identified and fought on many different issues: medicare, unemployment insurance, civil rights, a national pension system, immigration and refugee policy. We've fought for the preservation and strengthening of Canadian sovereignty, whether it was fighting for the flag, or proposing measures to make it more difficult to take over ownership of Canadian companies. *The Star* has fought to have the broadcasting act include provisions for Canadian content and Canadian ownership of the broadcasting media. So that's very much a part of our history and we believe that our readers understand and appreciate the fact that we are a crusading newspaper dealing with issues that we think are in the public interest.

When it came to the Free Trade Agreement, our argument was that we saw this as an important national issue which we had an obligation to explore in great detail, and where we had an obligation to encourage and bring out the policy debate and to provoke public discussion. So, from the first day the issue was raised by the Prime Minister, we started to write about it in our editorials, to set out what we thought the issues to be, why we were concerned about this issue being considered, and what the alternatives were. There was no pretence on our part, on this or on any of these other issues. When we think back to the history of medicare, *The Toronto Star* strongly endorsed the need for medicare many, many years ago. We had many editorials, many op/ed pieces, lots of insight pieces, we sent our reporters to Sweden and other countries to see how it worked. In the process of that, we reported the objections of the medical profession, we reported the objections of private life insurance companies that sell health care coverage to business. We reported the concerns of Mitchell Sharp as Finance Minister of the country, that we couldn't afford these things. But then we went out and examined what the people were saying. The doctors on that issue were saying that you can't have medicare because it would destroy the doctor/patient relationship. We sent reporters to other countries to find out what had happened to the doctor/patient relationship where they had medicare.

If Mitchell Sharp said it was a good idea but we couldn't afford it, we sent people to examine how other countries afforded it. I think that is a useful and positive activity and a contribution that a newspaper can make to society. Likewise with the FTA, when people said that this would create 200,000 new jobs, or whatever the number, we would go out and examine the economic research done by the Economic Council and talk to other economists, and ask "what do you think of the methodology employed by the Economic Council?" When people said there was no way that cultural industries would be affected, we went out and asked, "what were the possible risks to the cultural industries?" and spoke to people in those industries, and those in the academic world who follow cultural policy. We examined all of the assumptions and the assertions being made in the selling of the agreement.

I'd say that's a very important role for a newspaper, and we put a lot of emphasis on that. We felt a special need to do that, because of the government's own communication strategy, which Rick Salutin discusses in Chapter Three, and which was revealed in our paper. The secret memo said that the government was to rely less on educating the public than on getting across the message that the trade initiative is a good idea. We assigned reporters, columnists and editors at great expense and in numbers far greater than any other newspaper in this country, to get at this story from every possible angle. We dedicated more space in our pages to free trade than any other newspaper in the country, but it wasn't done on a hit and miss basis. We had many different approaches to doing this. We had, for example, two special eight-page sections which were prepared to explain the deal. One by Carol Goar, after the first outlines of the agreement came out, another during the election.

We had many outside experts from both sides of the issue, who asked to contribute to our paper. During the election campaign we set up a special free trade hotline to answer readers' questions. That in itself was quite revealing, because we really couldn't keep up with transcribing questions. It was revealing in a number of ways, one of which was, in spite of all the coverage, the main complaint of people phoning in was that they didn't understand the deal, and yet felt that they had to make a decision. They obviously were thinking very seriously about it, despite the comments made by Robin Sears in Chapter Three, and others, that people have only a passing, interest in what's going on in society. I was struck by that because I was the one who had to read all the transcripts of the questions revealing people's intense feelings for this. Not simply whether they were for or against it, but the importance they attached to being able to decide whether they were for or against it and the frustration they felt on this difficult issue.

I think the single biggest message was that there was this deep level of interest. We had several thousand phone calls during the election campaign, which may not sound like many, but I think it was quite a few. The first weekend we ran it, we ran out of all our tapes. The first weekend we had five hundred phone calls on a wide range of issues. People felt there was nowhere else they could really go, to get the answers. We had a free trade forum on our op/ed page. We had one rule and that was that no person was allowed to have more than one article. We had over one hundred fifty articles submitted; in the end we ran 49, twenty-eight opposed the deal and twenty-one in favour. At the same time, we had on our business page something called the Business Forum. We had dozens and dozens of articles on that page, not just during the election campaign, but the year or two prior to that: the vast majority of which were in favour of the free trade deal.

We had a wide range of columnists who were free without any outside interference to express their view. I had one view, Jack McArthur had another view, Carol Goar had her view. Tom Harper, our religion columnist, wrote two columns very strongly in favour of the agreement. Richard Gwyn, while he wrote a book advocating free trade, ended up writing columns opposing it, because of the details of this agreement. We were struck by the huge volume of mail received on the issue, for our letters page. We had to bend or break away from our standard practise in publishing letters, which is to publish letters in the same ratio as they are received. The vast preponderance of mail was against the agreement and for some weeks up to ten to one against. But we ran on a three to one ratio just to bring out more discussion.

In our presentation to the Press Council, we made the point that while there was a role for crusading newspapers, a crusading newspaper nonetheless had an obligation to make sure that people had the information from the other side. We did that in many different ways, not only through outside contributions. We had to fairly report what was being said by the proponents of the deal, which we did. When Brian Mulroney gave a speech in the House of Commons on the trade deal, it was our practise to publish the text on our Insight page, as with the text of advocates of the deal during the parliamentary hearings. We even made the decision that excerpts from the presentations of people for and against the deal would run in our paper every day. We were the only paper that consistently covered those hearings. Day in and day out, with our own staff, we provided that particular readership service.

In the end you can look at our overall coverage using the kinds of accounts people talk about, of how many articles you have for, against or neutral, and this kind of thing. Although I have a great deal of scepticism about the value of those things, if you want to use them, we had more articles against than for. But I would argue that in the final analysis, a reader of *The Toronto Star*, who had read faithfully *the* coverage in all our sections, prior to and during the election campaign, would end up being as well informed as she could possibly be from reading any media in this country.

We received a lot of criticism at *The Star* - we were said to be biased because we were against the agreement, although those who actively supported the agreement were not considered to be biased in favour of it. There was a lot of pressure put on us from time to time to sort of 'cool down' our coverage. One of these pressures was the complaint against us to the Ontario Press Council, because the person who made the complaint discussed it with the Conservative Party, tried to develop a strategy to have the complaint heard in the midst of the election. They tried to have it set up in such a way that it would be a public hearing with outside witnesses. This just would have been a chance for every pro-free trade group in the country to come down and try to criticize *The Star*, and inhibit or discredit our coverage during the election. We made the decision that we weren't going to appear until after the election was over.

We had people in public speeches, from Simon Reisman and John Crispo to members of the government, saying our coverage was unfair because we were critics. There was a lot of effort to try and discredit our coverage, but in the end I look back at it and I think,
-- well obviously there were some stories we could have done better, some headlines that could have been better, some stories played differently, -- but overall I think we lived up to our responsibility and served the reader in a responsible way. I was pleased that the Press Council came to the same conclusion.

Steven Langdon:

I'd like to make an important point about this city, with *Windsor Star* editor Carl Morgan sitting here and able to enjoy it. This city is perhaps the one place in Canada where there is one dominant newspaper, which because of the importance of the American television networks is also the central organ of communication throughout the entire Windsor and Essex county. This particular newspaper took a strong editorial position in favour of the free trade deal, and I think the results in Essex-Windsor were that the Conservative Party got 8% of the vote. Here in Windsor West I think it was about eight to 9% as well and with respect to Windsor Walkerville, the level of support reached a really quite dramatic, near-breakthrough level of thirteen or fourteen percent, if I remember correctly.

I have two things that I want to say. The first is that when we talk about Thatcherism and the crisis of the left, and anachronisms, even if those anachronisms are in the end rescued in Peter's speech, it's important not to fall into the trap of expecting that what exists at the moment is what will continue to exist, or is what represents the future.

The last four years of politics have demonstrated that the so-called crisis of the left does not exist. Instead we see a situation in which democratic socialist approaches to how a society should be organized, are receiving far more support than has ever been the case historically. When we look at the broad sweep of the last four years, this is going to prove to be the historically important and enduring feature of what's been taking place in this country. Eventually, this is going to show itself in a proliferation of different approaches to the media. Approaches which will come out, as they've started to come out in local community newspapers, local community communications. In cable television networks which are focused very much on the local community. In fact, the anachronisms and dinosaurs may turn out to be the very huge chains which themselves are over-reaching themselves, and quite rightly as some of the research Peter referred to suggests, losing touch with local communities and local readership. So I predict that we're seeing the last vestiges of a process rather than something that is ascending or becoming dominant. I suspect we're going to see new initiatives like CBC Newsworld, the all-news channel, a proliferation of cable outlets; we're going to see a variety of media.

Secondly, I hope this is not a conference on a sort of 'instant history'; that it's not a conference designed to look at the last election campaign and to draw some conclusions and see why it was that free trade came to pass in Canada. Instead I hope this is a conference which is the first stand in a much more successful, powerful and effective challenge to that Free Trade Agreement in the next election campaign. The reality is that the next election is going to be one in which people are not voting with respect to abstractions. They will not vote on what might happen; they will instead vote on their assessment of what has happened, and for their assessment of what has happened they are going to look at the thousands of jobs that have been lost. They will look at the attacks which have already taken place on our social programs. They will look at what's happened just in the last few weeks in terms of cut-backs in regional development in poorer parts of Canada. With these realities presented not just in parliament but outside parliament, by groups like the Council of Canadians, it's going to be possible to win that next fight. I hope that's what this conference is dedicated to achieving. If it is, I wish the organizers of this conference tremendous success in taking this first step.

As you look North at the Detroit skyline, have some sense of how, psychologically, Windsor and Essex County feel dominated by that skyline, and have some sense too of why it is that despite that psychological dominance the reaction right across Windsor and Essex Country was to reject the Free Trade Agreement in the 1988 election. It will be the same in the 1992 election.

Herb Gray:

I do want to begin by commending the Council of Canadians and the Department of Communication of this university for organizing this conference. I think it is of some significance that this conference is taking place here in Windsor at this university, and I might add the riding I represent. There's no doubt that unlike many other parts of Canada, people in this community are able to make judgements from their own life experience, rather than through information provided by the media, about what an issue like free trade could and would mean to them.

But this is not to say that the same thing would apply generally throughout the country, if one looks at the election and the debate involved on the free trade issue. I wanted to look upon this conference as something of a post mortem. On the other hand, generally speaking, you don't perform post mortems on corpses that you're pretty sure are going to get off the dissecting table and be walking around in a very vigorous way before too long. I'm convinced this is the case with free trade issues, even though the impact of the Mulroney trade deal on the lives of Canadians generally, may not be quite as evident as some of us might like it to be in time for the next election. However I think the impact *will be* sufficiently evident for the trade deal and its impact on Canadian life to be very much an issue in the next election, and that's why this post mortem, if I may call it that, is especially valuable. What's going to get off the table and walk around, is a new form of Frankenstein's monster, something very much to be chased around by the media in the next election.

Now I had to subject myself to my weekly effort to get into and out of Pearson Airport, and therefore I missed the opening words of Peter's speech, but I thought that it pointed out some of the very real concerns that should be in the minds of Canadians, as we move to the next election. One thing that struck me listening to Peter's speech is that while I noted in the list of participants in this conference, a number of very distinguished and experienced journalists, I didn't recognize the names of a lot of publishers. Now I don't know if there are going to be publishers here tomorrow in any great number and whether they're going to speak, but it seems to me that unless one takes a look at that side of it, a lot of the effort in this conference, while very interesting, will not be totally realistic. While there no longer will be the kind of independent newspaper entrepreneurs that made journalism so colourful in the last century, and in the early years of this century, it doesn't mean we won't be seeing an increasingly heavy hand of the media owners. Even though they won't be out front in quite the same way as the Hearsts and the Scripps and their ilk.

One example of what I mean is what happened at *The Montreal Gazette* in the closing days of the election, when after a very strong anti-free trade position had been taken by the working journalists on the editorial side of the paper, the publisher waded in with a signed front page editorial saying, never mind what the journalists have been writing, this is where I stand on behalf of the owners of this paper.

One can also take a look, and I'm not sure if this is on your agenda, at the way the anti-free trade argument was totally absent from the private, French language media, in the last election in the province of Quebec. Those of us involved in the debate across this country in both official languages, were very troubled not just by the extent to which the pro-free trade side was featured and favoured in the French language media, but by the difficulty, almost the impossibility, of getting the other side covered.

Another indicator of the future that I find troubling is the advice, if we can call it that, given in the editorial of today's *Globe and Mail* to the CBC, on how to live within the straitjacket of restrictions to be imposed on the CBC in the latest Conservative budget. That advice was that not only should the CBC lean back and enjoy what was going to happen to it, the way to enhance that enjoyment was to do such things as eliminating local newscasts where there were alternative newscasts offered by private stations in the same community, and in fact to do away with CBC stations entirely where there were private sector alternatives. So if people think there's some comfort to be taken in the future existence of the CBC as it is today, as a source of alternative views and voices, I hope they're right but at this stage I can't be totally optimistic.

Another disturbing harbinger of what we may see in the future is the trumpeting by Robert Maxwell of his desire and intention, to enter into the Canadian media scene, with the sweeping away of the current restrictions on foreign ownership. At the same time, I suppose one can't end some remarks like this without some note of hope and optimism. I would like to think that in spite of the economic pressures that Peter talked about in his speech, *The Toronto Star* with its circulation increasingly going beyond the confines of Metropolitan Toronto, will continue to offer an alternative voice to the media trend we are aware of. I also hope the kinds of journalists Peter spoke about will, whatever the pressures and risks to their career, continue to try to do their job to provide a multiplicity of voices, in terms of ideas and the recording of events.

I hope the Windsor experience has shown that Canadians will continue to exhibit a healthy degree of scepticism; not just toward their politicians, but also toward their media, such that they will judge issues like the trade debate on the basis of their own life experience, whatever the media do. But for that to happen, conferences like this are especially valuable. I hope this kind of conference will strengthen the resolve of its participants and the public, to maintain a commitment to a point of view I share with the Council of Canadians. In spite of the increasing concentration of media ownership in a limited number of hands, with purely commercial objectives, there will still be an effort by people like yourselves to provide a multiplicity of voices and ideas. In the end, this will lead to our survival as a sovereign independent nation, capable of developing its own values and applying them not only for the benefit of Canada itself, but the world in which Canada is and must be, a vital part.

Howard McCurdy:

Windsor has been cited as a place by Steven and by Herb whose resistance to the free trade debate was complete and utter; but there's a reason for that. And it's not that we're intimidated by Detroit or our proximity to the United States; it's not that they're particularly foreign to us. My wife is American, she's sitting over there, I have four children, all of whom are American, and there's hardly a Windsorite who doesn't go to Red Wing games and Tiger games and Piston games. Americans are our friends, and we know them better than most other Canadians do, and we are very much familiar with the kind of society that characterizes the United States. That experience of the dramatic differences between Canada and the United States, which we see every day of our lives, constitutes the basis of our fundamental opposition to free trade.

Now my two colleagues used up almost all of my time, but I share their concerns, as Herb said with respect to attention being given to the role of the publishers, and the identification of the ownership of newspapers with those commercial interests which fought for free trade. But there are a number of other elements of the process that occurred in the last debate, that I hope you will consider.

What we should be asking is, what is it about Canada that motivated those who supported free trade? What was the failure in our society and the nature of our economy and our people, which continues to throw us in the direction of dependency? For too long this country has been dependent upon our resources, because it was so easy to enrich ourselves and to ensure our short term security. What is it about this country that makes us incapable of seeing what is required for us to achieve greatness, in the next century, independent of the United States?

If you look at every other industrial country we are supposed to compete with, there are clear characteristics with which we have not come to grips, and that were hardly discussed at all in the election debate. Not by politicians and not by the media. Now I've heard mention of *The Toronto Star* and I've had correspondence with David Crane over the last couple of weeks over this issue. And this country has not come to grips with the fact that those with whom we compete are totally committed to creativity and innovation and the use of technology, not to exploit but to build, and none of that was said. We talked about the attack on our social programs; we talked about the market orientation, all of which were aspects of the philosophy underlying free trade and which are important to us. But we did not say anything about how one really builds a thriving economy, which not only can compete in the world of economics, but can compete in the world of social justice.

This would demonstrate that a civilized country devoted not only to economic growth, but to social justice, can establish a new kind of leadership in this world, and that to me was what the free trade debate was all about. And the debate failed us all. We did not ask how, in the context of our social democratic traditions, we can build a country absent control from the South, while at the same time being able to compete with and give an alternative model to, the good old U.S.A.

The *Windsor Star* almost every day has statements by the Mayor and the businessmen of our community telling us that free trade represents a real opportunity for Windsor; oblivious to the notion that if we had the slightest degree of confidence in our ability, we could have just as successful a relationship with the United States as free trade could ever have promised. And we would not be in a position of listening to propaganda, and living in dependency. And I know that Herb Gray and Steven Langdon and I and many in this room, are not going to let the free trade debate die in the next election, but by God, I hope they'll talk about the things we should be talking about. And I hope you'll be writing about the things you should be writing about. Rather than superficialities that mean tomorrow, next week or next year: we should be talking about the next century.

***

CHAPTER TWO

FREE TRADE IS GOOD/BAD FOR YOU

Introduction:

In this chapter we examine the evidence on, and perceptions of, media coverage of free trade. Our participants are from varying backgrounds, and hold differing ideas on our topic: a journalist-turned-politician (John Harvard), a journalist-turned-academic (Anthony Westell), a business reporter (Brian Bannon), and a political scientist (Fred Fletcher).

John Harvard argues that the media just served to confuse the public in the free trade debate, and didn't serve the country well at all. Public confusion was due to simplistic media coverage which showed one side saying, "free trade is good for you," and the other side saying, "free trade is bad for you." No wonder the public was confused. Studies analyzing media content indicate balance in coverage because they just tend to count numbers and don't get at the subtleties in coverage.

Tony Westell says the argument by media theorists such as Jim Winter (see Chapter Eight) is that the corporate elite owns and uses the news media to advance their values. Thus, the media would necessarily support free trade. However, content analyses conducted since the election indicate that the media didn't support free trade, but were balanced. Hence, what journalists are doing is merely reporting on institutions in a society which happens to be a capitalist one.

Brian Bannon opines he's yet to see any evidence linking corporate concentration and ownership of the media, to bias in reporting. From his analysis of *The Windsor Star* headlines on free trade, out of almost 1600 stories, his figures were: 95 positive, 118 negative and the rest were fairly neutral. Mr. Bannon says, in fact, there is actually a bias toward the negative, black-and-white arguments of the doomsters, the Parliamentary opposition and groups such as the Council of Canadians. These groups tend to get their stories and statements placed better in the newspaper, and they are better remembered. That's just the way the news operates.

Fred Fletcher argues that TV has made a profound difference in the way in which election campaigns operate. Parties organize their campaigns around it and use it to get their message out. However, TV allowed some players to get some messages across, for example legitimating business spokespersons, who were quoted four times as often as labour spokespersons in national TV coverage. A content analysis reveals that the pro-free trade side of the debate got much better coverage after the debate than they did before. This surprising finding may indicate that the media pulled out all of the stops to ensure a victory for the big business side of the debate.

John Harvard:

I was with the CBC until August 9th, 1988, when I declared my candidacy for the nomination of the Liberal Party in Winnipeg St. James, and so I can tell you a little of my experience at the CBC during the free trade debate, up until that point. And I can tell you, and I feel quite strongly about this, that insofar as the CBC in Manitoba was concerned, the CBC was massively indifferent -- it really didn't give a damn about the trade agreement. It wasn't until pretty well the launch of the election campaign itself that people got a little bit more interested in the free trade story. Unfortunately, by then it was pretty well too late. The news media should have been doing their homework way back in January, February, March and April and they weren't. There are a couple of reasons for that, particularly in television, and I think I have to point out here that more Canadians, get their information, unfortunately, from television than from any other source. That doesn't reflect well on Canadians and that doesn't augur well for the future. To be well informed you have to use all the media and not just television.

There are a couple of reasons why there was this indifference. One is that television doesn't take on issues of this kind very well. It likes pictures, it likes action and the trade agreement is not that kind of story. When you're talking about subsidies, or harmonization, or privatization, or deregulation, or continentalism; those things don't lend themselves well to pictures. Perhaps those who were against the trade agreement would have been better off if we staged massive rallies and demonstrations over and over again, week in and week out. For example I find it interesting that in the last two, three weeks, the media all around the world have been fascinated with what's been going on in Tiananmen Square in Beijing, China, and why? Because you know the story is right there; it falls into the laps of camerapersons; it falls into the laps of journalists; they can just stand there, sit there, talk to a lot of people and get those pictures. You can't do that with the trade agreement and that's a fault particularly with television.

The other thing is that when we finally got around to doing the story, it was so darned late in the game that what did we resort to? We didn't resort to any kind of deep investigative journalism, and coming to some kind of independent view; independent analysis of the trade agreement. What did we do? We took Ann Smith who was *for* the trade agreement and gave her a minute or two minutes or ten minutes to speak and then we gave Harry Smith on the other side equal time to speak against it, and that's a hell of a way to deal with a story, because it leaves the audience and the readers confused. I can tell you that as a candidate in the election campaign, day in and day out, door after door, voter after voter said they don't understand the story, that they were confused. The reason why they were confused, was they would watch Barbara Frum or they would watch Peter Mansbridge on the National, and they would get these stories that were so diametrically opposite: it's good for you, it's bad for you, it's good for you, it's bad for you. Well my God, most of us don't understand economics, we don't understand commerce, in fact, we don't understand continentalism. We don't understand these very deep, deep issues that go right to the root of what this country is all about. So no wonder there was an enormous amount of confusion. And we didn't serve this country well at all. I'm not suggesting it would have been an easy task; it would have been an enormous task. But we didn't do it, and I guess because I've been out of the media for such a short time, I still talk as if I belong to the media.

I read an analysis by that wonderful right wing think tank, The Fraser Institute, telling us that Barbara Frum, the CBC, and a lot of other organizations were against the Free Trade Agreement; they weren't for it at all, so what's all the bitching and screaming about? Well I am not absolutely sure, and I don't pretend to be an expert even though I spent 31 years in the media and 18 at the CBC. I'm not too sure whether we have measured the performance of the newspapers that well. For example, the *Winnipeg Free Press*; we all know that it was a great booster of the trade agreement. I'm sure that if you go through the columns and the articles and the newspaper stories in the *Free Press*, you will find just as many stories against the Free Trade Agreement as those in favour of it. But is that the measurement? Days after the television debate, *The Free Press* carried an unbelievably horrible photograph of John Turner; a photograph that showed a smiling Brian Mulroney, a somewhat thoughtful Ed Broadbent, and a John Turner with no teeth; no teeth in his mouth. That photo showed up not once in *The Free Press* but several times. Now I don't know how you measure this, but that was not a very good photograph.

How do you measure the use of words? It's not just a perception on my part that when *The Free Press* was putting together its headlines, it used wonderfully powerful words to promote the trade agreement, and weak headlines against it. They always took the stories against the trade agreement and put them below the fold on the front page. Very often they would start off a story with paragraph after paragraph of support for the trade agreement, then you had to flip over to page 19 or page 23 to find that there were some comments *against* the trade agreement. I don't know how you measure that, but all I can say is that if you simply count up the lines, you count up the stories, that's not good enough to measure how the media performed when it came to this issue.

Anthony Westell:

When Jim Winter called me about this conference a couple of months ago, he said it was going to be about the media and free trade. As my colleagues and I were doing some research in the area, we thought that we would have a contribution to make. Now it has widened and become the media and democracy and free trade, and I find that a difficult subject to address, particularly in five minutes.

You have two background papers before you. One is Jim's own sort-of paper on how he perceives the media and democracy and the role the media, or journalists, play. (Chapter Eight) The other analyses are about what happened in the test case before us, which is how the media covered the Free Trade Agreement during the election campaign.

Jim's paper presents a familiar argument. In short-hand, it's basically that the corporate elite own the news media and then use the media to maintain the values and beliefs of a capitalist society, and that the journalists they employ are unable or unwilling to challenge the values of the corporate elite. And so the media, in the crunch, with journalists doing the work, always come down on the side of the corporate elite. This explains (says Jim in my reading) why the media have supported free trade in the election and, by implication, why the Conservatives won the election.

He offers no evidence for this and neither do any of the theorists that I'm familiar with. They accept that this is the way things are. There's nothing wrong with that; one just has to realize that this is an assertion and not evidence. In this test case, -- how the journalists performed in the free trade debate -- we do have evidence in two attempts at content analysis. Content analysis is extremely difficult to do. First, you have to try to determine what the writer was saying, and secondly, what the reader got out of it, and almost by definition you're going to be into an area of subjective judgement.

Our finding is that, on balance, the media coverage tended to be unfavourable rather than favourable towards free trade. So the evidence which emerges from this contradicts the theory which Jim has advanced. He concludes that because the corporate elite own the media, the media will support free trade, whereas in fact they didn't.

If you look at the evidence and it doesn't support your theory, then you've got to have another look at the theory. And I want just briefly to offer you an alternative theory about the way things are. The corporate elite own the media, I think, for the most obvious reason, the same reason they own supermarkets, shipping companies and whatever you want to name. They own media to make a profit. They may from time to time want to intervene to make their voice known on the editorial page. But fundamentally, they are in the business of making money and their papers will publish whatever will make them a profit. There are examples in Europe of highly successful profit-making capitalists who have owned newspapers which promote socialist views.

The Toronto Star is a case with which we're all familiar; it is extremely unpopular with the business community. But it is also a highly successful, profit making enterprise. Also, if you think that ownership really dominates the media message, you have to explain why it is that the CBC which is state owned and not profit-motivated is fundamentally the same as CTV which is privately owned and profitable, and fundamentally the same as *The Glove and Mail.* Why is that? In my view it is because the content in media is not dictated by the corporate owners but by journalists.

A lot of the values of journalism are not very good and perhaps they ought to be changed. But that's where the prime motivating force comes from. What you read in the newspapers comes from journalists. There's a sort of "culture of journalism"; we all agree on what news is, and how you present news. That's why you find the same sort of news and the same sort of presentation in all media. They may be differently owned but they're all run by people who share similar notions about what should be in the media.

I don't know anyone who said this better than Walter Lippmann a long time ago, but you have to understand that there is a difference between news and truth. Any society sets up a series of institutions to do its business, from public institutions like government, to private businesses which operate under the rules made by the public institutions. Basically what journalists do is to report the actions of those businesses and institutions. They can't go out and cover everything that happens; they position themselves at various institutions, and what those institutions do is what fundamentally constitutes the news. In doing that of course they legitimate the society; they make it appear normal. They make it appear that this is the way life should be conducted. If they worked in a socialist society, they would legitimate a socialist system.

You can't really expect them to do otherwise. As Lippmann said, we're quite good at recording news, which is the record of decisions - some of which you have to dig out to find the hidden news. What news means, is a matter of opinion. And journalists are no better than anybody else on those questions.

You should not look to journalists to find the truth: you look to them to find the news. They might do it a lot better, but that is their job. Do not blame them for legitimating the society which does exist. Can you imagine that journalists should ignore the society and the institutions which exist, should invent a different one in their mind, should go out and report it and in that way legitimate it? They are not capable of doing it. It's absurd even to think about it. They just report what's there, well or badly, but that's what they do. So don't look to journalists to be the agents of change. It's not their business.

If you don't like the way the democracy operates don't blame journalists, don't blame the news media, don't blame the corporate elite. There are all sorts of ways of changing society. Just don't expect too much. Don't look to the media for truth; look to the media for news.

Jim Winter:

I'd just like to make a couple of remarks in response to Tony's comments. If I understand what you're putting forth, it's what I would call the "sociology of news" perspective. This holds that the professional values of journalists are responsible for media content, and we can essentially ignore the role of corporate influences. Well, I think that this is a naive perspective, but be that as it may. You say that those of us who make these latter arguments about corporate influence, such as I have done in my paper, have no evidence to back us up.

There are a number of things that I can say about this. First of all, in looking at your own words, if I may quote them back to you, in referring to your own study you used words such as "a content analysis," "test case," and "evidence," whereas you referred to my research as something like, "Jim's own sort-of paper." There is a tremendous difference here, and these are the kind of not-so-subtle differences in media content and language, which we should be looking at.

What I've done, very simply, is to analyze your words in a way in which social scientists such as ourselves have not been doing in our quantitative content analyses of media. And this seriously damages the evidence that we've been able to come up with, because the differences are subtle and they require these kinds of techniques. As you've said, content analysis is very difficult to do, and it's extremely difficult to do well. I think the disparity between my argument and your evidence is a reflection of the regretful state of some social science research today, and its simple and facile methodology.

There are people in Europe and North America who are using discourse analysis to come up with the kind of intensive evidence which goes along with some of my arguments. I have done this type of analysis, in fact, and I have very different evidence from your own. You say that we are "providing an assertion and not evidence." Well, we are beginning to provide evidence in accordance with our assessment. But let me remind you that your content analysis is only evidence and not "truth."

You also say the corporate elite simply owns the media to make a profit. What you fail to point out is that same corporate elite also owns other businesses. Ken Thomson owns *The Globe and Mail* but also The Bay and Simpsons, and so forth. So not only will Thomson's forty newspapers publish whatever will make *them* a profit, but they'll serve the other corporate masters as well. This is all part of serving Ken Thomson's interests. If free trade is seen to be good by, and for, this small group of corporate giants who run Canadian business, including its media, then the media *will* promote free trade to that effect. And the public weal generally, and professional journalistic standards, can and do go to hell in a handcart.

The pro-free trade perspective either will become a part of your "culture of journalism," or the offenders will be purged: witness *The Globe and Mail* example and listen to what Lorne Slotnick has to say about that. And Lorne isn't a media theorist like Ralph Miliband, or even Jim Winter, but a front line working journalist. Or listen to Geoff Stevens or Frances Russell, *et cetera.*

As for your last points, the media *don't* just objectively report institutional news, they selectively report on selected institutions, and there is a whole sociological literature full of examples of this. I don't know how you manage to reconcile your two views that: a) journalists objectively report the records of institutions, and b) journalists legitimate capitalism. The social movement to which Rick Salutin refers in Chapter Three, is an institution too! Why isn't it reported? On the other hand, if journalists are agents of legitimation, then clearly they are *not* objective, which is my point.

Rick Salutin:

I just want to enter a demur with one point of this apology that Tony has made. I am not in the least surprised that the media behave in the way they do, but to say that they simply give the news and report the decisions of institutions is absolutely false. They report the decisions of institutions like the BCNI. What I point out in the next chapter is that the biggest unreported story of the last three years was the emergence of a popular political movement, which had a near-decisive effect and yet you can't find this reported anywhere. So it's not that they "just report the news" and this is a very deceptive way to put it. They just report *some* of the news.

Tony Westell:

I've already had my say and so I won't add much. But, if we're going to do a semiotic analysis of what has been said I would object to Rick saying that I was apologizing for anything. I don't think I was. I don't think it is true to say the efforts of the anti-free trade lobby were ignored. I think that's totally wrong and that there was a lot of coverage of it in the media. Maybe not the coverage you would like. I don't really know what Jim means by....well, I know what discourse analysis means, and all that I can say is that in the absence of it the evidence we have is three content analyses. That at least is some evidence: you have opinion, we have some evidence.

Brian Bannon:

I'm not really going to try to discuss the general argument that has been made that corporate concentration and ownership in the newspaper business and the media in general, automatically leads to bias in reporting by reporters, and presentations in news, because it's not a new idea. The same thing was said twenty years ago, but I have yet to see any evidence to link the one with the other. It's like discussions I used to have with my father about God. His argument was that there is this wonderful world that works out there, therefore there is a God, and I would always answer "well, where is the connection?" and after a while I just realized it's a matter of faith. So I'm going to accept too that it's a matter of faith with people who believe that connection, because if over these years and decades there was real systematic evidence of this thing, we would have seen and read about it by now. That's all I'm going to say about it.

I only really want to make one point on this, about objectivity, but I'll use a couple of examples. I was quite irritated by the coverage of the free trade debate too, but for other reasons. I cover economics basically and business. Every day I'm talking to economists and business people, most of whom are in the export business; accountants, lawyers, bankers, all these types of people. I had a pretty good idea from quite a while back what the free trade idea was and the agreement as it unfolded, and technically what it meant from the economic point of view. *The Windsor Star* sent me to Washington when the agreement was in its early stage, just to find out if those guys down there were really protectionists -- were they serious.

The Star also got a group of us together to do a series on free trade before the election was called. It was not a new subject to me. I kept running into ordinary people, neighbours, relatives, and even though we'd done this series and there had been plenty of good stories on the free trade idea and the agreement, they kept asking, "why is everything we read in the paper, in all the media and on television, why is everyone against this agreement? Why are you all saying it's going to be terrible, there are going to be thousands of jobs lost, our social programs are going to be ruined, we're going to become part of the States? Why is everyone saying that?" And I really wasn't surprised, but I got more and more irritated and I'm going to try to explain why I think this happened; why people got that impression.

No one, by the way, in this conference has really addressed the question, the facts, the data in the Carleton study, or the Fraser Institute Study about the positive and negative stories and the breakdown on free trade. I did one of my own too with *The Windsor Star* between the date the details of the FTA were published and the election. We ran almost sixteen hundred stories with the word free trade in it. I just punched it into the computer and I got all the headlines. I went through them briefly, and picked out the headlines that I felt obviously tended to give a negative impression of the free trade deal. My figures were 95 positive, 118 negative, and the rest were fairly neutral. So the corporate agenda that people are alluding to, and the bias of the newspapers and TV in favour of the Free Trade Agreement - it just doesn't come through in the facts. I wish someone would address these data. This is the third sort of survey that's been done and no one has even addressed that, and I wish they would. Tell me in what way were the media were so pro free trade?

Now the point I wanted to make was, I'm going to just describe what I saw on television last night about this conference here, the coverage on the local CBC television station. I missed the meeting last night, the dinner and Peter Desbarat's speech, so I wanted to catch what happened. Well, they didn't interview Peter, they didn't even show Peter, he was in the background. They interviewed Maude Barlow and Steven Langdon and, typically for the local television, they didn't do it while they were speaking, they pulled them afterwards. The excuse always is, we've got to cover two things, we've got a deadline for evening news, so they just pull these people before or after the speeches and maybe they interviewed Peter too, but he didn't get on. After reading his speech today I think I know why. Because Maude and

Steven came on in these very short, very punchy, emotive statements, they are black and white, no equivocation about what's happening. Yes the FTA has been really terrible, it's not over yet, it's going to be terrible, the media have done a terrible job. All this within ten or twelve seconds.

Peter's speech, from what I've learned today, was a more broad ranging speech that touched on several topics. It raised some interesting points, but Peter didn't start stomping, banging on the table, and Peter I don't want to say that you're not a sexy speaker but I would say that you're more calm and reasoned and you're probably not as used to those clips, giving that punchy ten second or fifteen second bite as are Steven and Maude. That is a good example of how the Free Trade Agreement was covered. For example, after this the TV people aren't here today, they aren't really covering this conference. There is a print reporter here, and what is he going to do, who is he going to interview after this conference is over? I don't think he would interview me. I'm just trying to describe the mechanics of how reporters operate. I'm not going to go out of my way to make myself available to that reporter, because I don't enjoy being interviewed, I don't have a real good presentation and this reporter is much more likely to turn around at the end of the conference looking for someone to interview, and low and behold by pure coincidence, a couple of politicians will slide in beside him. Not only that, but if he talked to me, he would get me saying things like "well, I'm not really in favour of the Free Trade Agreement, my argument was really about the subtleties in the way reporters operate."

It's not good print or TV. Whereas, some of these other people who are very committed, see things in black and white: there's no equivocation and they know how to capsulize things in a short time. I can remember when I was covering the Free Trade Agreement, one time a banker came into town, president of one of the big banks and I asked him about free trade. He said "From the banking industry itself, it's not particularly good, I think it's slightly negative, but for the economy in general we think it's slightly positive. So we're going to support it, hoping the economy gets a little extra boost". I just cringed because that's not something you can make a story about - that kind of response. I asked him "how many new jobs do you think it will make?" He said "I don't know, in fact it may not be any jobs, in fact in some instances you might lose jobs". "What about social programs," I said. He said "Oh, it's very remote that it would ever cause deterioration of social programs or cultural sovereignty, very remote". I said "then there is a small chance"? He said, "Well, anything's possible".

That kind of response from someone is just murder to write about in a story. I tried to make it interesting, but it's back in the back pages somewhere and very few people read it and those who read it don't remember it. But I'll show you another story that came up on September 24, 1988, and I didn't write it. It says: "McCurdy Says Free Trade Deal Bad For Minorities." During the election campaign MP Howard McCurdy stood up in front of a group of local black people, during a black heritage day, and said "if you vote for free trade you're going to wind up in black ghettos like in the States." Now if you were a reporter who went up to ask him afterwards, his attitude would be completely black and white. There would be no doubt about it, he would use emotive language -- it's just what a reporter wants.

This story was placed well. The reporter may have had a bit of a bad taste in his mouth about the moral integrity of making this statement in public, but from his point of view it's a fantastic story. It's punchy, people are going to read it, remember it. That kind of influence on reporting is far greater than who owns the newspaper, what your publisher's politics are, any of that kind of stuff. It's getting your editor and the reader to think your story is sexy and that is 99% of the motivation for reporters. The problem of course is that reporters have to work much harder to get both sides of the story which is not as sexy and which is not emotive or outrageous, and that will make the headlines.

What is depressing is that sometimes you have to sit someone down for a half an hour to find out what their argument really is. You work hard and try to write so it's interesting to the public and will get read, and often it doesn't really get good play, it doesn't get read, it doesn't get remembered.

Rick Salutin:

I just want to make a contribution on this vexed question by Brian Bannon, of why the content analysis studies produce a lot of negative stories on free trade by the coders.

I'll suggest a simple explanation - it's a very bad deal; there's almost nothing good in it. Specifically I take you to the communication strategy of 1985 when the the Conservative government said: "It is likely that the higher the profile the issue attains, the lower the degree of public approval will be." That's absolutely right and they stuck with that all the way. If you read the government literature on the deal, there were huge amounts, and it's almost all fatuous statements of optimism, almost no specific references. I ask you to do a content analysis of *that* literature, for Christ's sake. See if you can *find* any content. I think what's amazing is the relatively large amount of positive coding that you wind up doing on these content analyses.

Brian Bannon:

That's not the question I asked, really. What I want to know is, why are people here saying the media were so pro free trade, but the data came out with more negative stories? That was the question and I think from my point of view, negative stories always get played more than positive stories.

Jim Winter:

If I could just interject one thing, part of it has to do with the nature of the studies as well. I'm thinking of the Fraser Institute study, for example. They left out *The Report on Business* in their analysis. What kind of effect is that going to have on your portrayal of *The Globe and Mail,* leaving out the ROB? We know what its perspective is going to be! Is it any wonder that conservative, business-oriented "think tank" found *The Globe and Mail* opposed the FTA? But what validity does a study have which omits the ROB section from *Globe* content?

Geoff Stevens:

The other consideration is that during the election campaign, of course, you had two political parties campaigning *against* free trade and one in favour. On any newspaper during the election campaign there is a formula that you try to give equal coverage to the three major parties. On any given date probably, you're going to have two anti-free trade stories for every pro-free trade story.

Fred Fletcher:

I'd like to introduce a couple of observations that are specific to the impact of television on public debate, especially during election campaigns.

It's important for those of us who are concerned with effective action, in influencing the way in which the media cover a particular public debate like the free trade debate, to understand how the media operate; to try to correctly analyse the factors are involved in determining the kinds of coverage that exist. It is important to say some things that have a theoretical context, although I'm going to try to be specific and pragmatic. I'm going to start with a question that really is central, which was raised in the background paper by Tony Westell and Alan Frizzell: Has TV changed our political life? Does television make a difference?

I'd like to argue that it's made a profound difference in the way in which election campaigns operate, and the way in which public debate takes place in this country. It's made that difference because of audience penetration and voters' increasing reliance on television news and public affairs to get their information about politics. It also is important because party strategists rely primarily on television to reach uncommitted voters. Studies of past campaigns have shown that their reliance is justified; that television does reach more uncommitted voters, and is more persuasive of voters than the print media.

It's difficult to find definitive evidence of the independent effects of television news coverage on the outcome of elections. However, it's very easy to demonstrate that television affects the nature of the public debate. Also, we can talk about how the parties organized their campaigns in the last few elections around television; how they used it to get their messages out. I've written a paper where I make a long argument using various kinds of survey data to try to show that television made quite a bit of difference in the 1988 campaign, and I'm going to make just a couple of assertions without offering the evidence, because of the time limitations.

John Turner was able to use television. Indeed, most observers would agree that the televised debates changed the course of the campaign. Turner accomplished that, as Rick Salutin says in Chapter Three, by crystallizing the unease that many people felt about the Free Trade Agreement, and by making himself, at least temporarily, the most credible alternative to the Prime Minister. On the other hand, the Conservative Party was able to use television to undermine the linkage between Mr. Turner and this unease about the FTA by attacking his credibility and his motives. The internal party polls tend to support the proposition that the counter attack which the Conservatives mounted, primarily through television, was very effective in destroying the link, and undermining his credibility.

All of this prompts me to assert that television is extremely important and leads me to a second question: In the 1988 campaign did television permit the people participating in the debate to get their messages across? In general terms, the answer is yes - but it allowed *some* players to get *some* messages across and that's what is significant. In order to become a part of the public debate as defined by television, the players have to have legitimacy in the eyes of the people who make decisions in television news and public affairs. And what does legitimacy mean? It is accorded to official sources and to leaders of the major political parties and to spokespersons for certain kinds of interest groups. Therefore, just to take an example, business spokespersons were quoted four times as often as labour spokespersons in the free trade coverage on the national television networks. This is not unusual. Indeed,it is typical of the coverage of issues in which "big business" has a majority stake. Social movements that are new, like the coalition against the Free Trade Agreement, have difficulty establishing their legitimacy unless they go to extraordinary lengths to attract attention.

The second part of my example has to do with the kinds of messages that can be communicated on television. The messages have to fit the television format. We've heard some discussion of that already: they have to be simple and personalized, and fit the 'two-sided' model of conflict. So that some actors, some messages can get across. There is evidence to support the notion that when a player got attention in the free trade debate, most of the time the message communicated was the kind of message they wanted to communicate. That is, when a spokesperson in favour of the Free Trade Agreement was quoted, the item tended to be favourable to the agreement in almost all cases. When someone got attention who was opposed to the agreement, most of the time, that whole item was unfavourable to the agreement. So the issue became: What do you have to do to get attention?

There are a variety of other things I could say about the nature of the coverage which reflects the limitations of television, and about the importance of the electoral regulations, which gave predominant access to the Conservatives, and about election spending. These are important with respect to the third party issues, but I'd like to leave them to later discussion.

I want to make two other observations. There was a dramatic change in the nature of the coverage. All of the content analyses (for all their faults) pick up the fact that fully half of the items in the major media about the Free Trade Agreement occurred in the last fifteen days of the campaign, after the debate. This is the case in my sample and in others I've seen. And there was another shift which requires explanation. The anti-free trade groups did have a modest edge in the coverage up to the debates. It would seem logical that since the debate focused attention on the opposition to the Free Trade Agreement, we would expect the coverage to favour the opposition, with a great deal of attention occurring after the debates. My numbers show that there was actually a shift in the balance, and that the pro-free trade side got much better coverage *after* the debate than *before*.

(*Editor's note*: It could be that prior to the debate, the media could afford the "luxury" of providing coverage for the opposition. After all, Mulroney appeared to be heading for another easy majority government. This was not the case after the debate, when the Tories plummeted in the polls and it looked as though free trade might be defeated. Now, all of the stops would have to pulled out to ensure a victory for the media's big business owners.)

(*Speaker's response:* An alternative explanation involves the notion of "campaign effort." It is arguable that the pro-free trade side made only a modest effort to promote their cause in the media, until the post-debate polls gave them a fright. Then, they blitzed the media not only with advertisements but also with speeches and other public relations activities. This represented a level of financing which their opponents could not match, lacking comparable resources. The coverage, according to this argument, reflected in general terms the level of "campaign effort" of the opposing sides, not simply the economic interests or ideological preferences of media owners, though this was undoubtedly a factor as well.)

There is a conservative tendency in the media, private and public, which is easily identified in long term studies. But it's important to remember that the media are not monolithic, that there are all kinds of working journalists making a serious effort to cover all perspectives in an issue. And I think that Bob Hackett at Simon Fraser University puts it clearly. He said that: "There is a certain monolithic quality to the media, which supports the status quo, but there are cracks in the monolith." And if you're interested in influencing the debate, by challenging the rules the media establish regarding the legitimacy of participants in the public debate, you have to look for those cracks. You have to find those ways into the system to get them to pay attention to issues or perspectives that aren't supportive of the status quo.

***

CHAPTER THREE

PAID AND UNPAID MEDIA

Introduction:

In this chapter we hear from playwright and freelance journalist Rick Salutin, well-known political advisers Robin Sears of the NDP and Patrick Gossage of the Liberal Party, and Montreal *Gazette* political cartoonist Terry ("Aislin") Mosher.

Rick Salutin says that the government communication strategy on free trade leaked to the press in September 1985 was explicitly anti-democratic. Its goal was to "rely less on educating the general public, than on getting across the message that the trade initiative is a good idea, in other words, a selling job." The government never wavered from this approach, and the media colluded with it. He says the government intentionally set out to mislead and disinform the public. The media were aware of this and yet reported government disinformation as factual. A popular movement or coalition which included everyone except big business, scored a victory for democracy by smashing the government's communication strategy. They did this with an anti-free trade booklet which went out as paid advertising. The media largely ignored the event and the movement.

Robin Sears says that in comparing paid media (advertising) to unpaid media (news coverage), paid media is the most important political tool in North American politics. As such, the Tories have an enormous advantage, as the Party of big business. He says that he and other Party strategists are guilty of presenting media and the public with pictures, zappy one-liners, photo opportunities, and leaked polling data on our candidates. We do this at the expense of explaining issues.

Patrick Gossage argues that TV isn't print and as a medium it isn't good at analysis and issues. He says the Liberals lost the TV war in both the paid and free media. They lost in the paid medium because they couldn't change their advertising quickly enough and didn't have the money, the will and the coordination to do it. The team had fallen apart. The Liberals lost in the free (news) medium because Turner wouldn't get off his set free trade speech and the press got extremely bored with it. Turner became a "broken record," who got good responses from audiences with his emotional attack on Mulroney, but the journalists got tired of it. The people loved him but the media got bored.

Terry Mosher says the Toronto *Star* seems to be doing it right. Every time someone would mention the *Star* during the election campaign, Brian Mulroney would stop looking like Ronald McDonald and he would go into that nervous Quebec City Irish two-step. It really upset him. But isn't that the media's job? In a way, Mosher thinks of the media as the official opposition. Better that, than going to 24 Sussex Drive and having lunch with the Prime Minister, with some piano player from the Holiday Inn playing in the background.

Rick Salutin:

I'll make just a few remarks and I'll try to focus on the subject of democracy. We know explicitly that the government had a media communications strategy which was leaked to the press in September of 1985, which was an absolutely explicit anti-Democratic strategy. Surely everyone here knows that document. To me it's the key document of the last three years. The document from the Prime Minister's Office said, in September, 1985,

> Our communication strategy should rely less on educating the general public than on getting across the message that the trade initiative is a good idea. In other words, a selling job. The public support generated should be recognized as extremely soft and likely to evaporate rapidly if the debate is allowed to get out of control,

so as to erode the central focus of the message. At the same time a substantial majority of the public may be willing to leave the issue in the hands of the government and other interested groups, if the government maintains communications control of the situation. Benign neglect from a majority of Canadians may be the realistic outcome of a well-executed communications program.

This is an absolutely explicit anti-democratic basis for their approach to the media. It seems to me that the media colluded with that -- the government never wavered from it and the media colluded with it; not only until the end of the election but to the present. At certain points the strategy broke down, but not because of the Parties or certainly not because of the media. Nobody mentioned the fact that the free trade issue was out there prominently for two years before the election. There never was a national televised debate about free trade; either among politicians or among partisans who are not in the Parties. That's astounding, it seems to me. And people said right through the election and until election day and after, that they felt uninformed and confused. That was exactly the result the government, with its communications strategy, was aiming for.

What I find astounding in a way is that the media, and I'm thinking of the mainstream media, had the communications strategy in their hands for three years and simply ignored it. You have the government saying explicitly, "we are going to mislead and misinform the public," then they go ahead and do it. They float all kinds of bullshit about what's going on. The media have this damned thing in their hands and they pretend that it never happened. You have a government announcing they're going to issue disinformation, issuing this disinformation, the media already reported that they said they're going to issue this disinformation, and then the media report this disinformation as if it's absolutely factual.

After the deal, what happened? Within about a month, reporters were saying that they thought the country had free trade fatigue, which in reality described the reporters. Up until the end of the election the people kept saying "give us more information." After the election, what happened? Well, I would say we still are in a situation where free trade is not debated. So my criticism is that the media were in bed with the anti-democratic communications strategy of the government, all along. Then, where was democracy in the free trade debate? It seems to me it did happen and it happened through the popular movements. There was a coalition which coalesced in this country in a way that has never been seen before. And it included virtually -- the best way to describe it is, take away business and it included everybody else. Almost everyone in this country was in this popular movement, and that movement worked for three years solidly.

All I want to say in this context is that if you had read the media, including the learned study by Tony Westell and Alan Frizzell, you would have no idea that there was an unprecedented intervention by a popular movement. And it's not just Westell's paper: in all media, in all journalistic coverage, there was almost no mention of this popular movement, this progressive coalition. There were many significant things that happened that were not reported. Let me also say that when this coalition published a book called *What's the Big Deal*? and 2.2 million copies were published all across the country, and we had a press conference about it, there was no response in the media. There was no mention of it. When the Business Council on National Issues, hiding under the cover of the Alliance for Job Opportunities, announced they were thinking of publishing a four page ad in the newspapers, it was covered in every newspaper and mentioned in every newscast.

Let me just say something about the TV debate, because I think it's pertinent. As I say, there never was a debate on free trade. What happened in that famous interchange between Turner and Mulroney, of 90 seconds or whatever it was, they were not debating free trade. Go back and look at it. Turner was demanding a debate on free trade and Mulroney was saying one had already taken place. They were debating about debating Canadian free trade; that was as far as it ever got.

Now anybody who thinks that the chaos that broke out in the last three, four weeks of the election, after the debate, was because Turner got juiced up for 90 seconds -- which is apparently what most journalists and journalism professors seem to think, is, -- well, you must believe in the tooth fairy. It's clear what happened. Let me point out there was a Gallup poll the day before the English language debate, which said that the country was now running 42 to 34% against free trade. It was the first time in a year that the gap had been broken. And it was because the work of this popular movement was successful, culminating in the booklet which went out and which was eventually acknowledged as having a serious effect. But that was the result. Before the debate, people had turned, by a significant plurality, 42 to 34% against the deal. It wasn't the debate, it wasn't what Turner did, as Allan Gregg understands and very few people in the media understand. Turner simply provided the people with a positive voting channel for their concerns about free trade.

American journalists were stunned by the effect of that book and what they said again and again was they couldn't believe that something in print could have such impact in the age of television. I just think that one of the things we learned was that people are not stupid, they're just deprived of information, and once they get it they respond intelligently.

Let me conclude by asking if there was a victory in this election. I think there was -- a victory for democracy. The victory was that popular movements in this country smashed the government's communications strategy. Now we had significant losses. We lost the election; we failed to stop the free trade deal, and in all probability the country will not survive. Let me put it differently. I think that if you were a betting person, unless you got very good odds, it would be silly to bet that Canada will survive under the FTA. I think the thing can be beaten, but the odds against that happening are very serious. I'm not being sanguine about this. I think there was a real, significant victory on the democratic agenda. This thing broke open and the government saved it, not by a policy of benign neglect, but by lying, which was not their preferred way of doing things. But it would never have happened if it had been left to the opposition parties or the media.

Robin Sears:

I'd like to spend just a couple minutes on the paid media before dealing with the unpaid media, as we rather uncharitably refer to advertising and news these days. Paid media have become the most important political tool in North American politics, and it is exclusively, in terms of any serious devotion of time and money and resources, a tool for television. We all spend a little bit of money putting nomination meeting notices in newspapers, and things. But basically we're talking about television advertising, and in this country, less than in the United States, national television advertising or at least regional television advertising.

The importance of this cannot be overestimated, when you're attempting to analyze the impact of certain types of information on voter opinion. To look at television news, without considering the advertising that surrounds it in an election campaign, and these are skilfully produced political messages, distorts the picture that a viewer is receiving at home in the evening. And it is a problem I have with media analysis as we're attempting to do it today. You have to look at what happens at 9:58 on the CBC during an election campaign and 11:02, which is to say to include the advertising minutes that surround the newscast, to have an impression of the impact that both types of media have on voter opinion during a campaign.

I won't go into the long public policy debate about how access to that should be structured, *et cetera*, except to say that anybody who doesn't think that the Tories had an *enormous* advantage in this campaign by being able to outspend Patrick's colleagues and mine by, depending on what you count and what you don't, a factor of two or three to one, doesn't understand politics. We need to look again at the issues we addressed in 1974 when we set up the Election Expenses Act, which was an attempt to deal with this problem, because it's not working any longer. The Tories will always have more money than their two competitors, particularly now that they've become more clearly the party of big business in Canada, whereas it was the Liberals who used to aspire to that throne. And that presents a problem in terms of having fairly equal choice of opinion out there in an election campaign.

Enough said about advertising. I must say that I can't resist the temptation to pick up on a couple of things that were said in the previous seminar because I think they do reflect very much on what the problems are with the role of unpaid media, that is to say television news. I think Tony Westell as a journalism professor and long-time Canadian journalist reflected very well, in Chapter Two, the majoritarian attitudes of his generation and of his approach to journalism in this country, which I would characterize as mouldy. That is to say, Walter Lippmann has something interesting to say to your generation Tony, about how opinions are formed. He has much less to say of interest to mine; and much less of interest to say to a culture where print journalism is largely irrelevant in the formation of political opinion by voters. We don't all agree about what is news.

What you say, quoting Lippmann, is "News is the record of decisions made by institutions". That is not my judgement of what news is. It's not the judgement of many people in this room. It is a fundamentally anti-Democratic view of how news should be structured, if it's to fairly reflect society as it exists, which is the test you set up. Hattie Dyck, in her comments in Chapter Six, said "this is a democracy, after all, there are two sides to every story." To which one could add the word "only" in the middle, as an explanation of what's wrong with the rather two-dimensional view of society and political choice.

This is what made coverage of the trade debate so terribly painful for television journalism. I participated in a number of discussions about this and with a number of the CBC and private sector executives who are involved in making these decisions. To be fair to them, the disciplining constraints of the medium they operate within made it structurally very, very hard for them to do much more than they did, and by the standards of their profession they did this debate and this set of issues better than they do most. And if you don't believe me, think about the treatment of Meech Lake. The free trade debate got a very intensive and multifaceted coverage on television by comparison with the kind of coverage television usually offers on complicated issues, which is, I concede, a low standard of judgement.

There is a dilemma on television which is even more sharply focused, about who gets the right to say something, and about how a complicated issue is depicted. Mark Starowitz made an observation with respect to the Meech Lake debate, and *The Journal's* efforts to cover it seriously. *He said that when the politicians decided not to talk about it, The Journal couldn't cover it.* This may seem strange to you, but it reflects the fact that the television medium, and to a somewhat lesser extent now, the media in general, *needs* politicians to talk about political events. That's one of the disciplining constraints of the business. Rick Salutin cannot appear by himself or even with businessmen, on a Journal panel, very often, because the constraints of television news are that political news is made by politicians and that was a problem with the free trade debate.

One of the gurus of political coverage at the CBC made a very interesting observation about the problem of an election campaign as opposed to a non-election campaign period for television. The rules change the moment the writ is dropped. It becomes a requirement that people like Fred Fletcher, when they're analyzing the behaviour of television networks during the campaign, in toting up the minutes allocated to each party and each party's spokespersons, that the Fred Fletchers come up with relatively equal totals for all three. That's not a normal approach to news judgement in a non-election period. And it means therefore that everybody has to change their frame of reference on both sides. Politicians don't have to deal with the news agenda as seriously. Frankly, the New Democrats know they're going to get a fairer slice than they would in a non-election period, and journalists resentfully recognize that they have to squeeze the stories that they want to cover, into that framework.

The last thing I want to say about the institutional structural problems within the media themselves and particularly with television, is this: it's just not possible to say a great deal in 90 seconds, and it doesn't matter how powerful the pictures are that go behind the words. That length of time, which is a long period of time on television, is a very complicated problem for television journalists, even if they're committed to trying to be as balanced and multifaceted as they can. And I don't know what the answer is to that. There'll be some improvement as a result of the airing of CBC's "News World" later this year, which will give the newshole of television news some greater capacity. But I can tell you that as a political strategist it will be the minutes between 6:00 and 6:15 P.M. in each time zone, and the minutes between 10:00 and 10:15 and 11:00 and 11:15 P.M. later in the evening, on the major networks in each market, that we will still focus on. Within those very small quarter hours there's not a lot of time to say a great deal, particularly if you're also trying to cover the rest of the world.

I want to say something self-critical about politicians and political strategists in this respect, because I think the sort of exchange we had in Chapter Two - "it's your fault, no it's your fault, so's your old man," is not all that revealing. Political strategists and politicians have gotten into a framework for discussing and planning elections, and presenting issues, in the last ten or fifteen years. They've been heavily influenced by American experiences and behaviour, and by the demands of television. Basically these can be summed up, if I can paraphrase slightly, one of George Bush's media advisors, who said, "Look all we've got to do to make sure we get a hit, is present you with pictures, punches and polls."

They provide some graphic of George Bush in front of a flag, some cheap shot at an opponent that contains a zappy one-liner and some leaked poll data that indicates the momentum of their candidate. When we've done that we know we're going to get a good position *vis a vis* the competitors, on the news. I confess to being guilty of having fallen into that kind of structure in my thinking about the planning of the campaign, at the expense therefore of trying to explain issues and offering the opportunity for candidates to comment on things that don't fit into that paradigm. If we don't find a way to break out of that, we're going to have an even more primitive characterization of the *impact* of the free trade debate on television news in the next federal election than we had about the *prospective* impact of it in the last one.

Patrick Gossage:

Well maybe I can help Robin exorcise some of that guilt, because I sit here quite amazed at this sort of pre-television generation lashing out at television, as if it was the wicked eye in our society that sort of evilly hovers over us waiting to scrutinize our every action and waiting to reveal us as we really are. I'm amazed too that television is always judged on the same basis we judge print. Television *isn't* print and there's no reason to feel guilty about the fact that television isn't good at analysis or at issues. It *isn't good* at analysis or issues and that's that; it's just a different medium. And by God, we learned that, didn't we Robin? It's a different medium, with its own disciplines and its own demands and its own requirements, both for politicians and for the popular movements that are so well represented here.

I'd like to suggest that perhaps the popular movement, which I'm very sympathetic with, and the anti-free trade forces outside of the official politicians, didn't use television well enough. Perhaps in their concentration on helping Canadians understand the "issues," they neglected to use the popular medium that could have pushed them over the top. Now the Liberals lost the television war in ways that Robin has helped us to understand very well. We lost the television war in the paid and free media. We lost in the paid medium because we couldn't change our advertising quickly enough and we didn't have the bucks, and we didn't have the will, and we didn't have the coordination; the team had fallen apart. We lost in the free medium because Turner wouldn't get off his set free trade speech and the press got extremely bored with it. Turner could not get off that track and it became a broken record. He was getting good response from the audiences as he travelled around the country because it was always a new audience for his really rather impressive, personal attack on free trade and on

Mulroney, but it was not carrying through into the media; it wasn't carrying through into the nightly newscast, because the journalists tired of it. Those were major reasons why we lost.

Let me talk very briefly about television as a unique medium because I think curiously it hasn't been done and I don't think it will be done by anybody else. I actually am a television person who grew up as a television producer and was brought in by little Jimmy Coutes to try and improve Trudeau's television image! What a joke! But the best I could do from across the room was to remind him to brush down his bushy eyebrows. That's one of my more important contributions to Trudeau's television image. But anyway, it's important to remember that television is about perceptions of personality and character. Television is about talking to your eighteen year-old daughter who's sitting right there and you're trying to explain to her in the three minutes before she goes off to meet her friends, what the free trade argument was about. That's what television is about. It's not about drawing her diagrams, it's not about showing her a fancy pamphlet with very well-organized headlines about what free trade is about. It's trying to convince her that free trade is in fact going to damage our country and damage the way we live, and in fact represents a real threat to the kind of life she's grown up with. That's what television's about.

So it has different requirements. One of the requirements, curiously enough is eyes, you know, and somebody said that I started to look better, on the tube, well, one of the reasons was that I started to know how to use my eyes. I started to know where to look and how to make these things communicate, just the way I try and communicate with my daughter who's going to sleep after I've talked to her for about three or four minutes. It's not that mysterious. I have a great story about Newfoundland Premier Clyde Wells, whom I went to spend a part of a day with to try to get him up for a debate. We were sitting in his rather nice sun room in St. John's and he was sitting behind a coffee table and he was rehearsing his opening remarks rather effectively. Boy, Newfoundlanders sure know how to communicate. I was the camera so I said "I'm the camera, you look at me", so he did it very well and he's got terrific blue eyes, you know he really does have great communicative eyes, like Trudeau's steely blue eyes, which were very important for his television image. I said to Clyde "You know you've really got terrific eyes, and you've really got to use them," and I gave him a few little tips. And he said "Well thank you Patrick but you're the first man who ever told me I've got good looking eyes!"

So anyway, it is about character and it is about personality and television does scrutinize individuals in a very real and effective and telling way. It's very hard to fool television and frankly, until Mr. Turner actually found it in his guts to believe that this free trade deal was a crock, he couldn't communicate it. He finally found it within himself, and then he was able to do it with effect, with the camera in front of him. Just the way I'm sure he couldn't have convinced his daughter Elizabeth that he was anti-free trade, three or four months before the campaign, but I know damned well he could convince her during the campaign. He got it, he found it, he found the commitment and the conviction to be able to get through that tube and into the audience.

Now let me just disagree with Fred Fletcher that you have to be an official spokesperson to get on television. I mean that's just total horseshit. The fact of the matter is that an unemployed worker or Marjorie Bowker herself, or the famous woman on Parliament Hill -- do you remember her? She told Mulroney off when he was trying to de-index pensions. These are ordinary people whom television can bring to a national audience, with tremendous effect. And you know, you can actually stage these kinds of things and you've got to learn these things, Rick Salutin. You've got to learn how to stage events for television because that's how we're going to win this bloody debate in the end. I assure you! Actually Robin and I are available for free consulting, I guess.

There is another interesting thing about television. People look at Peter Mansbridge and they think "This is the great television personality". This is *not* the great television personality. Peter Mansbridge is deliberately bland, because when you're conveying somebody else's message you have to be bland. He can't afford to show emotion. He can't afford to show anguish or anger. He tries very hard not to. He is deliberately bland. But that doesn't mean that television transmits blandness. Television actually transmits the committed. Television transmits people well who believe things, people who have intensity, people who are thoughtful, people who are expressive, people who are good at transmitting *themselves*. Television helps them transmit well. It isn't a mystery and you can learn it.

Of those speaking to date, the very guy who was the best communicator was Rick Salutin. He was terrific. I haven't seen enough of Rick on television, and I don't know if he really dislikes the medium. I really think it's because he moved in on you, he was very calm, he was cool, he spoke with great conviction, he was articulate, he knew that he spoke from his guts. He wasn't bullshitting you. That's the kind of stuff that works on television.

Robin Sears:

You contradicted your own thesis, Patrick. If official spokespersons aren't the only ones who get on television, then why isn't Rick there? Why *didn't* he get on?

Patrick Gossage:

No, Rick isn't there because, well we could talk about that, but what I would like to know is what problems the popular movement had with television? That's what I'd like to know, because I didn't see enough of it on television and I'd like to know why. Because I think really, the future of this country is at stake, the debate isn't over. I think the extra-parliamentary opposition to this bland and bloodless, right wing agenda that we have overwhelming us out of Ottawa, has to be fought and has to be fought with every tool at our disposal. And I really am distressed that the popular movement is going to put out another pamphlet. I think the bloody popular movement should be going back and forth across the country, with its absolute best spokes-people doing the report card on free trade on radio and television.

Terry Mosher:

There has been a drawing up of lines over this free trade thing, and unfortunately I think some friendships have been lost. Yet, I still have one or two good friends who are Tories. But what has evolved is interesting. Jennifer Lewington talks in Chapter Six about the sudden interest of the United States, in Canada, and I think it happened everywhere. We had phone calls here from Peru: "The Canadians are angry", from Turkey: "The Canadians are angry", from Quebec: "The Canadians are angry".

I just wanted to say that I've gotten to know Maude Barlow but she doesn't know me all that well. I have a bit of a reputation as a loose canon. So it's nice of her to ask me to speak. Usually people just say to me "Look, just sit in the corner and draw your cartoons and here's your cheque but keep your mouth shut for God's sake". I do have that habit, of sometimes speaking like I'm drawing a cartoon.

It's nice to be in Ontario. I came into Toronto and was waiting around for Rick Salutin, and I went into the Classic book store. It was great. I went by the popular psychology section where the "How To Die Gracefully With AIDS," "How To Drive Your Man Crazy in Bed," "Time Tested Techniques of Dealing with Nervousness," and right beside that it was "Nausea" by Jean Paul Sartre. Some poor bastard is going to pick that up, figuring he's going to deal with his nausea.

Coming down Eugene Whelan was on the plane. I had forgotten all about this, but of course Gorbachev spent ten days here in Windsor, in the very capable hands of Eugene Whelan and he was telling us tremendous anecdotes. Gorbachev was constantly asking question after question and apparently at one point he asked Whelan: "Who makes sure the farmers go to work in the morning?" It could be that perhaps the whole movement of Peristroika and Glasnost was really started right here in Windsor, Ontario.

When I came in last night it was fun. After all of that, there was my old friend Peter Desbarats, who wrote the introduction to my first book years ago, denouncing *The Toronto Star*. It seemed kind of ironic right here on the border of Detroit, with all of these trucks in the background slowly bringing in stuff over the bridge. I was thinking what is in those trucks? It's no good whatever it is. They were so patient, waiting, bumper to bumper, all the time knowing, "It's O.K., it's under control now."

I'm biased against the free trade deal and that's allowed. I should talk about it because I don't fall into the classic role of the journalist. I see it working within the media, but as a satirist; not as a journalist. *The Toronto Star* for example, seems to be doing it right. Every time someone would mention *The Toronto Star* during the election campaign, Brian Mulroney would stop looking like Ronald McDonald and he would go into that nervous Quebec City Irish two step. It really upset him. But isn't that our job? In a way, I think of the media as the official opposition. Every once in a while we seem to do it right and we bag a cabinet minister, we get them. I think that's good. Much better than going to 24 Sussex Drive and having lunch with the Prime Minister and some piano player from the Holiday Inn playing in the background. I'd rather be a little more scurrilous. I like that sort of thing.

Peter last night mentioned *The Toronto Star* and I liked what he said about having more room in the media for off-beat opinion. I thought he should be maybe a little more careful about what he was saying about *The Toronto Star*. After all, he's got that nice teaching position, but he might have to find real work again. He has tenure! What if they forced him to go out and find real work every four years as opposed to a sabbatical? They sort of get down there out of the windmill and try to give Don Quixote help, then they get right back into the windmill fast.

Anthony Westell quoted Walter Lippmann and I asked him outside if it really was really Walter Lippmann, and he quoted the book and the page number. Probably a lot of people have used Lippmann as the classic example of the 'disinterested journalist' or the 'disinterested man,' in trying to define what a journalist is, as excluding feelings. I don't think anybody has gotten it right yet. Even Lippmann had a mad, atrocious affair with a woman in his late forties and broke down and said something like "Wouldn't it be fun not to have to be a gentleman all of the time?" He began to become a little more like Henry Mencken, who was just a crazy bastard who wandered through life having fun. I admire that side of it and I wish there was more room for that sort of thing.

The Toronto Star was really quite gentle. I've got front pages from *The Montreal Star*, which was the most influential paper in 1911, for anybody who wants to look at them. This is scurrilous stuff: "Faced by Certain Defeat Reciprocity Forces Become More Desperate". There is also a front page letter to the Canadian people from Rudyard Kipling: "It is your own soul that Canada risks today." It's marvellous stuff. And it's not too far from some of the stuff that's in our booklet that we had a lot of fun with. Things don't change in Canada, they sort of go on and on.

A satirist is interested in emotions and feelings and how people are reacting. How the little guy in the restaurant is reacting to the hockey game last night, or what that cabinet minister did. Not facts because, whose facts are they? Duncan Macpherson described it very well. He saw his role as standing on a soap box and yelling back at the machine for the little guy. I like that concept because very few other people are doing it for them. A sense of humour is essential to a healthy human being; it is the same with society. They throw people like me in jail in Central America, because what we do is a testing of the system. Mitchell Sharp once said, very dryly: "Political cartoonists are something we allow in a democracy".

Actually I wish we had a lot more of it. I don't see much written satire consistently printed here in this country. It would do us a lot of good. It's a terribly important aspect of any society, to have a healthy cynicism. Francis Bacon talked about satire as saltiness rather than bitterness. I don't think we are very good when we become righteously indignant. We start to bore people. I think people in this business understand that we are just human beings, like everyone else is. Since the first political cartoons appeared, the idea has been a concern for the little guys and the unfairness of things. I can't remember ever going into work in the morning and saying: "I'm going to crucify some poor people today". So yes, there is a bias there. The fatter the cat the more you're going to try and do it.

The nicest definition I've ever read about cartoons is a suggestion of the hoot of the slum kid who has just tossed a snowball at the rich man's hat. I think that is the court jester role we play. At the same time, there is often an element of truth there. There is that great story about Muhammed Ali taking a flight, and the stewardess said to him: "Please do up your seat belt". Ali said: "Superman don't need no seat belt". She returned with: "Superman don't need no plane either". I think that's what we try to do with Brian Mulroney or whoever happens to be there. We become very popular with the opposition. The NDP guys happened to phone me a lot and say I'm the best cartoonist in the world. If they ever get into power they're not going to think so. That's the nature of the game. Before 1976, the Parti Quebecois in Quebec thought the light shone out of every orifice I own. They don't think so anymore. It's sort of that gadfly role.

The business of ethics doesn't apply. *The Gazette* came in with an ethics policy and they suddenly looked at me and said "No, this doesn't work. He puts words in people's mouths and in effect exaggerates". So it's quite a different kettle of fish.

Rick Salutin wrote the text for the booklet, most of you know that, and I did the cartoons. It was an interesting situation because as opposed to sitting back, as we ordinarily do, and shooting off in every direction, I took a stance on free trade and it was a very conscious and deliberate one. I think when Donald MacDonald asked us to take a leap of faith, that was the key point and that was a number of years ago. He wants me to take a leap of faith with guys like Simon Reisman and Alan Gotleib and John Crosby and Brian Mulroney and Conrad Black. I wouldn't let my daughter marry one of those guys. Barbara Frum might, but I wouldn't. It's a rich man's deal, negotiated by rich men, for rich men, in my estimation.

I'm not against free trade, I'm not anti-American. Maude Barlow and George Bush and I spend summer vacations within one mile of each other in the United States, so it's not a question of being anti-American. It's just very pro-Canadian. I don't like the deal and I'm very suspect of those guys. In effect, I was very above board with *The Gazette* and said "Look, I'm going to give these cartoons to any anti free trade group for nothing. Do you want *The Montreal Gazette* credit on it or not," because they in effect buy first rights. They said "Well we don't know". I said: "Look, if I ever do any pro free trade cartoons, the pro free trade groups can have them for nothing too, O.K.?" They said, "Well yes, that makes sense."

Producing the booklet was a very exciting operation and an eye opener for me and a lot of other people. The nicest thing that happened was hearing from people. Such as a woman in the Okanagan Valley who had a sudden trust in people, that we were trying to deal with these things and thanking us for trying to do something. That was very rewarding.

***

CHAPTER FOUR

CAPITAL THREATENS TO STRIKE

Introduction:

To examine the role of labour in the free trade debate, we hear from Peggy Nash of the CAW, Lorne Slotnick, former *Globe and Mail* labour reporter, Manitoba freelance journalist Doug Smith, and Winnipeg union activist Susan Spratt.

Peggy Nash says there was an unprecedented involvement of the labour movement, in the free trade issue. Aside from local community media, the biggest success they had was with paid advertising. First, they took out two full page ads in 42 newspapers across the country, in 1987. Second, they published the Mosher/Salutin booklet, distributed in newspapers during the election. Why did labour lose the election? Nash says it's because "we didn't have two million bucks in our back pocket."

Lorne Slotnick reveals that as the labour reporter for *The Globe and Mail*, he asked to be taken off the beat, because they changed it into a "free trade oriented labour beat," which is just propagandizing for business. As for reporting during the election campaign, he says reporters at *The Globe* were told and were subtly made to feel, that stories which made the free trade deal look bad were not welcome.

Doug Smith says business leaders effectively threatened to strike, by withholding capital and investments, if the FTA was defeated. If Bob White, the CAW, and the labour movement had taken similar actions, had threatened to strike unless the FTA was defeated, they would have been roundly denounced in editorials. Smith documents a sample of biased coverage, in the Winnipeg *Free Press*.

Susan Spratt argues that labour has to be inventive and to stop bringing the same old complaints about, "jobs, jobs, jobs," to the media. Of course, jobs are important, but as was said, the media get bored. The FTA fight brought together labour and other organizations, in an unprecedented fashion. This is what needs to be continued over the next four years. Popular movements must pull together and provide their vision of this country for the political parties to see.

Peggy Nash:

I wanted to say first of all how pleased I am that the University of Windsor and the Council of Canadians decided to include a workshop on labour's role in influencing the public debate on free trade. It's wholly appropriate, given that we are in the city of Windsor where many thousands of CAW members keep the auto industry going, that we have this kind of a conference on the free trade issue. I noticed, ironically last night that none of the politicians,, even from the Windsor area, last night mentioned labour's role in the free trade debate. I know they worked with the labour movement here and had a number of high profile events especially in Windsor.

I wanted just to take a few minutes and look at the campaign that labour ran, and the activities we participated in throughout the debate leading up to the election. In the CAW we began to debate the free trade issue in 1985. We began leadership training, we issued brochures, pamphlets, held seminars, did a tremendous amount of education work with our membership and local leadership. The CAW was probably the most active union on the free trade issue, but I have to say that there was an unprecedented involvement of the labour movement, I don't know of another time when so many unions participated in a political action issue. Unions that perhaps normally don't do the job they should in communicating with their membership, or getting involved in any kind of political action, really did get involved in printing materials, in organizing meetings, in participating in coalition work, as they've never done before.

We proved that we were right not to underestimate the intelligence of our membership. Even late in the debate leading up to the election, people were saying, "it's such a complex issue and I don't understand the issue." And to be sure, there are a lot of intricacies to the Free Trade Agreement. But we found that when you explain things in everyday language, when you give people information, they are fairly intelligent and can make their own decisions, and make up their own minds. And we found that rank-and-file union members, people coming out of auto plants, or out of aerospace plants and a number of other locations, were going to public debates, they were going to city councils and they were talking about omnibus trade legislation and countervail. They found that they really did know a lot and our ground work with our membership paid off, because when we got into these debates, we often found that our side was better informed, that we could make our case much better than the other side could.

So that grass roots work was very effective, and it paid off in a number of ways. We had people speaking to resolutions at city councils; getting city councils to pass a resolution in opposition to free trade. We had inventive examples of what people felt would happen under free trade. In London Ontario, we had an example of street theatre, where a person dressed up as a box of Kellogg's Cornflakes, somebody dressed up as a bottle of Labatt's Blue beer and they were on the street corner in London, illustrating industries that would be vulnerable under a Free Trade Agreement. So they not only took the information, but localized it, personalized it, and I think they did a good job in raising public debate.

The other key thing that happened during the free trade campaign was not just the amount of information and education work, but the unique example of coalition building: the number of organizations that came together. Unions that could never sit around the same table, were doing so. The Women's Movement and the Catholic Church found common ground; seniors, farmers' organizations, social agencies, churches, native people's organizations, cultural groups, and many other groups. Getting together, sitting down around the same table and finding where the common ground was on this issue, and being able to get some concrete activities done. What is most notable, and again, the point was made earlier by Rick Salutin, this was given very little coverage, very little interest by the media.

The success we did have in the media for the most part, aside from maybe local community media, the biggest success we had was in paid advertising. In the CAW, in the fall of 1987, we took out two full page ads in 42 newspapers across the country, listing the shortcomings we found in the FTA and calling for a Federal election. Up until that point, there hadn't been much public debate in the media, there had not been a lot of attention given to the free trade issue. Our biggest fear was that this thing would just slide through. The Tories would follow through on their plan of selling the deal and there would not be any public debate. When we put these ads in the newspapers across the country, our phone was just ringing off the hook, there was a tremendous amount of media attention given to that. So that was our first experience with paid advertising.

The second was the booklet that Rick Salutin referred to in Chapter Three which was really a paid ad. I mean, we got the idea from Loblaw's flyers. How does Loblaw's get its information out? They pay for the advertising and stick it in the newspaper and so we printed two million copies of this and of course it caused a tremendous stir. So much so that it forced the business community to come out with their own, pale imitation in the form of their own booklet. And because we did have to rely on paid media, of course it's very costly. Our pockets aren't as deep as the business community pockets. Somebody said "Why did we lose the election? Because we didn't have two million bucks in our back pocket." There's some truth in that. That if we had been able to do more of that in the days leading up to the election, we might have had a different outcome.

As well as not doing the job that I would have liked to have seen on the coalitions, the media in some cases either failed to understand the significance of some events, or chose to ignore them. I just want to give you one example. During the election campaign I had a call from a national TV reporter who asked me for a visual example that he could shoot, of what would happen under free trade. And he asked if we had a group of retired workers that is having a rally, where he could get some footage. I said well, our retirees in fact would be very avid. I'm sure I can find a rally of retired workers but I said, listen, there is something else that has just happened. There is an auto parts plant in London, Ontario which is closing down and moving to Mexico. He said "So?" And I said well, you know there's a little bit of history to this plant. This plant is called *Fleck* and in 1978 the women who worked in that plant waged a war, not only with the company, but with the police force, in order to get the right to join the union. The provincial government spent a fortune; more than they had spent on any strike, in police force salaries, in order to defeat those women. The police lost, the women won and they got their union.

Ten years later, Jim Fleck the owner, who was a Tory politician and who had been on a government advisory council promoting free trade, decided that he was going to move this plant to the Maquilladora section between the U.S. and Mexico. This allows those products to be imported into the U.S. practically duty free, which of course under a continental FTA means those parts can come into Canada. And even though those women were working for very little money, in spite of the fact that they had a union, they only made about seven bucks an hour, the workers in Mexico could be paid five dollars a day, so obviously it was cheaper for Fleck to move down there. So I went through this long explanation, and he said "Well, I don't see how that connects with free trade. Have you got a group of retirees for me?" And he did not want to cover the Fleck story and he did not cover the Fleck story. So that's the kind of thing we were up against.

The second part of our question: what can we learn for the next phase of the fight? Well it's true that there is a next phase now, the ground has shifted, the deal is passed and it's fair to say that the government feels quite confident, almost cocky, about imposing a neo-conservative agenda. We see changes in our taxation system, changes in unemployment insurance, we see the beginnings of the erosion of universality, and these are all very significant beginnings because they will build on this. We are going to see some significant changes -- so what can we do?

The language of the debate has shifted; instead of social programs being a sacred trust, the language now is the threat of inflation, global competition, and the deficit. Just like free trade, these are powerful buzz words for people, and that's the new language that we have to deal with. What worked before, and I think it did work for us, was the membership education, getting to our membership, the rank-and-file of the labour movement, popular communications, speaking in plain language to people, and getting rid of the gobbly-gook, and working in coalitions so that we're not isolated. Clearly there are a lot of people who feel common ground and a harmony of interest with us. So this worked for us before and we'll continue to do it.

We're where we were three years ago in the free trade debate. We have to start again from the ground up and build with the rank and file of the labour movement. It was mentioned earlier, this whole process is called democracy. That democracy is not just about casting a vote at election time. Real political democracy is when people participate in the political life of their society. I disagree with what John Harvard said, that the media lead this. I don't think they do. It's people themselves. They don't need the media to speak for them. People themselves can exercise that political democracy.

Some people are saying it's very depressing, things have changed, we've lost. I don't feel that way at all. We've learned a lot and I'm excited about the debate we're going to have over the next few years, leading up to the election.

Lorne Slotnick:

I was the labour reporter for the *Globe and Mail*, and I was doing that job until April, 1989. I had been doing it for four and a half years, and as people here who read the *Globe and Mail* know, the *Globe and Mail* was, I would say, nearly hysterical in its support for the free trade deal. That affected its news coverage in a way that we haven't seen very often at *The Globe*. I've been there for ten years and it has been a place where the news coverage has been somewhat independent from the editorial line, and from the views of the people who own and publish the paper. That changed during the debate and we're continuing to see changes at the paper.

The reason I'm not covering labour anymore is, *The Globe* has changed the labour beat to make it into almost a free trade-oriented labour beat. They said they wanted stories of how companies were doing good things with their personnel policies, to get Canada in shape for the competitive world economy. That was just a way of propagandizing for a certain view of reality and wasn't really a labour beat and I asked to be taken off it. As an aside, at *The Globe* there was an outright effective ban on stories that made the free trade deal look bad, and there still is. Perhaps that's too strong: it isn't a *complete* ban, but reporters were told and were subtly made to feel, that stories that made the free trade deal look bad were not welcome in *The Globe and Mail*. There was a definite orientation in the news columns and there was concern about this in the newsroom.

I want to say a couple of things about the role of the labour movement in the coverage of the free trade debate, because I think it was important, particularly at the initial stages. The labour movement is the richest and most well-financed opposition group in our society. Canadians pay about half a billion dollars a year in union dues and unions have the resources to fight battles that other groups in society don't have. Because the labour movement is well-financed and because it has the legal ability to disrupt the status quo occasionally, through things like strikes, it tends to get covered more by the media than most opposition groups. Now I'm certainly not going to say the labour movement gets covered adequately, because it doesn't -- less so all the time. But it does get covered more than groups like the Women's Movement and the Farmers' Movement and other parts of the coalition that have been referred to. So the labour movement does tend to get covered, as an institution, probably more than other social movements.

In 1985, when free trade first became an issue, not so much in the public consciousness, but among the politically aware elite in the country, the labour movement was in on the ground floor. It decided this was going to be a crusade and did have a fairly major impact, because it started spending money on publicizing its opposition to the deal. The labour movement did have an impact in getting this issue some publicity and in getting away from the attitude Rick Salutin was talking about, where the government was just going to do a selling job without educating the people.

But what I saw as an observer of the labour movement and of the free trade debate, was that the labour movement could only go so far because unions have a pretty bad image problem in this country, they have a bad credibility problem with the media, with the public and even in many cases with their own members. The result is that when unions speak on an issue like free trade, not too many people listen. Or when they do listen, they listen in the wrong way, or they listen in a negative way. Unions are often perceived as narrowly self-interested. They are perceived sometimes as very ill-informed and prone to overblown rhetoric and threats, and they're often seen as institutions where the leadership is not really in touch with the members. In the free trade debate, that meant the sector that should have had the most potential to stop the deal and have some impact, couldn't really do the job by itself. Aside from the political impetus to form coalitions, that's one of the reasons the coalition had to be formed. Because the labour movement on its own didn't have the credibility to do the job,or the public support it needed.

Now why isn't the labour movement able to get its message across with credibility, to the media? Part of the problem is the media's problem. Despite the fact that labour is sometimes covered in an organized way, with specialized reporters, most media managers are basically only interested in what unions have to say when it's an issue at the bargaining table, a workplace issue. Unions have some power to disrupt the status quo by pulling people off the job, and it's a very common conception in the media that trade unions are just meant to deal with those kind of issues -- narrow bargaining issues. That's not the way a lot of unions see themselves, but that's certainly a media conception of unions, which in turn is portrayed in the media. Consequently some union members themselves feel that their own organizations don't have the right to talk about issues like free trade, or to support political parties, or to talk about issues like abortion or disarmament. Broadly speaking, the media tend to pay attention to unions only when there are strikes.

But while the media can be blamed for some of the problems with labour's inability to really have a substantial impact on the public, you can also talk about labour itself. Peggy talked about how the CAW, for example, did a lot of work educating its members on the free trade deal. Well how many unions *did* that? There weren't a lot. There was a lot of rhetoric, there were a lot of speeches made, but in most unions there really wasn't the attention to getting together with the membership, holding meetings, trying to draw people out, publishing stuff and really getting people *informed* about this issue. And a lot of unions just pay lip service to the opposition to free trade. I agree with Peggy that it was probably the biggest campaign unions have done on a political issue. But it wasn't enough to get that credibility with most union members. When unions blame the media for the public's lack of interest I can ask the question: "Why should the news media be interested in what unions are saying, when it's pretty clear that unions can't even get their own members on side on a lot of issues, whether it's support for the NDP or issues like free trade?"

If there's one lesson unions should learn and people should learn about unions, it is that unions must increase their efforts to build a movement among their members, to educate their members, and to counter the barrage of business-oriented news media. Unions cannot rely on getting their message across through the commercial news media, they have to build their own institutions. That way, their own membership will move forward with the union leadership, and they may have much more public impact.

(Editor's Note: The revamping of the labour beat at *The Globe and Mail* sparked considerable concern among the staff and the labour community. No one from *The Globe* staff would agree to take the new "workplace" beat, and *The Globe*, faced with a barrage of criticism, backtracked on its ideas and proclaimed it was interested in labour coverage all along. A new person was hired for the beat, which was subsequently again renamed as "workplace/labour."

Lorne Slotnick left *The Globe and Mail* in November 1989 to take a position with the Southern Ontario Newspaper Guild, a union representing newspaper employees. For a copy of a letter written by Slotnick to the labour community in April 1989, see Appendix I.)

Doug Smith:

Last night Peter Desbarats asked everybody to imagine the coverage of this election without the *Toronto Star*. Coming from Winnipeg, I can do more than imagine this; I can tell you what it was like!

I find today's topic a bit intimidating. During the election I paid attention to an awful lot of things, but I didn't specifically set out to analyze the impact the labour movement was having on the media, as distinct from the various other organizations opposing the Free Trade Agreement. In the short time that I've had to prepare, I really haven't been able to do any comprehensive survey of the coverage in Winnipeg. So I'm going to go about addressing this issue in a somewhat indirect way.

To me, one of the key questions which needs examining this weekend is, "was there anything different or unusual about the way the media covered the free trade debate, compared to the way it covers other issues?" My answer is "no". It was coverage as usual, only more so. And that, perhaps, explains why the Carleton University study concluded that the coverage was fair, because they would conclude that there was nothing particularly wrong with the way issues in general are covered in the mainstream media. There may be ways in which the coverage given the free trade debate deviated from the norms of day to day journalism, as we practise it. And Lorne referred to the *Globe and Mail* coverage being somewhat hysterical at times. But I think those differences only serve to reflect the underlying realities and values of the contemporary media.

The way the media treated the labour movement was pretty much the way they usually treat it; only perhaps more so. In general labour is viewed by the media as a narrow, special interest group. When its leaders address social questions which extend beyond the immediate bread and butter issues of the day, the journalistic impulse is to tend to dismiss this as little more than rhetorical posturing. More significantly, the media have come to view the labour movement as a relic of a bygone era and one that they need not cover anymore. In Winnipeg, for example, neither daily newspaper has a full-time labour reporter. Allied with this is the belief that the interests of labour movements lie in direct opposition to the national interest. For these and other related reasons, labour leaders are treated with suspicion. In labour stories there is strong pressure put on reporters to make sure that every story is properly balanced, internally. Even if it's only in sort of a perfunctory way: "Management representatives are not available for comment, or refuse to comment." The interesting thing is to try to see whether or not those rules apply when we look at the type of coverage given business, and the type of coverage given business during the election.

Now imagine if you will that in the weeks leading up to the federal election, Bob White had threatened to call a national strike if the Conservatives weren't thrown out of office. Editorials would have roundly denounced him for jeopardizing the national interest and holding the country up for ransom. Debates would have been raised about whether the rights of union leaders should be curtailed. But there was a very similar sort of strike during that period, which you very rarely saw referred to by that name. It was a capital strike and it took place shortly after the debate. Day after day, business leaders were paraded before us, explaining how they would be forced to rethink their investment plans unless the FTA was approved. We were told the stock market was going to crash. Instead of being treated for what they were -- men who were demanding that their personal and business interests be treated as paramount -- these business leaders were treated as if they were guardians of the national welfare. And they appeared to have almost unlimited access to the media. Here I'm going to talk about the type of coverage the *Free Press* gave the business community in November, 1988.

On November 1st *The Free Press* ran a top of the page article surveying the national business community. The thrust of the article was summarized by the President of the Canadian Chamber of Commerce, who stated that free trade is absolutely essential for Canada's continued prosperity. The next page of the paper quizzed a cross-section of Winnipeg business leaders, who reached the conclusion that much of the

Canadian business community's future prospects are linked to the deal. The day after that, some of the same business leaders were back in the paper again, explaining why the trade agreement was so vital. On November 9th, two senior officials with the Canadian Manufacturer's Association warned voters about the dangers of rejecting the trade agreement. The CMA president said without the FTA, interest rates will go up and the economy will sink. It is interesting to see what's happened to interest rates since.

November 12th was a particularly good date, as *The Free Press* ran stories about how Manitoba firms target export markets. Another article was titled "Official predicts trade deal best fits Manitoba". Another article on the same date was headed, "Backlash Feared if Pact Rejected". Two days later we read about how "Global impact feared if Trade Deal dies". The whole absurd performance was climaxed when, two days before the election, George Richardson, the president of James Richardson and Sons, told how he fears isolation if the trade deal is rejected. This is not to say that *The Free Press* did not run news articles where critics of the deal were allowed to voice their concerns, but in almost every one of those cases the paper included comments and rebuttals from free trade boosters. In the last week of the campaign, the paper chose to completely ignore a statement signed by twenty-five economists from three universities in Manitoba, who felt the trade agreement was not in the long term interest of the Canadian people. Only the business community's values and interests merited special treatment.

In none of the above -cited pro-free trade articles, was there an effort to get the sort of balance and opinion the paper seems to require whenever the critics of the deal were interviewed. Some playing fields as we have seen, were simply not meant to be level.

I've also been asked to speak about the way forward. The only useful thing I can think of saying in this regard, is in pointing to some of the many obstacles that lie in the path of those who oppose the agreement. To me, one of the largest is the fact that the language of free trade, whose underlying values might be something like "the market rules", has come to dominate public discourse. From a left wing point of view we have to grapple with the fact that not only do most people apparently not view themselves as workers, with primarily class loyalties, but they seem to see themselves as consumers rather than citizens.

The effect that this sort of thing has had on language is tremendous. When Rick Salutin talks about popular movements, I can't help but think I'm in East Germany. The phrase just 'clangs' in our ears. We can't talk about popular movements. It sounds like the Popular Movement for the Liberation of Canada. The media foster this approach in a variety of ways. Look for example at the way we treat the issue of financial security for the elderly. For every *one* article that appears about reforming the pension system to make it more generous and equitable, there's likely to be a *score* of articles explaining how to invest wisely in an RRSP. In other words, we look for personal and private solutions to problems, not for public solutions to problems.

In such a culture, sacrifice and solidarity are two other words that sort of clang very uncomfortably, but they are words which I think represent the guiding strengths of any labour movement, and they're made to seem irrelevant and probably absurd. Politicians are expected to deliver good deals. If the price rises too steeply, we shop around for another model. Witness what happened in Manitoba, when the Pawley government took the lowest auto insurance rates in the country, and made them into the second lowest auto insurance rates in the country: they were turfed out of office. Those who believe that the market should not determine all values are in for a rough ride, as under free trade we enter into the heart of the beast.

I'm also a little afraid when I hear people talk about the importance of preparing for the next election. The success of the popular movements has been that they have encouraged people to think as citizens and not simply as voters. Any political movement which hopes to have any long term impact should not focus primarily on elections, because you need something to sustain yourself beyond that. Finally, you can't afford to ignore the media. Any victories will be won only by strengthening and developing the types of institutions and coalitions which came into existence to oppose the FTA.

Susan Spratt:

There is life after Mississauga. Every time I go to Toronto I remind people of that. The labour movement itself is perceived very differently in different regions of the country. The messages that come out of labour centrals in Ottawa, for instance, do not reflect the needs of the rank-and-file in certain regions.

One of the things I want to say about the impact of the labour movement in the last election is that we took a clinical approach to the media. We don't do exciting things with the media anymore. We put out our terse and cursory press release about how the Free Trade Agreement is going to affect workers: namely, jobs, jobs, jobs, and we keep saying that. The labour movement has been saying that for a long time. It is an important point, but we're doing it the wrong way. The population gets tired of hearing labour leaders getting up and talking about the loss of jobs, jobs, jobs. What the media get tired of doing, as Patrick Gossage pointed out, is coming to cover the same story all the time. When the labour movement engaged in theatre during the last election and when they engaged in rank-and-file grass roots press releases about workers in plants and how they were affected, and how their families were going to be affected: it got press coverage. There was more of an impact with the media when we approached them that way, as opposed to when the leaders or labour councils came forward to speak on behalf of their membership. It's an important lesson that we have to learn. The rank-and-file need to have more of a voice, and they are the ones who should carry the message forward, in concert with the leadership, which has has been criticized as having lost the connection with the rank-and-file in the shops and on the shop floors.

One of the problems the labour movement had in the last federal election, and in some corners I'll probably be criticized profusely for this, is that when labour speaks they seem to be speaking on behalf of or in conjunction with the NDP. If the NDP speaks, it's assumed that's what labour's position is, because of the direct partisanship of the labour movement and its direct affiliation. What happened in the last election is the NDP let the labour movement down. The labour movement was looking to the NDP to carry the banner and to fight for all the social and economic issues arising out of the FTA, and they didn't do that. So it created a real schism for the leadership of the labour movement. They did not have the social and economic alternatives to give to the members, except to say that they should be opposed to the deal and vote NDP.

Some unions, such as the CAW, had a leading role in the education and the work that they did with their membership. But as Lorne has said, the vast majority of unions did not do the educational work, and looked towards the NDP to do it with their membership, and it just didn't happen. In Manitoba, in the last election, we had a hard time getting material for the labour movement, and material on the Free Trade Agreement from the NDP. For most of us who were working in coalitions from the labour movement, who were either critical of the NDP or who felt strongly that the NDP should be writing more about the agreement in their brochures *et cetera*, we were castigated, and we were called Liberals for fighting for strategic voting. Unfortunately we're still fighting some of that sectarianism within the union movement.

As Peggy said, what the labour movement did do was, for the first time, we worked with other organization across this country. It's historic to me, being affiliated with the Confederation of Canadian Unions, that we are sitting in a group with the Canadian Labour Congress and in Manitoba with the Building Trades and Labour Centre, (which did not come across nationally in opposition to the Free Trade Agreement.) It is a must that coalitions maintain their work, are not controlled by any particular group, and work over the next four years for educational purposes.

I found personally that people in my shops that I service were more interested in getting information from the coalitions than they were in getting information from our union. At first I couldn't understand that, and then what it led me to believe is that the Catholics were interested in knowing what the Catholic Church had to say, et cetera. It wasn't just the labour leadership that was talking, they wanted to know how other people felt about the issues. Basically, they were making everyone accountable for information on the FTA.

So over the next four years, the labour movement itself has to work more closely with other people in the Pro-Canada network and in other coalitions. We did not have a good experience with the mainstream labour movement in Manitoba, and as a matter of fact they are not a part of the coalition, which is unfortunate. I hope that in the next four years that can change, because I think it is a void that needs to be filled. The other thing the labour movement needs to do over the next four years is to talk about what the alternatives are for the working class, even if that means going out on their own and coming up with policy and demands that *exceed* what the NDP has to offer. We must set up our own vision, so that opposition Parties are coming to the popular movements for what our future vision of this country is, instead of us going to them for what their vision is. It is very important that politicians start listening to us. We will be voting in the next election as we did in this election, and they need to be accountable to us and not the other way around.

***

CHAPTER FIVE

THE NEW (CORPORATE) RIGHT

Introduction:

This chapter has contributions from Frances Russell, columnist for the Winnipeg *Free Press,* Federal NDP communication critic Ian Waddell, CBC Manitoba host and journalist Leslie Hughes, and former *Globe and Mail* managing editor Geoffrey Stevens, now with *The Toronto Star.*

Frances Russell argues that as a result of the great Canadian trade debate, journalists are defiling their principles and debasing their calling. Previously, she says, there was an overall balance through a competition of biases and perspectives. But as Mel Watkins has noted, regarding the corporate agenda, "The hand of big business is not usually seen. This time we saw it with glove off, fist clenched." Ms. Russell says she used to give short shrift to conspiracy theories, but what she observed in the pre-election coverage, the campaign and now the war on the deficit, has made her wonder whether we can properly fulfil our role as a free press in a democracy.

Ian Waddell says the media fell short in their lack of reporting on the pro-business, pro-free trade groups such as the National Citizens' Coalition. This group spent $850,000 on a series of national ads attacking the NDP. He asks who they are and where their money comes from? The NCC's efforts have undermined the Election Expenses Act. He says there is a corporate agenda for Canada which includes union busting, reducing social programs and undermining national institutions such as the CBC.

Lesley Hughes feels there is a public perception that the CBC is on the left wing of politics, but their normal tendency is to assume that the government line is correct and to follow it. Despite this over-cautiousness, the CBC is seen as a threat and is in the lineup of those Canadian traditions which are to be dismantled. She says we have adopted the language of the new right, such as "privatization," "deficits," and "rationalization." But we don't know the meaning of words such as "oligopoly," because it's not on the corporate agenda for us to learn about these things, about how our "freedom" has been circumscribed and reserved for a very small, very powerful group.

Geoffrey Stevens makes the point that there's nothing new about a corporate agenda in this country: what's new is its current potency, thanks to government support in Ottawa, and the extent to which the press subscribes to it. Newspaper publishing is the most profitable industry in Canada. Of great concern is the growth of marketing strategies in newspapers. He says this compartmentalization of readers, by demographics, and writing newspapers for advertisers ultimately will drive away readers. Mr. Stevens says *Globe* publisher Roy Megarry has a personal agenda: he wants to make *The Globe* into Roy Megarry's paper rather than George Brown's *Globe*.

Frances Russell:

In a sense the free trade debate was interesting because it seemed to turn things topsy-turvy. That was my observation of both *The Globe* and the Winnipeg *Free Press* which were the only two newspapers I had access to. The op/ed pages (opinion/editorial) were the real source of information about the free trade deal. The news pages, which were supposed to be the source of information, let the public down very badly. There are a number of reasons for that, which is why I want to talk more about the role of journalism generally.

It was the celebrated everyman Mr. Dooley, who according to a biography of William Randolf Hearst, said that the mission of a modern newspaper was to comfort the afflicted and to afflict the comfortable. Tom Wicker of *The New York Times*, famous for his coverage of the Attica prison riots in 1971, said that objectivity in journalism is the cover for the defense of the status quo. I come at this question of the role of the media in the free trade debate, both from the perspective of naivete, and twenty seven years' experience. The combination of the two may sound strange to you, as it would have to me a few short months ago. But as a result of the great Canadian trade debate, I've seen my job, and I now refuse to use the word profession, from a startlingly-different perspective. A perspective that makes me profoundly uncomfortable and dismayed. The old rules don't work anymore. In my opinion, we journalists are defiling our principles and debasing our calling. We have to rewrite the style book from top to bottom.

When I started at the now-defunct *Winnipeg Tribune* in 1962, I was taught about the five w's: who, what, when, where and why. I was taught about seeking out the facts, about fairness, balance, and objectivity. When I became a columnist at the *Tribune* after a two year stint covering parliament and Queen's Park for *The Globe and Mail*, I learned about the "h" word; the how. For me as a columnist, that meant I acquired an additional responsibility. I was to make the connections, forge the links, wire the circuits if you will. I was to help people put it together. Columnists in editorial pages dealt with the "h" word, issues and opinions. There was a bias but there was also overall balance through what I would call a competition of biases and perspectives. The news pages dealt with the five "w's" -- the facts.

But it all came apart with the trade deal. Some would say all that happened was that the implicit became explicit and we've heard about the corporate agenda, and so on.

In our society money talks. As Mel Watkins said in *This Magazine*, "The hand of big business is not usually to be seen. This time we saw it with its glove off, fist clenched". Let us not forget what we learned about who actually runs the store. I used to give short shrift to conspiracy theories, but what I observed in the pre-election coverage, the campaign, and now the war on the deficit, has made me wonder whether under current circumstances we can properly fulfil our role as a free press in a democracy.

We are a free press when the elites are in conflict; when respectable authorities oppose other respectable authorities. But when the elites, political and economic, come together, no dissent exists among respectable authorities and we become as monolithic as the elites we reflect. With apologies to Andy Warhol, everybody may be famous for fifteen minutes, but a few people are famous for the equivalent of fifteen weeks, or months, while the rest of us only get our fifteen minutes if we own dogs that have puppies with two heads, or if our house burns down in a forest fire, or if we do something heroic or criminal. The media have a V.I.P. fixation and are very deferential especially to people with loads of money or their spokespersons. The trade debate was a text book study of the class consciousness of the Canadian media. Anti-deal people, mostly the fifteen minute types, had to do things to get coverage. Even then, they had trouble getting people to cover their news conferences. Pro-deal people, the fifteen hour types, just had to be on the other end of the telephone.

Even our celebrated fixation with balance and objectivity went by the boards. We ran reams of copy on business people extolling the economic nirvana: jobs and wealth that would flow from free trade, without, for the most part, bothering to get rebuttals from those other ordinary types, and least of all union bosses. But no anti-deal organizations got a word out without some recognized authority, usually from business, saying how wrong they were. As a result my paper, and I think *The Globe* too, turned tradition upside down. The op/ed pages had more balance than the news pages. The media became so polarized in fact, that even some V.I.P.'s got marginalized, just like welfare mothers, because they were swimming against the tide and opposing the deal. Bill Loewen who has built a multimillion dollar computer business in Winnipeg, is a case in point. He was dismissed because he had an axe to grind. Well, didn't Alcan and Imperial Oil? So-called "objectivity" meant you refused to go outside the safe lines; into the streets for instance, to find opposition. That would be advocacy, radical journalism. So we allowed ourselves to become, in effect, propaganda agents for the authorities, just like the media in totalitarian states.

It's very interesting. We journalists are quite comfortable in the streets of Poland or Panama or China, but not in Toronto or Winnipeg. We are quite able to see class distinctions like workers and students, and to use language like "elites" and "propaganda" the moment we set foot outside the country, but not in Vancouver or Montreal. I don't need to go through the proof, but when the Liberals soared after the television debates, the media prominently reported that the Canadian dollar plunged in stock markets. The media were eager to pick up and even amplify the Tories' use of the word "liar" against John Turner and Ed Broadbent. But have they been so eager to follow the story through, in putting into context the cutbacks in social programs and regional development programs and the harmonization of unemployment insurance and the almost certain demise of the Canadian Wheat Board?

Has free trade died and gone to heaven? You'd certainly think so from the coverage of the Wilson budget; it's as though last fall never happened. The elites coming together, cutting off respectable opposition for an "objective" media to turn to, is however just the icing on a cake that was baked some time ago. The media, Edmund Burke's celebrated fourth estate, have in the span of my twenty-seven year career, gone from being an independent enterprise in a free society, to a compartment of one or two mega corporations. As a result of the rationalization which killed my former newspaper and *The Ottawa Journal* in a single twenty-four hour period in August 1980, there is now not a single city in Canada where the two major newspaper chains compete. The concentration of media ownership and the syphoning off of competitive viewpoints has spun off another trend: the narrowing of media access. The free enterprise, competitive spirit that used to animate a diversified media, meant that a lot more Canadians got the chance to put their views across. The 1988 trade election and its aftermath showed that access is now severely limited: some might say deliberately restricted.

The day I received the invitation to this forum, I watched *The National*. I heard earlier in the day that the Pro-Canada Network was holding a news conference in Ottawa to talk to Canadians about what it thought of the first free trade budget. *The National* had a story on Solidarity in Poland, it had a story on the corruption of Jim Wright, speaker of the U.S. House of Representatives, it even had a story on the twenty-fifth anniversary of the Mustang car. But did it have a story on the Pro-Canada Network? No. In fairness to the CBC, neither did my newspaper or *The Globe*. Why is the repetition about the deficit a continuing story, when the repetition about sovereignty as it relates to the trade deal isn't?

Why is it that there can be story after story, *ad nauseum,* on runners, jumpers and weight lifters taking steroids, but free trade disappeared as an issue the day after the election? Why are we covering street demonstrations in Poland and China but ignoring the citizen's coalition which is mobilizing to ride the rails to Ottawa to protest the Wilson budget? It's part of my job to read the Federal Hansard. Where is the reporting on the link between regional development cuts and the trade deal? Between the destruction of universality and the trade deal; between the cuts to unemployment insurance and the trade deal? The links are all there; they're in Hansard, they're being made by opposition leaders who used to be, at least, after all, V.I.P.'s.

What do we mean by being "balanced?" Why do we use the phrase "labour-NDP alliance?" Why do we not also use the phrase "corporate-Conservative alliance?" Why do we use pejorative terms to discuss Canadian nationalism, like "strident" or "wrapping himself in the flag," when we use terms of power and admiration like "tough" and "determined" to describe the nationalism of a Ronald Reagan and Margaret Thatcher? Why is nationalism only a deviant trait when it exists in a Canadian? Why did we prominently display the reaction of business to polls indicating the Liberals might win, but we didn't report similar shock and horror from grape growers or grain farmers or single parents or pensioners, when it looked like the Tories would triumph? In short, why do we show obsequiousness to any element in our society, least of all the most powerful? Isn't it our democratic duty to give full opportunity for the people to speak against the King, in whatever form he takes? What happened to reporting the news? What happened to the idea that every story has two sides and that an informed electorate has a right to hear both of them, regardless of the balance of money or power? Our society is becoming increasingly fractured between haves and have-nots. Between the influential and the helpless and between those with access and those without. That makes our task much tougher. If we continue to believe that the guy at the food bank is as likely to phone the managing editor and ask for access as the bank president, we are going to mislead our audience and fall short of our democratic duty of reflecting society back to itself. We don't have to become advocates; but we at least have to take off our blinkers and take out our ear plugs. The visible will be seen and the loud will be heard. It's our job to see and hear everyone else. For starters, let's pretend we're on assignment in Lebanon or Poland or China. I think the rest is self-explanatory. And let's stop comforting the comfortable and afflicting the afflicted.

Ian Waddell:

The corporate agenda in our view has had a strong influence on the media's handling of the trade deal and other economic issues over the past couple of years - that's obvious. That doesn't mean that all Canadian media, in my view and speaking more as a local Member of Parliament, are acting in concert with some kind of multinational corporate conspiracy. I think there are other interests at work too. A lot of rank-and-file journalists are quite progressive but it's clear that most of them are not specialists in economic affairs. They are vulnerable to the publicity and expert pronouncements that come from industry and corporate think tanks. Managing editors and news directors are closely linked to local elites. If it comes down to a struggle between local interests and some big, bad foreign company, they'd often take a populist line, but the news executives still take a generally pro-business perspective and our newspapers and broadcast media reflect this. You look at the sports pages, the travel pages, the real estate pages, the business pages and their equivalents in radio and television, and you'll see this. To a large extent they exist to provide unpaid advertising for local products and services, of course with paid advertising put in as well.

So while news reporters see themselves as objective and independent, the fact is that most of their employers are strongly committed to boosting local industry, without regard to the needs of working people or the environment. This applies to the oil industry in Calgary, the forest industry in Vancouver, the fish products industry in Halifax and as Jim Winter shows in Chapter Eight, the car industry in Windsor. Like most people who oppose the free trade deal, I got the impression during the election that the news media were lined up with business, but I didn't prepare a content analysis. I'm surprised at the Fraser Institute's content analysis, published last fall. I recall once when I was a community lawyer in Vancouver, the Fraser Institute did a big study which "showed" that tenants didn't favour rent control!

The force of the issue caught a lot of people, including business media, by surprise in the campaign, and organizations like the Council of Canadians were able to seize the initiative and they had a lot of success I believe, in getting this message across. But regardless of how many Pro-Canada sources were quoted during the campaign, it's clear that the media themselves did a very poor job in reporting on the actual ground rules of the debate. The New Democrats and their allies levelled charges and various pro-business groups responded on behalf of the Tories. But one of the questions we had was "who were these pro-business groups?" The media were in a unique position to find out and they never told us the exact truth.

One example we were unable to speak about during the election, I'll speak about now, and that's the National Citizens' Coalition, which spent $850,000 dollars on a series of national ads attacking the NDP. The question is, well who the hell is the National Citizens Coalition? Where does their money come from? How much of the coalition's money comes from American-controlled companies? How much comes directly from outside Canada? How is the National Citizen's Coalition connected with other groups like the Business Council on National Issues? Are they the little brother or little sister to the Business Council on National Issues? Or the Fraser Institute? Do they share the same mailing list or the same donors' list?

It seems to me what we have here is a potentially very sinister development for Canadian political life and I believe the media slipped up in failing to expose the National Citizens' Coalition for who they actually are. There was some editorial condemnation of their "red scare" tactics. There was a feeling that perhaps it didn't hurt us that much, but one couldn't tell down the line in the crucial, final stages of the trade debate and the election, how much that unaccounted for, unaccountable media advertising hurt us.

One of the institutions that's at stake in any discussion of third party campaign advertising, is the Election Expenses Act. This act was passed in the Commons in 1974 when the New Democrats held the balance of power. Its aim is to ensure fairness in federal election spending. The Election Expenses Act requires public disclosure of any political contribution over one hundred dollars. It also imposes spending limits on parties and candidates. It regulates the allocation of television time for political advertising. The law has been called a model for other countries to follow. But I think it's developed some loopholes.

In 1985 the National Citizens Coalition won a court decision which said that any effort to restrict third party advertising during campaigns was a violation of the Charter of Rights. You should be aware that this Alberta Court of Appeals decision was influenced by the United

States decision to bar any restrictions on election spending. So now the National Citizens' Coalition can take money from anonymous donors, to advertise on behalf of the Conservatives. And to add insult to injury, as has already been brought out, they are allowed to deduct from advertising expenses for income tax purposes if it's pro-free trade advertising, but not if it's anti-free trade advertising. Talk about rewarding your friends. My party is trying very hard to close these loopholes. We're proposing amendments to the Elections Expenses Act. We just don't think its fair to have one group which can spend bushels of money and other groups like the Council of Canadians can only spend a handful. Plus we have groups like the National Citizens' Coalition, which is totally unaccountable as to who they actually are and where their money comes from.

I believe as well that there is a corporate agenda for Canada. It includes the busting of unions, reducing social programs and undermining national institutions. If we look at the example of the deficit, we see this agenda reflected in the news media. During the election, our NDP media watch reported that only the *Financial Post* and a few columnists were interested in the deficit as an issue. Obviously it was a question that would embarrass the Tories in the context of their lavish campaign promises, and business and most news media overlooked this. Compare this with the last few weeks: business is now on the warpath over the deficit and we see the media coming through for them.

I got a special report on my desk from the *Ottawa Citizen*, just before the budget. Here are the headlines: "Our Crushing Deficit -- Some dire warnings about the future"; "From Stimulant to a Millstone"; "The Way of the World"; "Thirty Billion Fantasy"; "Chaos When A Country Goes Broke". You know, we're not a third world country. "Canada dropping behind major industrial countries"; "Black Market Thriving"; "Failure to tackle the deficit with Britain and Canada"; "The Auctioning Off of Canada"; "Get set for the Axe", and so on. Well, that's pretty heavy and that's step two after free trade. The fact is, of course, that government spending is lower now as a percentage of gross national product, than it was in 1964. The deficit is lower as a percentage of the GNP than it was in 1985, but all of a sudden the deficit is a big issue.

What are the solutions? I don't have magic solutions. The news industry is mostly in the private sector and is very resistant to any steps to make it truly accountable. We've already mentioned the CBC, the cutbacks -- $140 million over five years. They're making a drastic change in the CBC. It will become more like an American network. We also have to look again, as already has been mentioned, at the question of media ownership and corporate concentration. We have to trot out the Davey Report and The Kent Commission, the role of the CBC, CRTC and so on. I note that a lot of the best newspapers like *Le*

Monde, *The Guardian*, and *Le Devoir*, are produced by small companies and they're dedicated to the craft of journalism and not just the bottom line. So perhaps we could pursue that in the context of looking at those reports on mergers and corporate concentration.

We need to encourage a diversification of media ownership. We need more and better journalists. We need more specialized reporters so that when a government tries to stampede public opinion, someone will say "just a moment". We have a deficit problem in *this* area; we have a deficit in journalistic capacity and a surplus of political and economic deceit. I suggest *that* should form the basis for the media's agenda over the next generation. And it's an urgent agenda. I feel that the whole future of this country is at stake with the Mulroney agenda. It will change dramatically the nature of this country and make it what I see as a colony, a second rate colony if you like, that won't be worth living in. And so the media have a huge role to play in the debate over that agenda, which has just started now with the deficit debate.

Lesley Hughes:

I can sort of sum up my overview of the concept of freedom of the press by recalling a consensus of journalists from 220 countries at a conference in Prague back in 1982. I remember people agreeing on this idea, that: "In capitalist countries business tells you what to print, in socialist countries the government tells you what to print and in the developing world there is no money to buy the paper to print on anyway." It was a very cynical view, but it is interesting because it was a global view at that time. It actually does have a lot to offer. The idea of freedom of the press is connected to the concept of objectivity, but I have a problem with the definition of objectivity. I can't decide what the acceptable definition of objectivity is, because I experience it in a very schizophrenic way in my work. I cannot decide, and I honestly don't think the people at this conference know for sure either, whether objectivity means balanced coverage of issues or access to justice. If you want to talk about objectivity as balanced coverage, there is a lot of doubt. But if you want to talk about it as access to justice, well, it's absurd as far as the media in Canada are concerned.

I'll just tell you a bit about the kind of work I do. I'm a co-host and interviewer of a regional, morning public affairs magazine show. I get up at 4:00 a.m., we go on the air at six. We do a combination package of live material and taped material for three hours. Our show is called "Information Radio," and I hope you are familiar with your own version in your part of the country. And I'd like to tell you how I think when I go to work and how the people that I work with think. When I go to work I do not see myself as an employee of Brian Mulroney, although in some grand cosmic scheme I am. I don't see myself as an employee of the rich taxpayers, because of course I'm told such an animal doesn't exist. The rich don't pay taxes. I see myself as an employee of The People - capital T, capital P. I guess that would be the great crowd of working taxpayers and I have, I think, a right to that given my own background, which is quite distinctly working class.

I try to lighten up the morning in terms of tone, that's the sort of emotional approach to the work that we do, but our job on the show, and we constantly remind ourselves of this, is to make the day easier to take. We try to do that by demystifying the public environment. That is, explaining to people that it is possible to know what's going on, no matter how many people there are out there trying to confuse you. We try to do this by providing reliable analysis of events and ideas, again, we try to be the local interpreters of the national scene. At work I'm constantly reminded by my colleagues and the people who decide whether or not to continue to let me work there, that we must be *objective*, meaning balanced). We must be credible, and not be seen as attached to any particular point of view. We must be non-partisan, we must not have political connections. We must be balanced on all issues.

If Winnipeg or CBC Manitoba is any example, the CBC continues to see itself, as least on the front line, as a public trust. We do not believe ourselves to be accountable to any administration or government or government Minister. But it is generally our view that we are accountable to a popular mandate, which is to reflect Canadians to themselves in a cool, clear, calm and critical light, and I wasn't even aiming for alliteration there, it just came naturally - a cool, clear, calm and critical light, no matter what the circumstances. I'll admit under pressure that we may fail to do this. But the goal is there. CBC radio ethics have great energy.

There is an unfortunate error in the country and that is the public perception that we are somehow vulnerable to the left in political life. That's sad and funny at the same time, because the truth is that our biggest temptation, particularly at times like this, is to assume that *only* the government is reasonable. To assume that government is the norm and to follow that; to follow the government line is correct. Now free trade as a case study is a brilliant example of that. I personally was very distressed by many things that I could understand about the Free Trade Agreement early in 1988. I'd say it was maybe January or February, and that was already too late. I remind you that I'm the principle interviewer of the lead public affairs show, for the region of Manitoba and Northwestern Ontario. I was viewed as somewhat hysterical and dotty on the issue.

Until the great 90 second Turner turnaround which happened, you recall, during the English language leaders' debate, at least from that point, the CBC provided more scrupulous attention. We paid far more attention, particularly to the people who were originally perceived as radical, because I think like all the other media in the country it took us too long to understand that it was the government proposal which was radical, and not the opposition to it. That was a real fight for many journalists, to communicate just that, in this country.

In the final analysis, CBC radio played a responsible role in educating people. I cannot speak for television and I wouldn't. Radio played a responsible role in educating people, but you have to remember this: that we're never supposed to take an advocacy position on anything. It's very difficult to expect us to do that given our tradition. We are supposed merely to ask the right questions of the right people at the right time, that is the important time, and I think fundamentally we did this. I think most Manitobans would tell you that anybody who listened to CBC radio in Manitoba *eventually* was aware of both the promises of the government and the specific warnings of the opposition. It's interesting because you've got kind of a schizophrenic situation here. That is, there was this sort-of Jeffersonian principle, a lot of journalists fall back on. I do myself. I'm a big believer in the Jeffersonian theory that if the public has the right information, they will do the right thing. It is not our job to tell *them* what to do, but only to give them the information with which to make the right decision, the best decision for the greatest number of people.

Well, I think in Manitoba and in Canada, people *did* finally get the information and they did reject the deal, if the statistics we have are correct, if ultimately 54% of the population voted against free trade. At the same time they re-elected the government committed to bringing it in. Probably because of unappealing alternatives, but that was not the failure of the media so much as a failure of the opposition, I'm sorry to say. Now, because the CBC is operating in increasingly right-leaning times and it doesn't take a lot of work to figure that out, despite our over-cautiousness, and this is a problem in the CBC, we're still being seen as frightening. We must be because somehow or other we appear to be in the lineup of those Canadian traditions to be dismantled. That would be very sad.

So this is the point at which the CBC meets the corporate agenda. If we're right in assuming that in the end the government agenda and the corporate agenda are the same thing. I wonder if we can even question that. It remains to be seen who will come to the defence of the CBC, since we're very likely to get a chair or champion who will not have the sympathy, or the opportunity to be a champion for us. If the CBC is sacrificed to the corporate agenda, or to the deficit or whatever else you want to call it, our loss would be very hard to fathom. Because with all its warts and its irritations, it still manages to operate largely free from commercial pressure and free of the corporate agenda in this sense: the corporate agenda is the free flow of money and power in its own direction. At least we are not part of all of that.

Just a word about language. I just want to indulge myself for one second before I finish. All of us in the media and CBC included, are responsible for allowing people to be absorbed into the new language, the new language of the new right. And this is very upsetting. It has come to my attention and I'm sure it has come to yours, that we all have this new, glib, economic vocabulary. We know what "privatize" means, it means to sell, we know what the deficit it, we know it's bad. We know what to rationalize is, that means to fire, we know what efficiency is and that means profit.

How come we don't know what an oligopoly is? Why is oligopoly a word we're not acquainted with? An oligopoly is, if I remember correctly, a word used to describe a capitalist system when it has gone too far. When it has gone past the stage of the wonderful word "free", "free market" and it has gone to the point where freedom is no longer a commodity to which everybody is entitled, but to which a very, very small group of people in power are entitled to. Why don't we know that word? I suggest to you because it's not on the corporate agenda for us to iearn it or to be throwing it around with the same familiarity and comfort that we throw around the vocabulary of the new right agenda. That's just one example. Finally, I'd like to say that if the CBC is going to survive in the environment that I've just described, it may have to become quite a bit more radical than it has been imagined to be, in the wildest dreams of Brian Mulroney.

Geoffrey Stevens:

I'll do my best to get through this as quickly as possible, which prevents me from telling you what's really happening at *The Globe and Mail* these days. I'd like to pick up a point to start by referring to Ian Waddell's thumbnail description of the corporate agenda in this country. He talks about the corporate agenda as being involved in the busting of unions, the winding down of social programs and the destruction of national institutions. That is probably true; I'm not sure that it's particularly new. There has been a corporate agenda for a great many years. What has changed is first, the potency of that corporate agenda now, thanks in part to the support, tacit or otherwise, of the sympathetic government in Ottawa.

The second thing that has changed has been the extent to which the press subscribes to the corporate agenda. There was a day, I recall, twenty-five or more years ago when I started in journalism, when at *The Globe and Mail* we did talk about a public trust and about serving readers. I haven't heard that sort of talk around the newsroom of *The Globe and Mail* for a great many years. They talk a lot more about demographics, readership characteristics; trying to make sure that the content of the newspaper coincides with the perceived interests of our readers. I'm not at all surprised that newspapers should become not only subscribers to a corporate agenda, but perhaps engines of that corporate agenda.

It's inevitable if you take a look at the profitability of newspapers. One of the really striking things over the last decade or so has been the extent to which newspaper publishing has become an extremely profitable business. Newspaper publishing is just about the most profitable industry in Canada. Last year for example, the newspaper publishing industry showed a rate of return on capital of 22.1%, which compares to 14% for broadcasting, 18% for food distribution, 10% for steel, 18% for automobile companies. The chartered banks which are considered to be immensely profitable are only at 4.6%. The publishing industry is immensely profitable and within the publishing industry, the larger units of course are the most profitable. To give a different set of comparisons, within retailing, Sears Canada last year showed a profit as percentage of revenue of 2%. Canadian Tire was 4%, George Weston 1.2%, The Oshawa Group, 1.3%, Toronto Dominion Bank 1%, but in publishing, Southam, 6%, *Toronto Star*, 8.9%, Thompson newspapers 21%, as a percentage of revenue.

These are immensely profitable businesses and it is not at all surprising that the owners and managers of newspapers should come to share and sympathize with a broader corporate agenda in the country. Another relatively recent development in the newspaper industry in this country has been multinational conglomerates. You not only have the Robert Maxwells and the Rupert Murdochs but you've got the growth, particularly in the United States, of the Thomson chain, you've got Maclean Hunter, you've got the new, rapidly growing Hollinger chain - Conrad Black with the *Daily Telegraph* and now *The Jerusalem Post,* but also many dozen, small mediocre newspapers across Canada and the United States. Hollinger either has or will be reporting a profit last year of $78 million dollars in newspaper operations, which is a lot of money.

Given the profitability of newspapers, given the development of international newspaper enterprise, it's not really at all surprising that most newspapers, like most big businesses, would support free trade. I'm not satisfied that given the existence of the corporate agenda and the support for free trade by the owners and editorial pages of newspapers, that they actually influenced the news coverage in the election campaign. However it is a real danger, and it may even be inevitable that influence will develop. My only experience in the last election campaign is that I know that at no point did I as managing editor of *The Globe and Mail* receive any sort of instructions at all in terms of coverage of free trade or the election campaign itself. I never had any comment as to whether or not there was too much or little coverage of pro-free trade side or the anti-free trade side. My only sense in monitoring the news coverage was that because the newspaper itself was strongly committed editorially to free trade, it had to make doubly sure that the news pages had at least as much or more coverage of the anti-free trade forces and arguments. And that's what we tried to do. I had no comments from anybody or criticisms from anybody at that time. On the other hand, I'm not with *The Globe and Mail* anymore, so perhaps there is a lesson in all of that.

One thing which concerns me as much or probably even more than the corporate agenda, and which is shared by newspaper owners and managers, is the evolution of marketing strategy within newspapers. Toronto has been held up as some sort of international example: "Look, you've got three separately-owned daily newspapers, all of them making money, fiercely competing in the market place." Add to that *The Financial Post*, separately owned, in part, from the others, competing frantically, it seems, and not making any money, yet it may well have established a niche and be able to turn a profit later. All this competition - isn't it a healthy newspaper business?

Well in fact, I don't think there is competition at all in the newspaper business in Toronto. If there is competition, it is not competition for readers. It's competition in part for advertisers. What has happened in Toronto is that each newspaper has decided that there is a slice of the market that it can have. *The Star* has taken on the position of your broad spectrum, mass market newspaper in the middle. It's something for everyone. *The Globe and Mail* has gone sort of to one end of *The Star*'s spectrum with a newspaper aimed at the upper income, upper education business and professional people. It overlaps to a degree with *The Star* readership and that's quite accepted by both newspapers. *The Sun* is at the other end of *The Star* spectrum, at the bottom end, competing for readers who like lots of pictures. *The Financial Post* is there for businessmen with limited attention spans.

I don't think the papers are really competing for readers. There is no sense in the newsrooms that "by God you've got to go out and beat *The Star* on this story". We say "well, that's sort of a *Star* story, they'll do that one. *The Globe* will do *this* story". Or "That's not really *our* sort of story, that's a *Sun* story". The old competition I remember certainly fostered that sort of competition. Getting the stories first and getting them in the paper, that has eased off. You really try to be more of a newspaper which is going to provide the sorts of stories your type of reader is going to want and you don't worry about getting a story that perhaps readers of other papers might want. You're not really trying to get a *Star* reader to stop buying *The Star* and switch to *The Globe and Mail*. You are trying to hold *The Globe* reader and further develop *The Globe's* type of reader.

The problem with this is that the marketing strategy defines the reader in a way that is fairly restrictive. *The Globe* reader for example, is deemed to be a person who is above a certain income level, who is a business professional at a certain level. The pressure is on in the newsroom to produce a newspaper, news stories and an approach to the news which satisfies that narrowly-defined reader. The weakness in it is that there is no such thing as a typical reader. The reader is not unidimensional. This particular businessperson making $85,000 dollars a year and driving a BMW is probably also a husband or wife, probably a parent, probably has season's tickets to some sporting team, goes to the opera or ballet regularly, uses restaurants a lot, takes vacations, is a camper, what have you, and looks to her newspaper for more than just survival information that she needs for her employment.

There is a real risk with any newspaper, when you start servicing only part of your reader's interest, that you will drive that reader into the hands of other newspapers or more likely right out of the reading of newspapers. They can't get all they want, they're not prepared to spend as much time as they need to spend to get through all those pages, to read all the ads which we are telling the advertisers everyone wants to read. I noticed that on a small level in some of the magazines which are being distributed with newspapers. I started a little informal survey asking people had they seen such and such a magazine, did you notice such and such a story? They said "Oh yes, I saw the cover". I asked did you read it? " Oh no, I haven't got time to read the magazine." The magazines come in, I don't think they get read, they get set on a coffee table and they look good and at the end of the month they get thrown out. At some point that becomes evident to advertisers, that in fact, people are not reading the magazines, they're not seeing the ads. When that happens, the magazine is in trouble.

I think there is an agenda at *The Globe and Mail* and it's an agenda which calls on the editors of the newspaper to produce the sort of newspaper which the marketing people have deemed to be the best for selling advertising. Jim Winter quotes Roy Megarry, publisher of *The Globe and Mail*, in Chapter Eight. He said: "By 1990 publishers of mass circulation daily newspapers will finally stop kidding themselves that they are in the newspaper business and admit that primarily, they are in the business of carrying advertising messages." That's true. What's wrong with the statement is that it isn't simply publishers of mass circulation daily newspapers; it's publishers of *all* newspapers including *The Globe and Mail*, which does not consider itself to be a mass circulation newspaper. It considers itself to be a targeted newspaper, but indeed, *The Globe and Mail* is in the business of carrying advertising messages; that's what it is there for.

We used to say in the old days that the newspaper existed to deliver news to readers. The cliche now is that the newspapers exist to deliver readers to advertisers. I think part of the agenda is the tailoring of the newspaper more closely to fit the perceived reader. That means eliminating a lot of things which are deemed not to be of interest to the perceived reader, or items which might actually irritate that reader.

Hence, you don't have a labour reporter because you perceive the reader not as a labouring person, but as a businessperson who doesn't want to read a lot of news about strikes. You eliminate women's beats because that's all sort of radical women's stuff and that's not what the businessman wants to read about; he's got a wife and a daughter but they are not to be considered, any more than the businesswoman.

The other part is that the publisher has a personal agenda. He wants to make *The Globe and Mail* into Roy Megarry's *Globe* rather than George Brown's *Globe*. I think that process is going on and I don't know where it will end. The personnel changes are very much tailored to meeting the agenda which the publishers put in place. Martin Goldfarb makes the point in Chapter Seven that publishers choose people who reflect their views, and that's true. If the people publishers have, don't reflect their views or don't reflect them quickly enough, the publishers will put in people who do.

***

CHAPTER SIX

FUZZY FOLKS TO THE NORTH

Introduction:

This chapter contains the opinions of practicing journalists: *The Globe's* Washington correspondent Jennifer Lewington, CBC *Media File* host Ron Adams, Truro Nova Scotia editor Hattie Dyck, and *Edmonton Journal* columnist Satya Das.

Jennifer Lewington states that there was so little coverage of the FTA in the U.S. because Americans increasingly see their world in terms of external threats, militaristic or economic. By that criterion, Canada is not a threat at all. Still, she says, Canada's concern for "sovereignty" is matched by U.S. concerns about "national security." The FTA is important in American eyes as an example and precedent for U.S. foreign economic policy and relations with the rest of the world.

Ron Adams argues that the greatest single failing our media are guilty of is that the general population's understanding of free trade didn't improve much between 1986 and 1988. This is where they failed their audiences and readership. They failed in this because there is a low level of economic literacy in the media, which leads to frivolous treatment. Also, because there is no serious, popular economic journal which might have raised awareness. In addition, there was a general lack of interest among the leftist elites until the issue focused on cultural sovereignty. So all of us failed, but the greatest failing was among the media who missed what was happening: the radical new initiative of the right, the fundamental change that has developed between the right and the business community.

Hattie Dyck says that people on the East coast were well informed by their newspapers on the FTA, and that the media did a good job of reporting the debate. That's why voters in the Maritimes turfed out the local Tories in the election.

Satya Das argues that journalists were taken in by labels in the free trade debate. He says the Conservatives in fact are not "conservative." Brian Mulroney and the PC Party have undertaken to utterly reshape the economic structure of our country: hardly a "conservative" venture.

Jennifer Lewington:

I've been asked to speak about the U.S. perspective in the free trade issue and the debate, but I thought I would tell you as someone who has to live with that perspective everyday in Washington, what part of my day involves doing. I'm on the phone quite a bit and of course asking a lot of questions of people, but I spend a good part of my day spelling my name and also having to spell the name of the newspaper. They seem to think it's some sort of global men's magazine! I've had a new iteration of that just very recently after the Free Trade Agreement. I called up the Senate Foreign Relations Committee, they are the custodians of appointments that must be approved, coming down from the Administration, for foreign ambassadors. I had been fortunate in being able to sleuth out who the new American ambassador to Canada was going to be, so I wanted to check my sources on the Senate Foreign Relations Committee. So I phoned them up one day and got the secretary and I did my usual thing with spelling my name and spelling the name of the newspaper. It turned out that she was one of Jesse Helm's assistants. Of course Jesse Helm is the most vocal and conservative member on the Foreign Relations Committee from North Carolina, and so the secretary said, "what is that, a paper from North Carolina?"

So that's what I'm up against in Washington. I thought what I would try to do is to explain where I think the Americans are coming from, not only in terms of U.S./Canada issues but in terms of their relations with the world. It has some important implications, not only for how they've dealt with the Free Trade Agreement, but how they will deal with it in the future. The American perspective is shaped by two fundamental factors. The first is that they look at themselves and the world in terms of strategic external threats. We are increasingly seeing that coming to fruition on the economic side, in terms of how they view their relationship with Japan. There is a great, increasing sense of unease about Japan's role in the world and about the kind of impact it has on the United States. Given that, as a strategic external threat to the U.S., where does Canada fit? Canada by that judgement is not a threat at *all*, and as a result, that more than anything explains why there was so little American press coverage on the Free Trade Agreement. It was not seen as a threat to the U.S.

The other fundamental factor is the role of domestic constituency pressures in the United States. They have a far more open political system than we do, and as a result, voices are heard in a couple of very major ways. One is through Congress, where each member of Congress has a very powerful voice and an extremely important role in shaping public opinion. The second forum is what I would call special interest lobbying. This is primarily business groups as one formal factor, but it is special interests in a variety of forms; not exclusively corporate. This is where you have a tremendous influence on the political system, through Congress, in the writing of legislation and in terms of access to the Administration. In both these cases you have a very strong sense of the squeaking wheel being heard.

Now how does all this fit into the Free Trade Agreement? As I've mentioned before, Canada is not a strategic threat to the United States' perspective, but it's more than that. Canada is seen as a good thing. So to the extent that there was coverage, it tended to be on the editorial pages and not in the news pages. You had *Washington Post* editorials, closer to the signing of the agreement itself, waxing on about those nice fuzzy folks to the North. That was one example of Canada not being a threat, and of being a good thing. The second thing where this plays out as being important in American eyes, is as an example and as a precedent for U.S. foreign policy and economic relations with the rest of the world. This is particularly true on issues like foreign investment, intellectual property, services and so on. This is where the U.S. has a very explicit agenda, in terms of how it wants to deal with the next GATT negotiations.

In that category you had a different kind of coverage. There you again had editorial comment, *The Wall Street Journal* being probably the most striking example of this, with absolutely strident editorials about those neo-communists to the North who were really doing such terrible things to the U.S., because they set such a bad example. In all of this Canada is less important for itself, than it is as an example to the rest of the world. The fact that Canada had foreign investment policies in the late 70's and early 80's that were seen from the American perspective as nationalistic, that was bad. But what was really bad about it was: here was an industrial country setting an example for Brazil and a whole series of other countries in the developing world, for their own foreign investment mechanisms, which would screen U.S. foreign investments.

Secondly, on the domestic constituency interests, how does that play out in terms of the Free Trade Agreement? I can cite a number of sort of sexy issues but one which is near and dear to me because I spent many an hour and a day covering it, was softwood lumber. This was the great example of U.S. special interests having a very influential effect on the political process. You had a large segment of the U.S. lumber industry unhappy with the increasing market-share of Canadian lumber exports to the U.S. Rising out of that you had, on their side, a very well-financed and well-organized lobbying activity, thanks to some highly paid lawyers in Washington. You had the lumber interests working on Congress, Congress then working on the Administration, and a complete circle being formed. So that politically, it became inevitable that a second lumber trade action would be taken against Canada.

Another example is film. This gets into cultural issues, which were very significant. If one looks at the whole process of U.S.-Canadian relations, from time to time there would be these high profile meetings between the Prime Minister and the President -- particularly in the Reagan years with Mulroney. The Canadian government would get very excited about the fact that they were having a glitzy meeting in Washington. But the main thing on Ronald Reagan's mind was films. That's all he ever wanted to talk about with Brian Mulroney, was about the funny film production policy we seemed to have. That was the first thing that happened on two separate occasions of these Reagan-Mulroney summits. There were much larger issues at stake there, but from Reagan's point of view he just wanted to have a very strong anecdotal conversation with Mulroney about how this film policy must change.

This plays out in a number of other ways in terms of how the Free Trade Agreement got covered in the United States. This lack of coverage was stunning, compared to what one was seeing in Canada. But I would like to make a sort of sub-category of the kind of coverage that did go on. That the Free Trade Deal was not a national issue in the U.S., is not to say that it wasn't discussed at all, but it tended to be a regional issue. For instance, those who were very unhappy with the Free Trade Agreement and continue to be unhappy with it, are from very clearly defined geographic areas of the country, and very clearly defined resource sectors. Lumber is a continuing one, uranium, metals, and another which will be a problem in the future is autos. So from the U.S. point of view, you would have some coverage by local media, sometimes local television stations representing these areas of the country. You would not have that bubble up to the national level unless and until there was a crisis. This is something that explains a little bit of how the American system works, that is they are very crisis-driven in anything they do in their politics.

From time to time, things like the lumber issue did become "national" in scope, because they did suddenly get the attention of the national media, *The Wall Street Journal, The New York Times, The Washington Post.* Very rarely would it get on television. Nonetheless, when an issue would bubble up, it would only be there very briefly until the crisis had subsided. Probably the most dramatic example of this came with the Canadian election itself. The Americans hardly knew there was a Canadian election until about a week after the Turner-Mulroney debate. They suddenly realized those warm, fuzzy folks to the North might do something unexpected, they might vote against the Free Trade Agreement. On the American side, the press and just the ordinary American had no sense of what the agreement was all about. But they did understand crisis and conflict and that very much drives what the coverage was all about then. And Canada was suddenly top news, and everyone was sort of running up to Canada to do stories. I found that was really quite striking, in terms of this whole notion of crisis mentality.

I want to conclude with one other aspect, because I think this has some implications for the future. That is how the two countries look at the FTA and how they will look at each other in years ahead. This has to do with national outlooks. We have talked a lot about the issues of sovereignty and nationalism in Canada and how the FTA is a symbol of that concern. What is important to note in terms of the U.S. side, is that they worry in their own way about the same issue we do, but they define it differently. We talk about *sovereignty*, they talk about *national security*. You hear them talk about a whole series of issues, such as the increase in foreign investment and the threat that poses for the country.

If you look at the debate about the loss of control over economic levers, internationally, you look at their concern over what is happening in technology, these are all issues that for Canadians have been very important for the last thirty years. But what is discussed in the Canadian context in terms of sovereignty, on the U.S. side, is done in terms of national security. What we will continue to see with the FTA is the expression of these similar kinds of themes on both sides of the border. The U.S. will be expressing it in terms of the rest of the world; anxiety about Japan, anxiety about the European community, those people out there somewhere doing something. In Canada we are worried about it more exclusively in terms of the U.S.-Canada implications of the Free Trade Agreement. I can see parallel anxieties going on there, but they will be discussed in different ways. The Americans may never discuss free trade *per se* but they will discuss it in terms of national security.

Rick Salutin:

One of the things we haven't talked about is the media coverage when the deal was actually made in October, 1987. That was an extraordinary episode that deserves attention itself. The thing was played as high drama in the media. It was very tense. It was "Would there be a deal?" The run up to it left the impression that the Americans didn't want to give us this deal. We desperately wanted it and they didn't. It was going to be very unlikely that we could get it. Then, at midnight on Saturday, suddenly the trade representatives were called back. The impression was that this was a great coup for Canada. I think given the way we know the Tories' plan, and the kind of strategy they had years before, they had a strategy and that was exactly this: to create a lot of attention, to make it look like this had to be a good deal for Canada, because the Americans didn't want to give it to us.

It seems to me, as I remember your writing on that, you covered the round in that way. That it was unlikely that we would get a deal, there was a lot of pessimism on the Canadian side. If that is not so, please correct me. I ask as a general question, because I do think that is how it was covered: one of the coalitions sent a delegation to Washington that summer which spent a week there talking to all kinds of people in Congressional committees. They came away with an absolutely clear impression that for the Americans, things were going swimmingly. They were delighted with what they were going to get, and they were doing a certain amount of grandstanding for their own purposes. I think that was their genuine attitude and not the other. When they went to a vote in the U.S. Congress, there wasn't a single opposing vote. So it seems to me that all of this talk about how reluctant the Americans were and how lucky we were to get a deal, was propaganda. It was orchestrated by whoever was the source for Canadian journalists in Washington, and journalists played right along.

Jennifer Lewington:

I beg to differ with you on part of your premise. I think that when you assess what the media meant by "Americans didn't want the deal," from my own perspective, I would say that what they didn't want was a subpart of the deal. They wanted the deal and certainly I and a lot of other people were writing that, but what they did not want very explicitly was any kind of dispute settlement resolution which would abandon or in any way do away with existing U.S. trade law. In fact, the deal doesn't, as you well know. That was a very important distinction in this. U.S. interest in the Free Trade Agreement has to be broken down between sort-of public exposure on the issue, and private agendas. In terms of the public exposure on it: nothing was very observable in any serious way, throughout most of the negotiations, from the American side. When it did become more obvious was in the last five weeks before that October 1987 date. That's when you started to get American interest, both in terms of the media and in terms of the attention it got within the Administration and on Capitol Hill.

The other point in all of this is that ten days before the Canadians walked out, which I would argue, and we wrote at the time, was very much a staged event, I had written a story with my colleague Chris Waddell. I was absolutely convinced that this deal was going to happen. I had a discussion with the desk at *The Globe* about it, and they kept saying "Well, what proof do you have?" I only had a sort of sensitivity about it, having covered the issue for about four years. There was a great sense of inevitability about it. My prognostication powers were put to the test, because the Canadians walked out and that created the high drama and that was the falseness of what you saw. As far as the Americans were concerned, they very much wanted the deal and they didn't say very much publicly because they *did* want the deal. They knew that as soon as somebody opened their mouth in Washington, it would be seen negatively or it would be interpreted negatively in Canada. To the extent that they had a strategy, the strategy was that silence was more politically effective for them, because nothing they could say in terms of saying it is a good deal, would be very convincing to a Canadian audience.

As far as Washington is concerned, the only time in which there was any danger of the FTA not going ahead was when that surprising early vote came. This was a vote in about 1986, in which Congress had to give a green light to launch the negotiations from the U.S. side. There, once again, the issue was not free trade with Canada, good or bad. It was, "How do we hit the Administration over the head with the fact that we in Congress do not like what has happened to the U.S. trade deficit, and we don't like what's happening in terms of U.S. trade policy. We will use the issue of giving the green light to the free trade talks as a club with which to beat the Administration and embarrass them on a whole series of issues, of which lumber is one subset." That was the only time there was any sort of mini-crisis about what was going to happen to the U.S. interest in having the deal.

Ron Adams:

The degree of general understanding among the population of what free trade really was all about didn't improve much between 1986 and 1988. It's distressing enough that it didn't improve much in that time; it's equally distressing to me that it was so low in 1986. We've been hearing a lot and talking a lot in these pages about the coverage of the free trade issue during the last election campaign, and that to me points the finger directly at the greatest blunder, and the greatest single failing our media in this country are guilty of: the degree to which they failed their audiences and their readership.

The modern free trade debate began in this country around 1967, when the Ontario Economic Council published a piece advocating and setting out the case for free trade, and it was picked up again in the early 80's. It was in a hotel meeting room in Vancouver, just after Labour Day in 1983, when Donald Macdonald opened the economic Royal Commission hearings, and free trade began to be talked about there. I submit that you can draw a direct line from that, to the signing of the agreement just after Christmas in 1987-88.

By the time 1986 had rolled around, the fact that so few people in the country were aware of the issue, or understood it at all, points to one of the greatest failings of our media. We failed to recognize what was at work here. What was building was a radical, new initiative that doesn't really bear an awful lot of resemblance to 1911 and other cases. This time it was also linked with a kind of a social movement. What some people call Thatcherism, other people call the imported Reagan revolution. This time there was real impetus behind this; it was various people in various regions of the country who were speaking out about it. I'm skipping over all kinds of time periods and sign posts here, but there were a number of reasons why we failed in this, and I just want to mention two or three to try to stimulate some discussion.

First of all, there is a general low level of economic literacy among our media. There are very few specialists and this became clear to me in the period between 1983 and 1985 or so, when I was having great difficulty waking editors up about free trade. They never heard of it, it wasn't going on anywhere that they knew of, so they couldn't care less about it. It wasn't until it was launched as a government initiative and it moved into Ottawa and became an Ottawa parliamentary press gallery story, in other words a sports story, complete with tape, we had film at eleven on this finally, that it began to make some news. We had the usual question period sound bites. Before that, we ignored this story.

Another reason is that there isn't in this country any serious, popular, economic journal. Nothing that could have taken this issue, identified it early and raised the level of awareness. At least among the people who read other journals. We don't have that, and that's another thing to regret. Another thing is the general lack of interest among what I think of as the elites of the left. The people who came together later in what Rick Salutin calls "the popular movement". Anything that was about trade, was considered by most of those people as really a pretty boring and trashy issue. Those people got excited about this when it became an issue of cultural sovereignty: something they could understand.

I think all of us failed. The greatest failing was among the media, my colleagues and I, but we all failed and the people who, in the end, found themselves fighting so hard to prevent this thing failed as well. They didn't recognize that it was part and parcel of a fundamental change in the relationship between the right and the business community in this country. Like it or not, that was happening and we missed it.

Hattie Dyck:

I am the Truro Bureau Chief of *The Chronicle Herald* in Nova Scotia but I am also a reporter who is encouraged to seek out the real content of the free trade deal and this was very important for media people to do during this time. I thank the Council of Canadians for asking us here from the Maritimes, because the free trade deal will affect us very, very greatly, in the extremities of Canada.

May I first say my understanding of why we are here this weekend is to take a look at the media's involvement in the free trade debate, in the knowledge that this debate isn't over. The big issue of definition of a subsidy is yet to be dealt with; and so is the fallout from the signing of this deal, be it good or bad. But I hope we will not waste our time in non-constructive criticism that will serve no useful purpose today or in the future. If we did, we would be wasting a weekend that all of us need, to recharge our resources to deal with the effect of this historic agreement.

To give you my opinion and the opinion of my employer, *The Chronicle Herald* newspaper, journalists do have a social responsibility; one that we carried out with distinction during the free trade debate and one that we are still carrying out after it has been signed. I brought the goods to prove it. Here's what our newspaper published on free trade: several thick folders worth.

We can honestly say that if Nova Scotians didn't know about the Free Trade Agreement between the United States and Canada, it's not because we didn't inform them. And I believe they did. When you look at the results of the election in our province, we sent six Liberals and five Tories to Ottawa. One heavyweight Conservative went down, and one old timer who had what was considered a safe seat for years. In the Atlantic provinces we sent twenty Liberals and twelve P.C.'s to Ottawa. Our people received the message, they digested it and they voted accordingly. The people of the Atlantic provinces will in future be seen as prophets not of doom and gloom, as we were accused, but as against a deal that will strike a blow at our rural economy.

When you look across Canada you see 54% of Canadians voted against free trade, so I believe the media did a good job in representing that agreement for what it really is. This despite the fact that the Conservative government used our money to launch a huge advertising campaign to sell us only on the merits of free trade; they didn't have to be fair; they didn't have to be factual; they took our tax money and sold us only on the merits. They told us about the other side of the story. And this despite the fact that Thomas Aquino and his crew from the Business Council on National Issues (BCNI) spent millions more to support it, and I understand that they are going to be able to write these expenses off and the Council of Canadians' supporters cannot.

I congratulate Peter Desbarats on his excellent paper in Chapter One, in which he set the tone for this meeting. I also invite him and those who study the media field to take a hard look at the good job that some of the smaller newspapers did. Mind you Halifax isn't small, it's a major city and we cover a province of resource workers: farmers, fishermen, miners, the backbone of this Canadian nation. We are a major newspaper and we do have a lot of influence and this must not be overlooked in the West. As I've told my husband for years, and he's from Ontario, the world doesn't end at the Ontario border. I suggest the Council of Canadians and all other groups that have concerns concentrate in the future on getting that message out all across Canada. I realize that it's important here in the two big provinces, Ontario and Quebec, but it's probably more important in the extremities, because we will be hurt the most.

I would like to quickly touch on some of the points Jim Winter makes in Chapter Eight. I find it unfair to categorically say the media sided with business in favour of free trade. Canada is still a country where small business dominates. Our newspaper is a small business. It's a privately owned business; we don't own a shipyard, we're not looking for contracts; we don't have to be government licensed; we don't owe anything to any government. And even if we were pro-business for advertising reasons, as Winter infers in Chapter Eight when he lumps all media together, wouldn't we be a bit stupid to cut our own throats by allowing the very life blood of our existence to go down the tube? No one will disagree that we must curb the escalation of multinational media, but this is not something to be done over night. We have very pressing issues that we must deal with now if we want to keep our small business viable; if we want to keep our jobs under this free trade deal.

If I understand the issue of free trade correctly, it is an agreement that gives domination to the multinationals as opposed to small business. That is one reason why all employees and the unions they represent, must be alerted to the changes that take place when we enter the leaner and meaner free market system. Not that we can stop change, free trade or not, and not that we would even want to stop change. But it has been proven that we can't expect politicians to look out for our small businesses, to look out for our welfare, or to look out for our jobs. Collectively we'd better be prepared to do that for ourselves, or we really are dreaming in colour.

Our publisher Mr. Graham Dennis said at the beginning of the free trade debate in 1986, that you don't sell newspapers to the unemployed.

What has to happen is a collective cooperative effort. We don't have time to berate one another and let's face it; it doesn't take much intelligence to find fault with the media, the NDP, the labour unions and yes, even the Council of Canadians. We have the best health care system in the world we have to worry about. My daughter just had a major eight hour operation. Can you imagine what that would cost if she had lived in the United States, instead of Canada? Believe me, I'll never again complain about paying health services tax.

Down in the land of the far East where I live we have full communities headed for the unemployment insurance office, because of fish plant closures. We have jobs at risk in the port of Halifax over lost subsidies; we have seven hundred million dollars on the line. All our regional development programs are at risk and so are the transfer payments. So it's a time for cooperative effort to stop this destruction of our economy and the destruction of our standard of living. We have to protect our small businesses, our farmers, our fishermen, our everyday livelihood and if we fail we all know who pays the price and we all know how we'll pay it.

Satya Das:

I can't offer any great academic insights, but I would like to offer observations from the vantage point of one of the two editorial boards in the country that right up to election day wrote editorials against the Free Trade Agreement.

In regard to journalistic responsibility on the editorial page and in the newspaper in general, I would see our role as promoting the democracy of ideas. Unfortunately in this case, once one got to the marketplace, there weren't that many ideas to choose from.

There were quite broad, conspicuous thoughts in support of free trade, that almost verged on boosterism; and then the various positions against free trade, which ranged from the thoughtful to the emotional. But at times, reporters' national coverage of free trade was like watching a debate between George Babbitt and Horatius at the Bridge, so there's no wonder there's a good deal of confusion in the ranks. But the confusion also arose from fundamental misperceptions of things that were going on.

First of all, our journalists were taken in too easily by labels. They heard the Conservative Party call itself "Conservative" and failed to understand that it was in fact a radical party, because gauging the parties on how committed they are to the process of change, there is no doubt that Brian Mulroney and the Progressive Conservatives undertook to utterly reshape the economic structure of the country.

So once one heard the reassuring word "Conservative," and all that it implies: careful stewardship of the status quo; being extremely careful in moving away from what Canada is worth; and what it was built upon, that was the first misleading concept. Next was the equation of free trade with the Canada-U.S. Free Trade Agreement, which are entirely different things.

Free trade in principle is almost like motherhood; no one can disagree with it, but as the many futile years of GATT negotiation show, to try to achieve true free trade is a slow and laborious process and in fact, it hasn't been achieved anywhere. And in going through the Free Trade Agreement, one finds that it's really a prime example of managed trade. So starting from those two broad, if not false premises, journalistic coverage in our area took off in certain directions.

At *The Edmonton Journal* we tried to encourage any journalists who are covering free trade to read the agreement, unlike our Minister of International Trade. But to read it and understand it are two quite different things, because it is a very, very complex thing. And it's certainly not suited to twenty-five word encapsulations. The electronic media really weren't much better; the CBC radio morning program for instance. One had so-called pro- free traders coming out and saying that unless we have free trade all our best talent will move South, and no one thought about asking about the U.S. immigration laws. So those sorts of items were allowed to go on. In terms of covering it, we were far too swayed by the good-bad, black-white arguments and didn't spend enough time on the grey areas. When we tried to expose the grey areas in certain editorials, we were variously accused of being for free trade, against free trade, and somewhere in the middle.

In trying to take an analytical approach, issue by issue, we were very often in the middle because in principle we supported free trade, though we didn't like this agreement at all and rejected it. The good-bad tendency really was expressed in the electronic media, but in our part of Canada we really did not see very much thoughtful analysis at all. What we really lacked was independent critical examination by the media. We had some of it on the editorial page, but again it was from a limited perspective, like blind people trying to feel our way through the agreement, all the while being cluttered with a barrage of propaganda. It said "no don't look at this specifically," or "no don't look at that specifically," and every time we tried to offer a serious argument there was all sorts of white noise trying to block it out.

We did spend a lot of time fighting off those who were attacking our editorial position, because there were strong vested interests, but we did maintain it to the end, and our publisher stuck with us. It's a matter of reality that in a Conservative province which thinks free trade and a continental energy policy are wonderful, that ours was not a viable position. But it really was based on an analysis of the document, and not on doctrinaire, emotional opposition to the concept of free trade.

The other problem we had was that we had too much focus on the immediate, and what's happening now and what the effect will be tomorrow. We really didn't stop to think of the long term implications. We didn't stop to think that ten years from now it's not the United States but Europe and Japan that really are going to be the leaders of the world economy, and that we risk barricading ourselves behind the fortress of North America and thereby undermining our position. We didn't really think about the social implications ten years down the road, and I think as Peter Desbarats pointed out in Chapter One, the Opposition Parties didn't come up with a coherent alternative. Mulroney said that trade with the United States was a lottery and we're going to get the grand prize if we go with the FTA. Nobody really asked if we have to play the lottery at all, and what effect it would have on our standard of living? If we are to maintain a strong trading position, what are the steps we have to take? Can we achieve our goals through the GATT? Where should we go in trying to secure multilateral negotiations? These are questions we should have asked, that we didn't.

***

CHAPTER SEVEN

THAT CRUCIAL MIDDLE GROUND

Introduction:

Liberal Party pollster Martin Goldfarb opens this chapter with a defense of Canadian culture, and the role of polling. This is followed by questions from the audience, and by a panel on the same topic. Panel participants are: Alan Frizzell, a pollster and professor of journalism from Carleton University, NDP "spin doctor" Robin Sears, and Doug Baer, professor of sociology at the University of Western Ontario.

Martin Goldfarb argues that the media are the last bastion of Canadian identity, and he fears losing that identity through media concentration and cost efficiencies. The media trusts should be broken up. Corporate Canada *isn't* neutral, and laid its cards on the table during the free trade election. Pollsters, according to Mr. Goldfarb, interpret the issues for journalists and the public. They occupy the crucial middle ground between politicians, media and public.

Alan Frizzell says that if there ever was an example of ostrich politics, it's what has been happening at this conference. He is irritated about some of the things in Chapter Six, such as: 54% of Canadians voted against free trade. Dr. Frizzell says that's absurd; it's simply not true. When you look at the evidence from three independent national studies, everyone found this wasn't a free trade election. Everyone. Free trade is a highly complex issue, and people don't make their electoral decisions based on highly complex issues. They make them up on a constellation of moods and ideas, which includes style of leadership. Free trade was an important issue in the election, but he says we mustn't take issues out of the context of their meaning in an election outcome.

Robin Sears says the NDP mounted a very late effort in the election campaign to put the FTA into the context of issues which people usually vote on, such as medicare, cultural sovereignty, *et cetera*. As far as pollsters are concerned, there are a number of questions that Martin Goldfarb didn't address, such as whether a pollster should serve a partisan political client and a media client in the same election. As a broadcasting client, what do you do if you know the data you've been given are bad, and yet you paid $80,000 for the study and you have reserved the first five minutes of the newscast or the front page of the paper? This actually happened in the last election, and the news organization involved just ran the material and hoped no one would notice. And nobody did.

Doug Baer argues that there is a major structural problem in Canadian democracy: the will of the majority of the people doesn't translate into political power. This happened in Saskatchewan not too long ago, and when Joe Clark came to power in 1979, so it's not just one election. And, says Dr. Baer, this is a problem which has not really been dealt with by the press. Rather than majority vote determining who gets elected, it's a matter of whether or not they made it into power. There is no attack on the legitimacy of governments which do not have majority approval. People say, "Well, they won using the rules of the game. Let's not concern ourselves with the rules." Hence, there is a declining degree of political legitimacy in society: people are less and less inclined to believe that the political system reflects their will, and it doesn't. So, he says, what we have is an undemocratic process.

Martin Goldfarb:

The media are part of the heart of our society. As we move to a number of large trading blocks in the world, culture, and how we convey it, will be the only way of maintaining national identity. As we harmonize our economies into an economic marriage, the way the news portrays local, regional, and national events and issues will define and preserve that culture.

Each medium has its own role to play in society. The morals of society are expressed daily on television; it's an emotional medium. Newspapers function as the conscience of the nation; it's in print, it's there to see. In essence, newspapers are a mirror of yourself; you read about yourself everyday. You read about how you think everyday; you cry and laugh on the same page. Radio keeps us in touch with urgent events and pacifies our anxieties. How each of these media are owned plays an important role in how they perform their cultural role.

There are three economic trading blocs in the western world. There is the Western European common market, the North American market, and the Pacific Rim market, dominated by Japan. It's the emergence of these trading blocs over the last ten years that really precipitated the drive in Canada towards free trade.

There is a fourth market that we don't talk about; it's the Eastern European bloc. In real terms Western Europe needs it desperately and understands it better than anybody else, because the Eastern bloc has resources, cheap labour and a huge untapped consumer market desperate for consumer goods. Western Europe has a need for these resources; a need for all of this cheap labour, and it has an enormous capacity to produce consumer goods. It wants to produce those consumer goods for its own wealth. Our problem in North America is to figure out how we can play a role in the European commercial theatre. I see Western Europe beginning to break with American interests because the real economic opportunity for them is in Eastern Europe. I see it with many of our clients who are beginning to build plants in Eastern Europe: automotive companies, other technical companies and many consumer goods companies. We will slowly drift towards the Pacific Rim and free trade will drive us there. In real terms, for all the talk about the Pacific, it's very unnatural for us. In cultural terms, we are not comfortable with Pacific values. We struggle every time we deal with the Pacific; it's very natural for us to look at the Atlantic.

What does this have to do with the media and the role of ownership? In this country, a great deal. As we harmonize our economies, and as Europe becomes tougher for us, even tougher than it is today, and as Europe becomes tougher for the Americans, then our only hope is with the United States. And the harmonization of our economies will happen faster and faster and more aggressively than we had thought. In that sense, reduction of tariffs over time will happen, citizens will move across borders as if they do not exist. The media, as an art form which invades the culture of this country, will have an enormous role to play in maintaining a Canadian perspective on Canadian identity. There won't be a Canadian business ethic: there will be a North American one.

The evolution of media and how they are owned in our society will determine the values and morays, religious heritage and political structure, of our way of life. The media tell the story of what we are and what we tell ourselves about who we are. In essence, the media are our mirror; a reflection of what we are. As I said before, we laugh and cry in the same page and in the same thirty minute program, and if it's really effective: in the same thirty second commercial. Especially now that we have free trade with the United States, we must be committed to preserving Canadian media, because this is all that can preserve a Canadian identity. My fear is that through concentration of the media, we will lose local or regional coverage of major events, because of the pressure from national institutions, to reduce costs. And it is through this local coverage of national events that we express the regions which are the culture of Canada. I am quite concerned that this responsibility that the media have is the last bastion that can really maintain Canadian identity.

In an economic sense, even if we operate in Canada and even if we succeed in the Free Trade Agreement, the reality is, language will harmonize; institutions will harmonize. I'm not here to debate whether free trade was good or not; let's assume that it's here and let's assume that it will be good. Even last week or the week before last, we had eight major accounting companies in the country. There was one Canadian name; it's gone now. If there are no Canadian symbols, whether it be accounting firms, airlines, gas companies, if you only see American or other symbols, with no Canadian symbols, then what kind of Canadian identity will we have?

It seems to me that the media have an enormous responsibility to keep this country Canadian. I would also argue that the C.R.T.C. should allow for more and more independent television and radio stations, and we should let them be independent and not let them join or sell out to conglomerates. I think it's through the loss of local identity over time, that we will lose a little bit of national identity and that will be our biggest problem. It's not just elections that I'm concerned about. It's how we cover events and subjects like the environment, crime, drug abuse, I could go on and on. Yes, there are national perspectives to all of these, but there are local Canadian perspectives in different regions which have a different impact on how citizens respond. My concern is that the local press is becoming more national, and the national press will harmonize and become more like the American press.

I get calls to go to the Washington Press Institute to talk about the role of the press in elections. There is *no* Canadian institution that talks about what kind of press we should have in Canada; or teaches press people how to run Canadian newspapers. Our orientation is Washington; it's *not* Ottawa. All these things make me nervous. The Davey Senate report in 1970 touched on some of them, but it saw the problem in economic and nationalistic terms. I see the problem in the context of cultural survival.

In Europe, for example, because of 1992 and the E.E.C., there are small museums opening up at an enormous rate. This is an attempt to preserve local identity, this independent cultural identity, and I believe you will see this in the media as well. The media have a new responsibility. A responsibility to look within, to envision more local interpretations. What's happening in the United Kingdom is an attempt to preserve cultural identity; not just to restrict ownership, because preserving cultural identity in light of what's going to happen in 1992.

I was asked to talk about media objectivity and freedom of the press. I have no problem with freedom of the press, I think the press is free and that for the most part, the individuals who work for this press are independent and objective. But the owners select people to cover events who have points of view which mirror their own. So what you end up getting is individuals who cover the editorial point of view which the major shareholders want. In that sense, there is a problem and we really have to worry about that; I don't know what the solution is, but it is an issue.

In the next election, corporate Canada is going to face a different electorate. When Corporate Canada weighed in with all of its energy on one side of the free trade debate, it signalled for the first time, that it was prepared to provide its muscle to help a government get elected. My perspective is that the marketplace has changed, and it will not go back. Corporate Canada now cannot stand back and say that it is neutral again. Corporate Canada *isn't* neutral and it will now have to suffer the consequences, and I believe there will be consequences. They have chosen a position that is irrevocable and the average citizen will now stand back and say: "We'll do what's in *our* best interest, you do what's in *your* best interest," and there will be conflict here - conflict like you haven't seen before. I don't think Corporate Canada is going to get the ear of the average citizen when it comes to what Corporate Canada thinks: it just won't get the attention of the average citizen.

I was also asked to talk for a moment about polling and how it affects the media. Many of you know how I feel about that. I have written about it in a book with Tom Axworthy, and I wrote a chapter on it, so I'll only cover a couple of paragraphs on that. Polling has changed the nature of politics in this country. I'm not saying it's for good or bad, but it has changed the nature of it. It's also changed the nature of political issue management and the way we run a campaign. A lot of people resent me for saying that and a lot of people wrote nasty articles about it. But the reality is there when you reflect deeply about what pollsters do and what roles we play in the evolution of our society, and what ethics pollsters uphold. Because of this general lack of reflection, pollsters are seen as a fair lot, simultaneously revered and reviled, praised and blamed, mostly misunderstood by both their clients and the public.

For more than one hundred years politicians have looked at the print media as a source of insight. Journalists were supposed to keep an ear to the ground, supposed to sense, identify, express, interpret feelings, thoughts and desires of both average and extraordinary people. Journalists occupy the critical middle ground between the public and the politicians, who in turn recognize their potential to read the public mood. Journalists were the public pulse takers who could shape foreign content and public opinion. Thus, they were a vital and significant factor in the political equilibrium of society. Things have changed irrevocably. Pollsters have assumed a lot of the ground that was traditionally held by journalist,s and as a consequence, have assumed an important role in the political framework of our society. Print and electronic journalists today are often simply reporters. They tell us what has happened; they rarely tell us why. Journalists doubt their own ability to understand and express the public mood and public opinion. They speak cautiously about the news of the so-called "people on the street," information gathered through haphazard interviews.

Pollsters are not a source of information on the nature of public opinion because they ask questions and collect answers in an organized way, but because they gather information in a systematic fashion. They go beyond the simple collection of data, and tell us what this information really means. The result of this innovation has been phenomenal.

When you really analyze it in the perspective of the last ten or fifteen years, the public recognizes that journalists give us only the who, what, when, where, and they turn to pollsters to find out the why. Journalists understand it and that's why they keep reporting the polling numbers and why people keep saying it's only the numbers that count. It's easy to collect numbers. But it doesn't take a great deal of statistical talent to figure out how to dial random numbers on a telephone. You simply start with any number you want, in the telephone book, and choose every seventh or ninth number and keep going and chances are you're going to get a pretty good sample.

At election time, journalists describe the contents of the political leaders' speeches. But the pollsters are the ones who interpret the issues, tell us in effect, what the score card is. In fact, pollsters have become journalists. But journalists *must* come to grips with the basics of polling and so many journalists I have talked to really don't understand the difference, for example, between reliability and validity. It's *fundamental* if you're going to look at the questions; it's *fundamental* if you're going to look at how data are presented and organized, and what they really mean. The journalism schools have got to come to grips with polling as a core subject in reporting. Not just political reporting, but any reporting on economic matters, consumer behaviour, attitudinal structures. These are not all things that we had to study in the last fifteen years.

Newspapers and the electronic media consult us when they commission polls, to spell out the results of research.

To paraphrase McLuhan, the pollster has become the messenger, the newspaper is simply the delivery system. Pollsters occupy the crucial middle ground amidst the media, politician and public. We form the main link. This is a totally new development. It has transformed the media's perception and understanding of their own role in society. We shape self-awareness and comprehension of politicians, and in my mind this has redefined how society formulates attitudes and behaviour as voters and as consumers.

Pollsters possess an almost mythical mystique. Like alchemists, they are frequently seen as magical figures who share some mysterious secret. But in reality what we simply do is what my mother did in her grocery store. She didn't need pollsters, she knew every customer. She knew them by name, but in a mass society we need people who can organize data, understand, interpret and reflect on them and their historic consequences. Because in my mind, and from an anthropological perspective, culture is our *raison d'etre*.

Audience:

You seem to accept the harmonization of our country with the United States as a foregone conclusion. I think the consensus of the people here is that we are going to fight it tooth and nail.

Goldfarb:

I think that consensus is probably accurate. But when I say harmonization of our economy, it's hard for me to understand how you're going to fight when you're going to function in the North American economic environment. Whether you function from Windsor or Toronto or from Buffalo or Tennessee or Dallas doesn't matter, because you're going to market to the North American perspective. You're not going to market to Canada. You're not going to market to the United States, you're going to market to the North American perspective.

Audience:

Could you comment on *The Globe* editorial that suggested CBC stations should be shut down where private stations are providing local services. Does this speak to your problems of local identity and the regional roots of national identity?

Goldfarb:

Small towns make a country. Small cities make a country. Local identity is what culture is made of. If you went to any society that isn't as sophisticated as ours, the first place you'd go to is the small town, to understand the structure and how it works. You work your way out from the little hamlet to the larger cities. That's how you understand how a culture functions. It's the same thing in our society. Destroy local media and local interpretation of national events, and you destroy culture. The CBC has a unique role our country. It is the only place you have local interpretation of national events. It's a string that helps this country hang together and it's such a fine string, and it's so easy to tear.

Catherine Morrison:

Business competitiveness and ideological differences aside, is there any difference between what Martin Goldfarb does and what Alan Gregg does?

Goldfarb:

I think so. I think we're anthropologists and Alan is really a political scientist. We do look at data in different ways. We even organize the way we collect data in different ways. I have enormous respect for Alan, we've been political rivals but good friends. So yes, we have a different perspective. I would say that there is a role for both. We may come out the same way in the end, our strategies may even be identical but we approach it from a different perspective. When I was teaching I used to use this example: if you were sitting on the twentieth floor and a body came floating by your window, if you were a sociologist you would see it as a suicide, if you were a mortician you would see it as a client, if you were a medical doctor you might see it as a patient. Depending on your perspective, you see the absolute same event in a different way.

I approach political behaviour in an anthropological way: how it fits our culture and our way of life, which is a different perspective than Alan Gregg has. In our commercial research, we may do research for the Ford Motor Company, but I approach cars as an artifact of the culture. The benefits in any culture are the same, whether you're driving a car in Spain or in Costa Rica - you want the same benefit. But the artifact has a different role in each culture. So we market artifacts in the same way an archaeologist discovers artifacts and interprets their impact on society. That's our whole approach to the marketplace.

Ian Waddell:

I'm glad to hear about your anthropological approach. I always thought the difference between you and Alan Gregg was that he manipulated data for the Conservative party and you manipulated data for the Liberal party. I've learned something today.

Goldfarb:

You just want to be a pragmatist, that's all.

Audience:

In the last election, there were many polls, a polling feast. And the public announcement of polls tends to create a bandwagon effect or at least induces people to jump on a winning bandwagon. I'd just like to hear you comment.

Goldfarb:

With regard to the 'bandwagon' effect, you have to decide whether or not you trust citizens with information. I don't think anybody should have information that every citizen isn't entitled to. If the politicians are entitled to information, the citizens are entitled to it. If a writer writes and has influence by his or her interpretation of events, then the citizen is entitled not only to read the writer, but he or she is entitled to find out where the writer got that information.

I also would argue this: there is some evidence that there is an impact if there is a whole series of polls saying the same thing. It has to come two to three weeks before the vote. If you publish a poll three, four or five days before the vote, if the polling had an impact on how people were going to vote, the polls could *never* be accurate, because they would influence enough people to cause a deviation from the numbers you publish. So I would argue that doesn't happen. We have done both experiments, and our experience has been that an individual poll does not significantly impact on voting behaviour. A series of polls will suggest there is a mood in the country but I don't think it's just the polls that suggest that mood. It's all the other events that take place and are reported in the media, which contribute to that mood.

Maude Barlow:

One of the first very thoughtful analyses that I read of the Free Trade Agreement and what the polls were telling us, was by Martin Goldfarb. He said something that I have never seen or heard anywhere since. He said that people tend to hold different *values* on different sides of the issue. He said those who are not in favour of this agreement care about economic issues, but they also care about social issues. They care about issues of poverty, equality, social justice and culture. He said that when you look at the value system of the people who tend to be pro-free trade, it comes down to a bottom line figure. Values. It was a very important analysis for him to have made, and for us to have received. I'd ask Martin to continue making these thoughtful analyses.

Alan Frizzell:

I hope that I don't offend anyone's sensibilities, but I think that if I were a Tory and a supporter of free trade, I would leave this conference with a sombre expression, turn the corner into the main street out there, jump up in the air, click my heels and laugh my head off. If there ever was an example of ostrich politics, it's what has been happening at these meetings.

The fact is that there has been a lot of work done on what happened during the election. There have been three national studies on the vote, there have been two national studies on the media and media coverage. The studies have been comprehensive; maybe not great, but comprehensive. The other thing is the evidence about free trade and what it meant in the election, which has been largely ignored. I think you ignore evidence at your peril. I think you're taking a stand on issues, ignoring the evidence, that's even more silly. You must go beyond looking at the polling data on free trade, because it was all silly questions about whether you oppose or favour the free trade deal, and there are much more important questions to ask. If one looks at the data, they happen not to be very good. But they were collected at considerable cost to the Canadian taxpayers, by the Tories, ostensively through the Department of External Affairs. But in fact it was the P.M.O. that was using the data. And there has been very little change in the data since. Prior to the agreement, it was very different; it was something like a 72% approval rating for free trade. But it wasn't free trade, it was *negotiating* free trade. Since we've been collecting data, the country has stayed the same: roughly in balance between those opposing and in favour.

What is slightly more work from a data analysis point of view is that in 1986 the first question asked was: "Do you understand enough about the free trade deal to make a comment on it or to have an informed opinion?". Fifty% of the population said no. That was in 1986. During the election the same question was asked in an election poll. Guess what - 50% said no. So there has been absolutely no change. It's quite understandable, frankly, because it is a highly complex issue and people don't make their electoral decisions on highly complex issues. They make them up on a constellation of moods and ideas, which includes style of leadership. They don't make them on a specific issue.

It irritates me to hear some of the things that I have, for example, that 54% of Canadians voted against free trade. That's absurd; it's simply not true. When you look at how people make their voting decisions, and you look at the evidence from three independent national studies, everyone found this was not a free trade election. Everyone. All the data are remarkably similar in what they show. What does that lead us to assume? That one, there is a softness in the population about free trade, because they don't know what it is about; and two, that it didn't impinge in a decisive way on the last election, although it was an important issue. One of things, that we're going to have to look at, frankly, is did free trade influence voters, or did a voting decision influence your views on free trade? I'm coming increasingly to the latter view, that because of the softness of the issue, it was one's partisan disposition that influenced one's attitude on free trade, and *not* the other way around.

You know free trade *was* the issue in this election, there's no doubt about that. The last election, the issue was unemployment. But people didn't have a clue about unemployment as an issue, or have any solutions to it. What we've tended to do here is to take the issue out of the context of its meaning in an electoral outcome. The fact that some people are upset about the issue, or support it in a very emphatic way is not the point. But once you get beyond that and you start to say this issue is crucial, or that people were mislead because of the media, you get into a realm where you're just going beyond what evidence exists. And all that does is to give succour to those who oppose your position.

Robin Sears:

It is true that the election was not about the trade deal in the sense that 'about' implies a vote-determining issue. It is very true. It was one of my frustrations as a New Democrat that some of the criticism after the campaign was over of our approach to the deal, was a result of our late effort to put it into the context of issues people usually vote on, like the future of medicare, cultural sovereignty *et cetera*.

It is also true that it wasn't possible to frame it as a news story, in a two-sided approach, very coherently. I mean you could try to frame it that way. I don't know if any of you saw the bizarre debate between one of the lawyers who negotiated the deal and the opponent of the deal from Saskatchewan, Charles Ritchie and David Orchard. If you did, you realized that they might as well have been talking French and Spanish. There was no relationship to each other in terms of discussing the same questions, in the same vocabulary, from opposite perspectives. There was just too much material. When one side would push in a direction that was unsatisfactory, as a political response the other would change the subject and talk from a different perspective. That's very tough for a journalist and particularly an electronic journalist, to deal with. It creates a very good example of the dilemma of approaching a multi-faceted news story for any news organization.

I participated in forums on this topic on four or five occasions since the election and I really haven't heard much of a solution to it, much of an answer to the horserace, confrontational, event-driven style of journalism. It is so much the culture of journalism at least in North

America, that it's very hard even to conceptualize a way out of that kind of straitjacket. It is not only limited to economic stories. Think for example of the discussion of the Constitution, particularly in the 1980-81 round, but also in this most recent period. It's really embarrassing; this level of illiteracy and stupidity that passes for serious comment on either side of Constitutional issues, in serious news organizations.

Then there are the polls, and Alan will probably be unhappy about what I have to say, as will Martin Goldfarb. There are four or five questions that Goldfarb didn't address or addressed inadequately.

1) Is it appropriate for someone who has as lofty a position as Martin Goldfarb, to serve both a partisan client and a broadcasting client, in the same election?
2) Even if that were appropriate, is it not reasonable for the public to have some knowledge of that relationship, when they are considering the data being presented to them, as objective information?
3) Isn't it also appropriate for there to be some agreed upon standards for the design, conduct, structure, reporting and analysis of something as crucial to opinion formation as polling has become?
4) Isn't it curious that news organizations seem to be willing to give up a chunk of the front page to people who are not journalists, to write the main news story of the day, based on data they have collected and are being paid to collect? What happens if you know the poll is bad and you paid eighty thousand dollars for it, and reserved the first five minutes of the newscast or the front page of the newspaper?

This actually happened to a news organization in this last election. What do you do? Do you say "well, most of this is right but we happen to know that this province has gone off the map for some reason that we can't understand?" No - because that raises the question of credibility. Do you junk it and defend the expenditure of $80,000 to the bean counters? No. You just hope that no one notices. In this case, no one did.

Alan Frizzell:

The point you made about polls, I agree with. In fact, your last point was the most valid point of all: what are journalists doing? Paying money and making space available on the front page for the kind of polling that you get. I want to go further than that. In fact, the way journalists behave with polls really worries me, because they do not apply standards to polls that they would apply to a reporter in the newsroom. They would demand things from a reporter: "Are you sure your sources are correct?" "Have you covered all the ground?"

"Have you got X, Y and Z?" You don't demand that from the pollsters. I think there are two reasons why they don't. One, they don't know enough about statistics and what they're dealing with in the polling, to be able to make valid judgements. Two, you have to understand why media use polls in elections. It's not simply because they've got to have a story. It's not that at all. The media get them cheap, because almost all pollsters use the polls as loss leaders. But what the media get out of it, well let's take Southam News. They've got an election poll. What do they get out of paying Angus Reid for that poll? They've got it on every dinky little radio station across the country: "In the Southam News poll today..." It's very, very, cheap advertising. The fact is that they do not want to concentrate too much on what the poll says because they know they're getting a good deal out of it as it is.

Robin Sears:

What's happened since the election, which is even more troubling, is Southam has *bought* Angus Reid Polling. The relationship that Angus now has to Southam is that of an employee, and that raises an even more profound question about the relationship and the objectivity of the material one is getting.

Doug Baer:

I would like to extend the concern about polls a little bit and perhaps bring up a couple of extra points. I say this as someone who teaches statistics to graduate students who may be looking for jobs in polling, so I speak from an interested position and I'm going to argue against that interest for a few minutes. I think we have to look at polls in the context of what I would call the fractured and limited nature of political democracy in this country. If we take the so-called 'poll that counts', it is indeed the case that the majority of Canadian people who voted in the last election, regardless of Alan's arguments as to why they voted, voted for parties that had very explicit policies with respect to the free trade debate. That is to say they were opposed to the Free Trade Agreement. Fifty-four percent of the people who voted, voted for a Party which was against the Free Trade Agreement.

Let me say that there is a major structural problem in Canadian democracy, and the normal response that I might have to the pleas "well it is important not to restrain the press from publishing poll results", has to be seen in the context of this structural problem. That problem is that the will of the majority of the people in this country, frequently doesn't translate into political power. Even in an explicitly thematized election such as the one we just had. There have been other examples where majorities have been beaten out of Canadian politics. Some of them even in the case of elections that were fundamentally fought between two different parties. For example, Grant Devine's election, where he received 49% of the vote versus 51% of the vote for the NDP in Saskatchewan. Joe Clark received fewer votes than Pierre Trudeau did when he came to power briefly in 1979. It is curious that the Conservative party seems to have benefited from these instances. I'm sure one can find somewhere in Canadian history that other parties benefited as well.

Now as an aside I will say that in a lot of political questions, often it's not a matter of two choices. So the critique that in our political system the majority will doesn't translate into political power, gets a little more complex in environments where you have three contending choices, and I won't get into that here. What concerns me is that the whole question of how political choice gets translated into political power in the legislative institutions of this country really has not been thematized by the press. Indeed, if anything, it is not the majority vote that then becomes the legitimation upon which governments are based, but rather whether or not they made it into power. So there is no attack on the legitimacy of a government for not having popular support immediately after an election. People say, "well those are the rules of the game. They won using those rules. Let's not concern ourselves with the rules themselves."

In this context of what I might call quasi-democracy, I don't think we have a lot to be proud of in terms of how we translate people's desires to have a say in the matters that affect their lives, into some form of representative political power. I'm not arguing for direct democracy here. I'm just asking if there is some way that interests can get represented well in the bargaining and negotiations in the corridors of power?

In an electoral context, people have to second guess when they vote. Large proportions of people are unable to affect the democratic franchise. In some senses, to have any power whatsoever, they have to vote for Parties which may not represent their first choices. This is certainly going to be the case in a political system where parliamentary majorities are secured with a majority of votes. There have been very few instances in which there have been 50.1% majorities, or majority governments based on at least 50.1% of the popular vote.

Where this creates a problem, back to the question of polls, is that it makes the whole reporting structure in which there is an emphasis placed on the horserace, all that much more critical and important. I would feel better if we had a political system in which I knew that even though I represented only 20% of the people, in terms of my desires on a particular political question, that 20% of the representatives in power, would represent that point of view. If I knew that there had to be negotiations in parliament itself, because no one group is going to have a majority, perhaps I would be a little less concerned. But given the political structure we have here, as a voter I have to make some unfathomable choices. I have to say to myself, who am I going to vote for even if I hate them because I want to block some other party which might come into power, because they have 30% or 40% of the popular vote.

That's why, given the fractured nature of our political democracy, I would argue that something needs to be done about pre-election polls. Even to the extent of banning them. I buy the argument that banning pre-election polls creates a lot of difficulties. There is the whole issue of leaks; how do you deal with indirect sources of information. But it's very clear that from the standpoint of election acts, we haven't been successful in effecting legislation that provides a level playing field for different Parties. The classic example here is the business of the Election Expenses Act and third party advertising, which basically made the Election Expenses Act a sham. There is no Election Expenses Act, or at least there certainly wasn't one in the last election.

Another issue related to that, is the whole question of media objectivity. I would like to suggest that the question ought not to be whether a given media outlet A or B is objective, but what happens across the entire system. In some senses the objectivity bias, as I would label this thing, is worse than having newspapers going out and saying "well we're opposed to the Free Trade Agreement and we're going to take every single reporter off it." Or for those in favour of the Free Trade Agreement: "everybody just try to do as good a job as you can on it." At least then it's more apparent to the readers what's going on. Even *The Toronto Star* which came out against the agreement, felt compelled to justify its position as more or less news neutral, even though it did not follow a neutral editorial policy. I think this is problematic. I'm not suggesting there is an easy solution to this.

If we release newspapers from the objectivity constraint, my guess is that if we were to rerun the free trade election we would find the situation pretty bleak for the free trade opponents. I am suggesting that the objectivity bias, which implies institutional influence on reporters to report in the fashion they did in the last election, needs to be addressed in some way. It's not the press *per se* that causes the problem, but it's the press in the context of our political system, and I think some rather radical responses are necessary in this context. The press needs to pay more attention to the flaws in the democratic system itself, and this needs to be thematized as a major issue. In the absence of that thematization I think this country is in big difficulty. I should point out by the way, that there is some evidence, if we take a look at the various academic theses that have been done over the last ten years, of a declining degree of political legitimacy. People are less and less inclined to believe the political system reflects their will or that the people elected in the political system reflect their wishes or interests.

There is a precipitous decline that's occurred in the last twelve to fifteen years across surveys that I've seen.

Next, I would say that the press goes too far in giving legitimacy to governments elected with a minority of the vote. There is this implicit assumption that a government has legitimacy to rule, simply because it's won, given the flawed rules of the game, without in fact questioning the rules themselves.

I do not feel the same way about public opinion polls held between elections, given the flawed nature of our political system. This is one of the few mechanisms by which opposition groups in society can exercise any power whatsoever, in the face of a parliamentary majority. Question Period in the house and the occasional reports that the government is doing something that 70% of the Canadian people oppose, probably constitute two of the very narrow bases upon which any power whatsoever can be exercised by the disenfranchised majority in Canadian society. We have a problem and I think for us to sit around and smugly say, "Well that's the democratic process and it has worked out that way," presumes the process is democratic, which it is not.

Robin Sears:

There are two examples out there which I think would be worth considering, to pick up on Doug's point. One is the Swedish case (and as a Social Democrat one always has to use the Swedish example for anything). They have one polling institute and it does one poll and that's all the polling that is allowed. It's an academically funded institution, The National Institute of Public Opinion, I think it's called, and they do a poll about every two weeks, running up to the last two weeks before election day. The other experience that one might consider is the French experience which says basically, it's an open marketplace and anyone can do anything they like except in the last two weeks when they can't poll.

I have real problems with this operationally, having worked a fair bit in British Columbia during the period when they banned the publication of polls there. As a Party, you have an almost irresistible temptation to create a phoney poll of your own and if *you* don't, the hamburger guy who wants to boost hamburger sales will happily accommodate. In fact, one of the events we used in this last campaign was Ian Waddell and Ed Broadbent buying ice cream cones where somebody translated the hamburger poll into an ice cream poll. You really do have a problem there because they acquire, for even less sustainable grounds, a level of importance as a reading of public opinion which is really awful. Finally, you have the problem of people like me, walking over to Ron Adams and saying: "I can't show you, but I have in my pocket here a poll that would just blow you away. You should see the numbers we got last night!" And most often your colleagues would say:

"Really! What are they?" and I can say whatever bullshit I want. I don't even have to have a poll. There is a joke among political hacks that we should all stop doing private polls and just make up our numbers to feed to the media. I think each of those things becomes a more serious challenge to the credibility of any polling firm out there in the marketplace, if there isn't a cross-check of some work that Alan Frizzell or somebody else has done. I don't know what the answer to that is but it is an increasing problem for us.

Ron Adams:

Take the Swedish model for example. The experience in the last year or so has shown us that every once in a while, otherwise quite reputable pollsters can really put their foot in it.If we've only got one poll, you've got nobody else's numbers to compare it with. If they happen to come up with the so-called "rogue poll" (and I'll leave you to argue whether or not there is such a thing), but if they do come up with it, then they seriously misinform you. The other problem is of course, if you consider some kind of ban on media organizations conducting and publishing polls, I don't know how you can prevent the Parties from conducting their polls, and then you're left with a situation where you have decreed by law that the Parties will know more about what the people are thinking in aggregate than the people do. I'm at a bit of a loss to see how that's a more democratic solution.

Alan Frizzell:

Well that's interesting Ron because when you talk about the "One rogue poll" you're talking about the November seventh Gallup Poll. It's interesting because if you look at what happened during the election, I was on CBC's *Cross Country Check Up* and I couldn't believe the phone calls that were coming in. The depth of anti-poll feeling there was in this election was astonishing and the major criticism was that there were too many of them. I thought it was rather funny because during the last British election, which was four weeks in length but in essence a three week campaign, the first week parliament remained in session, there were, as far as I can recollect, 79 national polls in a three week campaign. We are probably one of the *least* polled countries in the western world. So we don't have too many polls by international standards.

One of the effects of that Gallup poll was that it caused a considerable flutter in the international markets. It wiped a fair amount off the Toronto Stock Exchange. Interestingly enough, the same thing happened in 1987 in Britain. Six million pounds were knocked off share prices in Britain by, guess what - a poll which was never a poll. It was a leak that went to some stock brokers and it was only rectified by the fact that there were constant public opinion polls coming out, and indeed the next day that flutter ended. But I'm saying the irony of all this was that you had to have polls to stop that nonsense from coming out. The problem with this is that we had an argument brought up that: "Look, we've got a fractured democracy." Well, whether we have or not and we can argue about that; I think it's nonsense. But let's say that we have a fractured democracy, it's an incredible leap from a fractured democracy to the influence of polls. The assumption is that polls actually influence people's behaviour. No one in this country can come up with evidence of how that happens. Is it a bandwagon, or an underdog effect? Is it something else? The fact is that none of the models have been shown to apply consistently to Canadian politics.

Robin Sears:
Oh sure, I can give you four examples Alan. They are not vote-determining, but they are crucial to a political party's capacity to deliver votes. It affects volunteers, it affects fund raising, it affects the morale and the enthusiasm of the people who are working on the campaign, and it affects the level and quality of the coverage.

Alan Frizzell:
One of your own candidates, Robin, told me the very opposite, said "when we get a bad poll it spurs my campaign workers on to greater effort."

Robin Sears:
Don't buy a used car from that man or woman!

***

CHAPTER EIGHT

DREAMING IN COLOUR

Introduction:

The following chapter was written by the editor as a background paper for the conference. It was distributed ahead of time to conference participants. What follows is an edited version of that background paper. The only major change is the addition of the case study analysis of *The Globe and Mail*, which was not completed in time for the conference.

Winter draws on the work of Harold Innis and numerous other authors, to argue that: advertising and crass commercialism of the press have had a devastating impact on public opinion and democracy in Canada; by virtue of their funding and who they are, the media represent corporate interests; so-called "professional" customs such as "objectivity" actually add to the media's corporate bias; the public, caught up with consumerism, is subject to manipulation and what Noam

Chomsky has called, "Manufactured Consent." Thus, we knew *exactly* from the outset, how the media would represent the free trade debate.

James Winter:

It may come as a surprise to learn that the man who has been regarded as Canada's greatest social scientist was named after a weekly newspaper, the farm publication called *The Family Herald.*

Harold (nee Herald) Innis of Otterville Ontario, near London, was named after a newspaper by his prescient mother. As a political economist he devoted the last dozen years of his prolific career to researching and writing on the press. His works included *The Press* (1949), *Empire and Communications* (1950), and *The Bias of Communication* (1951), as well as numerous articles and papers.

Innis is the fellow whom it is said, provided many of the ideas later popularized by another Canadian academic named Marshall McLuhan. I personally concur with those who hold that McLuhan distorted some of Innis's ideas all out of shape, but this is fodder for another paper. In dying of cancer in 1952, Innis wasn't privy to McLuhan's popularizations and extensions, which only began in earnest in the 1960s. As 1952 was the year television was introduced to Canada, Innis also missed this development.

He likewise missed the premature death of *The Family Herald,* which was victimized by lack of advertising support, despite its healthy circulation of over 400,000.[1] For those familiar with Innis's work, there is a cruel irony here, in that he was appalled by the crass commercialism of the press and its ramifications.

The crux of Innis's work didn't revolve around the concepts of time and space or the oral versus literal, in McLuhan's terms. Rather, what Innis boiled down to was a concern with individual free will and the role of public discourse in the path from materialism to knowledge. Most importantly, Innis was not a mere technological determinist, as some have claimed.[2] Innis argued that by the mid 1800s, newspapers had become mere stock in trade turned to profit. The development of a commercial press meant newspapers "the size of a blanket," in order to accommodate the display ads. For Innis, the lower penny price of newspapers meant that the new publishers who displaced editors could concentrate on sales volume to attract advertising revenue.[3] As Noam Chomsky points out in *Manufacturing Consent,* not only did the growth of advertising mean lower costs for newspapers with ads, but it meant that papers without ads were put at a disadvantage owing to higher prices. In effect, advertisers' choices now influenced media prosperity and survival, with a resultant decline in left-wing publications which advertisers were disinclined to support.[4]

For Innis, the entire goal of the 'development' of the press historically can be seen as an attempt to increase its efficiency as an advertising medium.[5] Although it is not often recognized, since this point back in the middle of the last century, newspapers have been written for their advertisers rather than their readers. As the Kent Commission and press critic Ben Bagdikian among others have noted, advertising has increasingly made up a larger portion of newspaper content, from half in 1945 to 65% or more today. So too has the burden of payment fallen increasingly on advertisers. Today, about 80% of newspaper costs are borne by advertisers, with readers accounting for the rest.[6] There is however an important caveat which Bagdikian documents: relative to 1940, subscribers are paying more absolutely, if not proportionately, and are receiving more ads and less news content in return.

A more important point about the role of advertising in the press is the way in which support of the larger circulation paper in the interests of market penetration and economies of scale has, in the words of the Kent Commission, "a tendency to favour or reinforce monopoly newspaper situations." [7] Bagdikian goes further, arguing that advertising creates monopolies.

Innis further argued that investment in capital equipment and the advertising system led to the development of "good will" towards business, or a tendency in newspapers toward conservativism.[8] This point has been reiterated by The Kent Commission.

> Because of the large amounts of capital required to put out a newspaper, the press became concentrated in the hands of big business. Diversity of opinion was placed in jeopardy. Freedom of the press ultimately came to depend on an increasingly restricted ability to publish or be published. As in old authoritarian days, the definition of truth once again risked becoming the prerogative of a few, now the few who had the power of money. [9]

Herman and Chomsky point out how the start-up costs for a newspaper in New York City in 1851 were $69,000; by the 1920s this had risen to anywhere from $6 to $18 million. [10]

The point was well made by that great journalist, A.J. "Joe" Liebling, when he indicated that freedom of the press exists for those who own one. Liebling argued that, just as Americans wouldn't have a free electoral system if candidates for Congress were required to have $1 million and candidates for Senate $10 million, (much as this may *de facto* be the case today) "In the same sense, we have a free press today." [11] Hence, ownership of the press is reserved for the wealthy few. And the few are becoming fewer. By the time of the Kent Commission Report, newspaper chains accounted for 77% of all dailies in Canada, an increase from 58 % ten years earlier. In Quebec, chain ownership went from 49% in 1970 to 90% ten years later.[12] Today, the Southam and Thomson chains control 50% of

Canadian circulation; 60% in English Canada, or if you include the cosy share swap and exchange of directors in the August 1985 agreement between Southam and *The Toronto Star*, in other words if you include *The Star* as part of the Southam chain, (or vice-versa) the two chains control 70% of English language circulation.[13] Three chains control 90% of daily circulation in Quebec.

For Innis, the "bottom line" was a concern over the health of democracy. Writing in a period shortly after the Second World War, he was concerned not only over the rise of dictators such as Hitler and Mussolini, but over the increasing length in office of administrations in democratic countries. FDR comes immediately to mind, of course, and in the current context: Trudeau, Thatcher, Reagan, and now Mulroney. The volatility of the electorate can lead to massive majority governments, as we saw with the Peterson government in Ontario in 1987, and the Mulroney federal government in 1984. Innis saw the decline in political discourse with journalism moving from "a profession to a branch of commerce" as partly responsible for both developments.[14] Shallow and frivolous information in the press has led to a subsequent decline in knowledge and increased susceptibility to manipulation. To Innis, eternal interruptions by petty topics meant the mind is compelled to flow in the shallows, losing intensity of thought and depth and magnitude. In effect, largely through the influence of advertising, the newspaper has become a portable version of the department store, with one price and a broad selection to please everyone. Hand in glove with other industrial developments, "Numerous departments were created to cater to the demands of special groups in a specialized society." To morning papers were added evening and then Sunday ones, in the 1850s in the U.S., but not until the 1970s in Canada. News space declined, along with opinions, while soft features, sports, travel and entertainment increased along with advertising.[15]

Innis was not alone in his concern for democracy given the role of the press. This was at the heart of the Kent Commission's concern,[16] and has been the major focus of press critics throughout this century. With good reason. Speaking of department stores, here is what James Batten, CEO of the Knight-Ridder chain in the U.S. said to his newspaper executives in a speech in August, 1988.

> In general, we can conclude we have not given our advertisers, year in and year out, the competent service and solicitous concern that they deserve...I have told some of you about a wise old newspaper friend of mine who liked to remind me that the success of a free press in the United States owes as much to the institution of the American department store as to the First Amendment. And he, of course, was right. [17]

The newspaper as a one stop shopping department store has seen the proliferation of "fluff," a.k.a. "revenue-related reading matter," or what one wag told the Kent Commission was "Pablum Canada." The incline of feature material has meant the decline of serious news. The Kent Report said,

> Many [House of Commons Press] Gallery members across the country told us that they had to struggle to get space in the face of marketing surveys which appeared to favour feature material over hard news and political comment.[18]

One reporter testified to the Commission,

> It's the depth that is asked of a reporter....[newspapers] don't want to, or they don't have, or they say they don't have, the money to create the kind of resources to give the public the depth of discussion it deserves....I have been told to think in terms of consumerism, [to] think of consumer stories.[19]

Despairingly, Innis quotes H.L. Mencken who wrote: "As a consequence, about the only subject newspapers are able to discuss with unfailing sense and understanding is baseball," while their "Large circulations [have] prevented newspapers .... from attacking anything but the man-eating shark." [20]

Since the decline of the (at least openly) partisan political press before the turn of the century, the press has paid lipservice to the notion of "objectivity," a topic to which I will return at greater length shortly. Again concomitant with advertising, this practice has exacerbated the problem of fragmentation of the news. In their desire to studiously avoid injecting "opinion" into their news stories, reporters and editors have failed to tie together related items. For example, concentration and monopolization of one industry is unrelated to developments in another. Industrial pollution and accidents are isolated and unconnected events. Blame is placed with individuals who are rotten apples in an otherwise O.K. system. To dig deeper and expose systemic weaknesses, to challenge the status quo perspective, is to exhibit a 'bias' which is anathema to journalists and their corporate sponsors. Thus, to hold a coherent view of events, to be able to relate causes and effects and to strive to truly understand our society, is to court the label of "ideologue."

Again, obviously, this is an anathema to the press. So deeply has the shallow and fragmented, one-day, ahistorical world view taken hold of the press and society generally, that anyone attempting to relate so-called "disparate" events is dismissed as belonging to the lunatic left fringe element. As Michael Parenti summed it up, We have noted the media's tendency to favour personality over issue, event over content, official positions over popular grievances, the atypical and sensational over the modal and systemic."[21] In short, in our materialistic consumer society, the news has become a commodity like any other. Or, more correctly, as Dallas Smythe points out, it is the audience which has become the commodity, as the press is in the business of delivering audiences to advertisers.[22]

As the Davey Committee, the Special Senate Committee on the Mass Media, noted in 1970,

> ...forget content because, in the strict economic sense, that is not what the media are selling. What the media are selling, in a capitalist society, is an audience, and the means to reach that audience with advertising messages...It seems harsh, but it happens to be utterly accurate, that editorial and programming content in the media fulfils precisely the same economic function as the hootchy-kootch girl at a medicine show -- she pulls in the rubes so that the pitchman will have somebody to flog his snake-oil to.[23]

All of the preceding discussion really boils down to a single point which is painfully obvious to some and yet to which many are oblivious: The news is business. Big business. This was apparent to the Davey Committee.

> And this leads us to what may be the Committee's most fundamental conclusion: that this country should no longer tolerate a situation where the public interest in so vital a field of information is dependent on the greed or goodwill of an extremely privileged group of businessmen.[24]

Nor has it escaped the notice of the publishers themselves. Here is what *Globe and Mail* publisher Roy Megarry had to say on the question.

> By 1990, publishers of mass circulation daily newspapers will finally stop kidding themselves that they are in the newspaper business and admit that they are primarily in the business of carrying advertising messages.[25]

Or, of course, there is the late Roy Thomson, father to Ken and the Thomson newspaper chain, who said "I buy newspapers to make money to buy newspapers to make more money. As far as editorial content, that's the stuff you separate the ads with."[26] And son Ken learned well from his father. He told the Kent Commission, "I believe in growing. I believe in growing in the newspaper business...I like to invest. I like my family's investments to grow...Newspapers I like very, very much." [27] Today the Thomson Corp. is a global publishing giant with sales of $5.8 billion in 1988, and 192 newspapers in North America alone.

So government through the Davey and Kent reports, and industry through its record and its publishers have been telling us that newspapers are big business for some time now. And of course academics such as Innis have been doing so as well. The late sociologist John Porter, in his classic text *The Vertical Mosaic*, included a discussion of the ideological system of the mass media. Porter noted almost 25 years ago that, "Canada's mass media are operated as big business. Many of them, particularly in the large cities, are closely linked with corporate enterprise."[28] Although Porter ultimately subscribed to the liberal belief in a pluralistic system of competing elites, he noted that a large portion of those controlling the major newspapers belong to upper-class institutions; are private school grads who belong to the same exclusive clubs as do members of the economic elite. Porter's student, Carleton sociologist Wallace Clement, on the other hand studied the overlap between media and economic elites and concluded that they are essentially one and the same. Hence, Porter's view of pluralist competing elites must be replaced with a highly monolithic elite structure. Clement's research showed that the media and economic elite generally are one and the same.[29]

In a *Content* magazine article, John Miller waxed nostalgic over the end of the era of newspaper builders such as Beland Honderich of the *Toronto Star*.

> These publisher-owners were important beyond their papers, and they are all gone to retirement or other ventures, replaced by young MBAs and financial managers whose souls reverberate to different drummers. Their first impulse is not "the story" but the bottom line. They talk not of powerful leads, stunning pictures and exclusives, but of return on investment, cost per thousand and targeted circulation.[30]

As we will discuss in more detail shortly, there is a tremendous contrast between publishers such as Beland Honderich, and Roy Megarry of *The Globe and Mail*. As The Kent Commission put it,

> ...since publishing a newspaper has become a complex business, it is natural that the publisher be first and foremost a businessman. The necessity of dividing work in the large media companies has brought about a separation of the editorial department from the business side, and has forced the publisher

> to delegate his editorial powers to the editor so that he can concentrate more on management. The result is that the publisher becomes more sensitive to the opinions of the business world; his point of view ultimately comes closer to theirs than to any other group's and it is altogether likely this will influence the paper's orientation. How could it be otherwise, since, as a rule, the newspaper publisher moves in the same circles and breathes the same atmosphere as other businessmen? [31]

Let us consider the point about the business connection made, and hope that in flogging this particular horse to its knees, we haven't lost too many of those mentioned earlier, for whom this is an obvious point. Now we come to the crux of the matter: if the media are big business, shouldn't it be obvious what position they will take not only in a free trade debate but on virtually any major issue facing society? This is where we get into the discussion of notions of "objectivity" and editorial independence, and so forth. For even if media-types are willing to confess to economic ties with big business, they steadfastly maintain that they remain "unbiased." In fact, in the U.S. and to a lesser extent in Canada, the media actually are accused of having a liberal if not leftist perspective which biases them against business! Most often such claims are based on the mistaken notion that mildly progressive personal views held by some reporters will be reflected in media content.[32] This view displays ignorance of an extensive and growing body of literature on the sociology of news, and an appalling lack of awareness of how newsrooms function.[33] Those who claim the media are leftist are part of what Herman and Chomsky describe as the "flak machine," organized by business to keep the fear of God (or at least mammon) in the media. Here we could include the right-wing Fraser Institute, with its publication *On Balance*, and in the U.S. such organizations as Freedom House and Accuracy in Media (AIM).[34]

Although these flak operations attack the media, the media treat them well, providing respectful attention and rarely mentioning their corporate links and propagandistic role. Of course with their sparse and cheap labour, the media are unqualified to challenge studies such as the one on media coverage of free trade, reported in the October 1988 issue of the Fraser Institute's *On Balance*. The study's methodological design excluded *The Globe and Mail*'s Report on Business, using only *The Globe*'s front section in its analysis. How might this design flaw have affected the finding that, for example, "...The Globe and Mail interviewed 60% who were not in favour of free trade as opposed to 40% who were in favour."?? The study would appear to be intentionally designed to underestimate *The Globe*'s strong bias in favour of free trade, especially in the conservative Report on Business section, a topic to which we will return at greater length.

Despite the myth of objectivity, the media are more like prisms than mirrors, in that they refract information and distort the picture of reality. But this is not the popular perception of the media. To provide but one example, CBC National News anchor Knowlton Nash has described journalism as "the hinge of democracy," and "the glue that holds together our democratic society."

> Our job is to try to reflect reality, not somebody's self-image-...I've always thought that the media are, in effect, an agent for the public in seeking out and providing information on what's happening, where, when and why....The heart and soul of our business is our credibility. We get that credibility, and the respect and power that go with it, only by being a socially and professionally responsible agent for the public...Our job in the media, be it television or radio or print, is to provide that news, and to provide a searchlight probing for truth through the confusing, complicated, cascading avalanche of fact and fiction. [35]

From an academic perspective, Altschull has summed up this view as the Libertarian or "Market" press model. In the market model, the belief system embraces the theology of the First Amendment, the code of objectivity, the idea that an independent press stands as a protection for the people against the abuses of power, and above all, as the centrepiece of the democratic assumption.[36]

But given its corporate connections, is the press "objective?" In his social history of American newspapers, Michael Schudson says that "Debunkers show that the claims of professionals about being objective or expert or scientific are really just attempts to legitimate power by defining political issues in technical terms."[37] Schudson argues that belief in objectivity is a political commitment, and forms the "dominant ideal that legitimates knowledge and authority in all contemporary professions," including journalism. Schudson argues that in the 1960s, objectivity became a term of abuse. Instead of an antidote to bias, it came to be looked on as the most insidious bias of all, representing a distorted vision of reality which refused to examine the basic structures of power and privilege. How does it do this? Schudson's critique of objectivity takes three forms.

First, he argues that humans are not value-free, and that all news story content rests on a set of substantive political assumptions which form the unspoken yet organic beliefs of journalists. These include a belief in God, Puritanism, the work ethic, but also capitalism, and the West, for example.

Second, he says the form of the news story incorporates its own bias. Reporters' laziness and lack of resources feed an "event orientation" which makes them susceptible to news releases and pseudo events staged by powerful institutions such as business or governments.

Third, the news gathering process constructs an image of reality which reinforces official viewpoints. Journalists essentially function as stenographers for authority, such as police, politicians, and executives. In this respect, journalists use "objectivity" to defend themselves against criticism, diminishing reporters' responsibility for the words they write. Thus reporters quote people in positions of recognized authority, and then, according to the "rules," can only evaluate what is being said by quoting another acknowledged authority![38] An example of this is contained in Figure 1, a clipping from the May 31, 1989 edition of *The Windsor Star*. With the heading, "Media giant's chief denies concentration," the article goes on to quote Maclean Hunter president Ron Osborne, testifying before the Canadian Radio- television and Telecommunication Commission. The occasion for his testimony was Maclean Hunter's $606 million dollar purchase of Selkirk Communications Inc., as the article points out. It also reports that Selkirk owns radio and TV stations in Calgary, Edmonton, Toronto and Ottawa, and Maclean Hunter owns the Sun chain of newspapers which operates in those cities. So, a publishing giant is purchasing a broadcasting chain, in a classic case of cross-media expansion.

But the article lead tells us that "Concentration and cross-media ownership will not increase" with the acquisition, according to Ron Osborne. Nowhere in the article is this patently false and glaringly illogical view challenged. The only other authority figure quoted in the article is the president of Maclean Hunter Cable TV, who makes his own contribution to this Maclean Hunter brand of Orwellian Newspeak. Apparently with a straight face, *The Windsor Star* and the Canadian Press are reporting that an increase in media concentration and cross-ownership is nullified by the statement or testimony of an "authoritative" source with a blatant conflict of interest. The justification for this would be that CP is merely reporting in an objective fashion on the testimony before the CRTC hearing. The outcome is a ludicrous absurdity posing as a hard news item. This does not represent great advances since the days of U.S. Senator Joseph McCarthy and his fabricated lists of "communist" subversives.

Figure Two shows a similar example, this time from *The Globe and Mail* of October 31, 1989. In this front page piece, the president of the National Firearms Association (NFA) is quoted as saying that government plans to outlaw imports of "assault rifles" such as the Israeli Uzi machine gun, will result in more, not fewer, violent crimes involving firearms. Firearms control, according to the NFA president, just serves to keep weapons out of the hands of law-abiding citizens, who are then unable to defend themselves, for example, through the use of "machine guns mounted on Jeeps." While it's difficult to ascertain just where the reporter is putting words in the NFA president's mouth, the point is that the man's specious arguments are unopposed and unquestioned in the article, owing to so-called "objectivity."

As Herman and Chomsky note, "experts" from outside of the corporate/political realm, such as academics, also have been put on the corporate payroll as consultants, or funded through research institutes, *et cetera*.

> As Henry Kissinger has pointed out, in this "age of the expert," the 'constituency' of the expert is "those who have a vested interest in commonly held opinions; elaborating and defining its consensus at a high level has, after all, made him an expert."[39]

Business has effectively bought many academic reputations, to add credibility to the corporate position. In the free trade debate, for example, University of Toronto economist John Crispo has criss-crossed the country in just such a role. This development would no doubt cause Innis to roll over in his grave, for having despaired of the press in the 1940s, he turned to an independent academia as the last hope for the development of knowledge and an informed public.

Thus, Schudson argues that subscription to objectivity represents a political commitment to personal and societal values, powerful institutions, and the views of recognized authorities. I would simply reiterate and elaborate a point made earlier, to add to this: the unconnected, ephemeral, ahistorical/here and now and quantitative, statistical focus of media content mitigates against all but the most superficial thought processes. Rather than concerning themselves with substantive issues, the media instead focus almost exclusively on "horse race" aspects such as: who is in front and by how much, what the strategies are, and how the strategies might affect the standings. Even with a crucial issue such as free trade, media content focused on these elements during the fall 1988 federal election, presenting a battle between two opposing sides, with media and public as neutral observers.

In the end, the media pundits were puzzled that the public could remain undecided and even confused by the issue in the face of so much "coverage." For their part, academics will quantify and measure coverage and fiercely debate whether in fact the media demonstrated "bias," in one direction or the other. In the process they will miss both the macro level view of how the debate was framed within the "objective" criteria outlined above, and the badly-needed intensive micro-level analysis of media content, rather than simply counting up numbers of "favourable" and "unfavourable" stories.

As for the public, they once again will have learned that "politics really is too complex for the layman," and is better left to the experts to understand and interpret, or as Innis put it: "to do our knowing for us." Thus, as John Kenneth Galbraith put it in a different context, we must believe we are unmanipulated in order to be manipulated effectively. Or, as Parenti expresses it: "The worst forms of tyranny - or certainly the most successful ones - are not those we rail against but those that so insinuate themselves into the imagery of our consciousness and the fabric of our lives so as not to be perceived as tyranny." [40]

We may sum up the discussion thus far as follows:

1. Advertising and the crass commercialism of the press have had a devastating impact on public opinion and democracy.
2. By virtue of their funding and who they are, the media represent big business.
3. So-called "professional" customs of the press such as "objectivity" actually add to their corporate bias. As such, journalism is the oldest profession, as identified by Upton Sinclair in his 1919 book, The *Brass Check.*
4. The public, caught up with the superficial, and what's "new and improved," is subject to manipulation or what Herman and Chomsky call "Manufactured Consent." In short, we are dreaming in colour.

How does any of this relate to free trade? In light of the above, we know more or less *exactly* how the media would represent the Free Trade debate of 1988, arguably the most important political debate of Canadian history. In the reciprocity debate of 1911, the media sided with business and opposed it. The smaller Canadian businesses feared being swallowed up by the larger American ones. But by 1988, the surviving Canadian monopolies were ready to take on the Americans, and indeed needed to look to the U.S. markets for growth purposes. The media again sided with business, this time favouring free trade.[41]

A major travesty in all of this is that the general public seemingly remains blissfully unaware of the corporate-media connection, or symbiosis, and further, subscribes to the myth of independent professionalism on the part of the media. It is thus, as the Quebecois say, that we are "dreaming in colour." Otherwise, we would take to the streets in protest over the way that we have been had.

It may be argued that exceptions to the pro-business, pro-free trade stance taken by the media constitute disproof of the above arguments. In other words, how do I take into account opposition to free trade on the part of corporate, mainstream newspapers such as *The Toronto Star*, or *The Edmonton Journal*?

First, one must put the free trade debate into perspective, from the business point of view. With 80% free trade between Canada and the U.S. as it stands, and all parties committed to some form or other of free trade, the battle was in contention but the eventual outcome of the war certainly is not.

Second, occasional exceptions such as *The Toronto Star*, do exist, as pointed out in Chapter One by Peter Desbarats and David Crane. *The Star* takes what former publisher Beland Honderich terms "a people point of view," in the long tradition of populist former publisher Joseph Atkinson. *Star* "policy" favours, for example, nationalism and public ownership.

Third, the media are not a solid monolith on all issues, only on some. Capitalism, "development," or "progress," technology, the entrepreneurial spirit, consumerism, these are a few which spring to mind. After all, opposing a particular free trade agreement is not at all like confronting any of these media sacred cows. And as Bagdikian put it, "The sacred cows in American newsrooms leave residues common to all cows. But no sacred cow has been so protected and has left more generous residues in the news than the American corporation."[42]

The press is unidimensional regarding the benefits of the capitalist economy and the status quo. The real test case would be if the press published an expose on itself, but for all of its opposition to the free trade agreement, *The Toronto Star* did not carry any headlines to the effect that: "Free Trade Represents Corporate/Press Interests." To do so, with its advertising base, would be to invite economic disaster. Relatively minor deviations from the official business party line are alright, but just don't challenge the system. Speaking out in opposition to the corporate plan is different from revealing it for what it is. The former may in fact help by keeping up the semblance of healthy debate and diversity. As Parenti notes, "A press governed solely by the desire to avoid all critical news that might reflect negatively upon dominant class interests reveals itself as an obvious instrument of class domination, loses popular support, and generates disbelief and disaffection."[43] Besides, as Antonio Gramsci pointed out, the ruling interests must act in the public interest at least some of the time. If they do not, this will lead to a decline in legitimacy and hegemony, shrinking their power base back to the police and military capacity, and resulting in a more overtly repressive, but more isolated and less secure rule.[44] In other words, we might suddenly and rudely awaken from our colourful dream.

Writing about Clement's thesis that the media function as legitimators for corporate Canada, John Porter suggested that a test case would be if a publisher kept a failing newspaper alive for ideological purposes. With the outgrowth of monopoly newspaper towns and excessive profitability of surviving newspapers, there has been no need: publishers can disseminate their views and profit by them handsomely. However, with news that Hollinger Inc. chairman Conrad Black has gained control of *The Jerusalem Post*, the possibility has been raised. Black owns *Le Soleil*, *The Daily Telegraph*, and bought 21 dailies and 59 weeklies in 1988, increasing his worldwide publications total to 156. In 1989, he paid $17.5 million for a money-losing company with a book value of $1.5 million. One disgruntled would-be purchaser commented, "It makes no sense at all, unless there is a political motive."[45] It would never do, however, to underestimate Mr. Black's ability to turn a profit.

One question arising from all of this is, what of the role of the CBC? To date, like Innis, I have for the most part referred to the 'press,' but would lump the broadcast media in with it. Being of an even more ephemeral nature and relying to an even greater extent on advertising, they are, if anything, "worse." And owing largely to its continued reliance on advertising revenue (at least for CBC TV,) coupled with its dependence on diminishing government largesse, the CBC is severely hampered as an "alternative" medium. In the main it remains an example of state capitalism, which is really little better than the private kind. Hope for its future rests with eliminating advertising on TV as well, increasing and guaranteeing funding for long terms, and distancing both the CBC and CRTC from the government. Of course, the Conservatives are heading in the opposite direction, in each of these areas.

As for the press, one would hope that recent developments at *The Globe* are not the forerunner for the industry as a whole, but they probably are. With a series of firings and appointments early in 1989, Canada's so-called "national" newspaper has drawn even closer to business. With the hiring of former Report on Business editor Timothy Pritchard as managing editor, and other changes, former staffer Murray Goldblatt commented: "(Publisher Roy) Megarry felt he could surround himself with more empathetic conservative elements ready to unveil a more business-oriented, Tory-minded publication..."[46] *This Magazine*'s Geoff Heinricks reported that industrial accountant Megarry's goal is to make *The Globe* into a "Bay Street Journal," targeted at an elite readership of managerial, professional class (MPCs) to the exclusion of "waste circulation," or people earning under $20,000 annually. Heinricks documents how Megarry and Co. have diverted resources from other parts of the paper to the ROB. In a holiday season memo to staff in 1986, Megarry noted: "The (new) business emphasis of *The Globe* will be reflected in news, features and opinion columns in the front section of the paper." [47] Journalist Walter Stewart has commented:

> The Globe is going to become, all the while denying it, Canada's Wall Street Journal, a slick and single-minded publication designed for and devoted to the interests of, a small, ad-buying portion of the community...We can anticipate more coverage of annual meetings and bigger slabs of the speeches written by PR

> men for the utterance of board chairmen. We will witness, if there is anyone in the country still bold enough to complain about the Free Trade Agreement, the ritual thrashing of the offender by one of Megarry, Thorsell or (ROB editor Peter) Cook -- the Trio Con Brio of the FTA propaganda parade.[48]

To this point, as Tony Westell and Brian Bannon comment in Chapter Two, there is a lot of theory but few "facts," or "evidence." What follows is an attempt at least to provide the latter, as what constitutes the former is in the mind of the proverbial beholder. At the same time, I would point out that there is extensive evidence supporting the general case which professor Westell sums up (disapprovingly) as: the corporate elite own the media and use them to advance certain values. Specifically, reference is made to the works of Noam Chomsky and Ben Bagdikian. What follows concerns the specific case of the free trade election.

Our case study comes from the performance of *The Globe and Mail* during the fall 1988 election. In keeping with the more intensive analysis of the single case study, we have examined a single issue of *The Globe*, for November 11, 1988. Our approach follows the traditions and methodologies of discourse analysis, rather than the traditional, quantitative content analyses used by most North American researchers.[49]

It is imperative that we address at the outset, one criticism advanced by those steeped in the content analysis way of thinking. Those used to quantitative sampling approaches and large numbers will argue that any 'imbalance' on a particular day will be offset by another day's coverage, and all will even out in the long run of the campaign. Certainly that stance has been taken, not surprisingly, at *The Globe*, where management and some staffers view their election performance as both balanced and objective.[50] On the contrary, it is our position that the intrinsic and pervasive biases evident from a careful analysis of one day's coverage - 26 stories - are adequate to prove our case. Claims to objectivity and balance aside, one does not entirely throw over the kind of deep-rooted biases evident from the analysis, from one day to the next. These are the very kind of biases which simplistic and extensive, rather than intensive, content analyses have been unable or unwilling to detect. One reason is that the very immense task of coding thousands of articles precludes careful individual examination, and in fact is almost always done by undergraduates, graduate students, or minimum wage clerks. Another is that the use of the individual story item as the basic coding unit means that articles are decontextualized. However, this is not the place for an extensive methodological critique and comparison.

What follows is a detailed, story-by-story analysis of *The Globe's* coverage. To begin however, we may sum up the findings by reporting that of 26 articles carried on November 11, which was near the end of the election campaign, 21 favoured free trade and the FTA to a greater or lesser extent. Four articles opposed free trade, two of which were of the single-paragraph "news in brief" variety, and one item on the topic was judged neutral.

Any favourable or unfavourable article about one of the three major political Parties was, by virtue of the Parties' clearly defined stances, also either in favour or opposed to the FTA. Hence, stories concerning polls, Parties, and the value of the dollar, were included although they made little mention of free trade *per se*. Each of the articles, headlines, and page locations are listed below, along with a brief description of story content and/or angle, and the author's judgement of story bias. The stories themselves are in Appendix II at the end of the book.

1. "Dollar leaps in reaction to the polls." (A1) This is about how the dollar was driven up by news that the PCs were recovering, to a neck-and-neck race with the Liberals. Reagan is scheduled to deliver a Washington speech defending the FTA. "Financial markets (are) clearly on the side of the free trade deal..." The money markets revived with the Liberals' "sagging fortunes." Following the TV debates Gallup showed the Liberals with 43%, whereas they had been "flirting with oblivion." This was the top story of the day. *Pro free trade.*

2. "Poll says Canadians want to renegotiate, not rip up trade deal." (A1) This is a direct slash at Turner, who vowed to rip up the trade deal if elected. The story reveals that while a majority of 51% opposes the FTA, 44% want to renegotiate rather than rip it up. Surely, the headline and emphasis here should be that, for the first time, *The Globe's* own poll shows a majority opposed to the FTA. Likewise, the decision to play the dollar leaping story above the poll story, is suspect. Furthermore, *The Globe* chose to emphasize that 39% "think cancellation of the agreement would be bad for the Canadian economy," instead of emphasizing the 48% who said cancelling the FTA either would be good or make no difference. They also carried a graph titled, "Environics Tracking on Support For Free Trade." Given that a majority opposed the FTA, one would think they would be tracking opposition rather than support. *Pro free trade.*

3. "Costs? What Costs?" (A6) This column by Jeffrey Simpson is an attack on John Turner and the Liberal party. He describes the Liberal Party programme as "voodoo economics." Turner is: "disingenuous at best, and mendacious at worst," for not costing his "hugely expensive" campaign promises. *Pro free trade.*

4. "A Stronger Canada." (A6) This is a strongly *pro free trade* letter from the president of the Ontario Chamber of Commerce, and was one of only two letters on the topic. The second letter also is *pro free trade*, scorning the FTA's influence on our culture.

5. "Would it be so hard to rip up the deal?" (A7) This "showcase" op-ed piece by Liberal Senator Philippe Gigantes is a strong column

against the FTA. Unfortunately, it is largely undercut by the headlines and emphasis on the front page, to the effect that "Poll says Canadians want to renegotiate, not rip up trade deal." The subtle message is that like Turner, Gigantes is out of step with the mood of the country. *Anti free trade.*

6. "One more kick at the can." (A7) This column by Thomas Walkom does everything but call former Liberal Minister John Roberts a "has-been." It does describe Roberts, a candidate in a Toronto area riding, as a parachute candidate who wasn't the first choice of the local Liberal Riding Association. He is "A Toronto carpet-bagger," who "hardly even knocks on doors." *Pro free trade.*

7. "Straight talk on free trade." This headlines four straight pages of ads favouring the FTA, sponsored by "The Canadian Alliance for Trade and Job Opportunities." While this study is about editorial, not advertising content, as Robin Sears points out in Chapter Seven, it would be foolish to ignore this material. *(Not in appendix) Pro free trade.*

8. "Mulroney 1st choice as PM, poll finds." (A14) This headline on the election coverage page, is accompanied by the kicker: "Turner moves to 2nd place." *The Globe* chose to emphasize in its lead and headline the poll result showing that Mulroney remains as first choice, even though he has dropped three points in the standings. Yet, Turner showed a twelve point jump since the October poll. Why not emphasize this in the lead and headline? Or, why not emphasize that Turner leapt by 11 points as "most competent" leader, and the leader with the "best ideas and policies?" Or, why not emphasize Turner's vast lead in the category of leader whose performance has most improved during the campaign: Turner 64%, Mulroney 12%, Broadbent 10%. What this story points up is that there are many angles from which to choose, and *The Globe* reveals its biases by its selections. *Pro free trade.*

9. "Broadbent unwilling to make a judgment on need for Bill 101." (A14) This is the only article dealing with Broadbent, and it is critical of him. It says Broadbent can't make a judgement in the Quebec case, although he was outspoken earlier in the year in his opposition to Saskatchewan legislation. It reports on the "apparent contradictions" between the federal and Quebec NDP wings. *Pro free trade.*

10. "Liberal Ads get go-ahead from judge." (A14) This was the only neutral item in the paper. It reports that Liberal ads taken from the TV debates can be used. *Neutral.*

11. "Books are open to Liberals, Mulroney tells party rally." (A16) Mulroney charges that Turner has all of the information needed to cost his campaign promises. "All he lacks is the courage to do so." It describes how Mulroney is sharpening his attacks on Turner. In paragraph 14, the article points out that Mulroney failed to mention that in the 1984 campaign he too said he couldn't cost his promises until he looked at the government books. It's not hard to imagine how this could

have been the story lead, if *The Globe* had a different perspective. Or, at the very least, it could have been pushed further up in the story rather than being buried in paragraph 14. *Pro free trade.*

12. "Wilson calls Turner liar, coward, defends national sales tax plan." (A16) Here, the emphasis is on Michael Wilson's charge that John Turner is trying to scare votes out of elderly Canadians. Hardly a "news" item as *The Globe* reported similar charges by Wilson on page 1 on November 1st, ten days earlier. Nevertheless, after 5 1/2 paragraphs of Wilson's attack on Turner, the article mentions that Wilson "was still somewhat vague" on the national sales tax. It's not just with hindsight that this could be viewed as a potential lead. Instead, *The Globe* chose to play up the anti-Turner angle. *Pro free trade.*

13. "Mazankowski offers to quit if deal a threat." (A16) Government House Leader Don Mazankowski tells senior citizens that if there is anything in the FTA which affects medicare or old age pensions, he'll resign his seat. *Pro free trade.*

14. "Metis favour NDP." (A16) Metis and non-status Indians fear the FTA will do damage to natural resources. But even the Metis' favouring of the NDP is qualified: the association "prefers" but "refuses to endorse" the NDP. This story is one paragraph in length. *Anti free trade.*

15. "Grit wants new deal." (A16) The Alberta Liberal leader would ask Turner to renegotiate the FTA if elected. He was attacked by provincial Liberals for his support of the FTA. Now he says it needs new clauses ensuring social programs will be unaffected. All of this amounts to a qualified opposition to the FTA. The story is one paragraph in length. *Anti free trade.*

16. "Tories set for effort to rebuild their lead." (A17) This story details the PC strategy for the last week of the campaign, towards rebuilding a majority government. Their strategy is two-pronged, hammering Turner's credibility, while Mulroney takes the high road of economic prosperity. Paragraph 12 mentions Liberal strategy as being opposed to free trade. The Liberals get two paragraphs. Paragraph 14 begins discussion of NDP strategy, with Robin Sears, again for two paragraphs. Why is the emphasis on the Tories rebuilding, rather than that of the current leaders? How about, "Liberals set for effort to maintain their lead" ?? *Pro free trade.*

17. "Trading status with US not at risk, Turner says." (A17). Here, *The Globe* manages to be so critical of Turner in his daily campaign story, that the coverage is bad for him. The story tells about how Turner tried to reassure a largely business audience that cancelling the FTA wouldn't harm ties with the U.S. In the second half of the story, we are told how, although Turner's speech was "generally warmly received," about 10 out of 70 tables remained seated when the crowd

gave him a standing ovation. The message is that Turner was suspect, unable to convince everyone of the integrity of his anti-free trade stance. The last five paragraphs are spent giving a Tory candidate's criticism of Turner, and pointing out a supposed-inconsistency in his tariff policy. On balance, this story does Turner more harm than good. *Pro free trade.*

18. "Queen's Park acts to ban export of water" (A18) The Ontario Government now has introduced three anti-free trade bills, one of which bans the export of water. Ontario will refuse to approve the export of water, despite the FTA. Factually reported, although the reporter inserts defenses of the FTA, for example, "The (FTA) agreement...does not specifically mention water exports." *Anti free trade.*

19. "Steel industry under pressure from US actions" (B1) With this, we get into the Report on Business section. This story says the Canadian steel industry has been charged with dumping by American counterparts, with more cases in the offing. If the FTA is cancelled, the Canadian steel industry's ability to deflect dumping actions will be reduced. It also takes the debatable position that the FTA dispute settlement mechanism is better than what exists under the GATT. (For a discussion of this, see Mel Clarke's piece in this volume). *Pro free trade.*

20. "Quebeckers counter-attack on free trade" (B1) Here we have the Quebec "captains of industry," the "cream of Quebec's business community," gathered in a show of force to support the FTA. They are reportedly "very disturbed" by the drastic change in popular support (read Conservative election chances) for the FTA. Included in this group is relentless FTA supporter John Crispo, and David Culver, President of Alcan Aluminium and chairman of the Canadian Alliance for Trade and Job Opportunities. Culver is, of course, quoted in the article, perhaps in return for the four-pages of ads sponsored by his group, in the front section of the paper. Very *pro free trade.*

21. "Free trade fears: zap, zap, zap, you're frozen." (B2) In this column, arch-conservative Peter Cook argues that Canada will suffer if the FTA is cancelled (another form of response to the op-ed piece by Senator Philippe Gigantes). Very *pro free trade.*

22. "Dollar soars on rally in fortunes of Tories" (B3) This is the more blatant, ROB version of the page one story. Somewhat directly, it states: "...the dollar staged a sharp turnaround yesterday in response to an apparent rally in the fortunes of the Conservative Party." Again, the message is that if you want the dollar and the economy to be strong, vote Conservative. Very *pro free trade.*

23. "Grain farmers to receive drought relief." (B3) Farmers will receive $850 million in relief from the federal government, as an-

nounced in four different provinces by groups of Tory cabinet ministers. *Pro free trade.*

24. "Free Traders, foes in frenzied fight." (B6) This article has the appearance of balance because to a certain extent it presents both sides. The problem lies in the balance. Just as the headline mentions "free traders" versus "foes," so too is there a bias in the story. A total of eight paragraphs tell the pro free trade side, versus just five for the anti-free trade side. Four paragraphs are neutral. The story is about the release of news analyses by both sides, on what accepting or rejecting the FTA would mean for multilateral trade relations. *Pro free trade.*

25. "Alberta may lose $14 billion in projects: IDA" (B6) Investment Dealers Association of Canada officials say Alberta could lose up to $14 billion if the FTA is scrapped. Growth rates are based on FTA acceptance. The FTA is needed to justify investment in Canada, to ensure free access to the U.S. market and to avoid countervail or dumping charges. *Pro free trade.*

26. "Signs right for stock boom in '89, IDA says" (B8) That is, provided the FTA is approved. The Investment Dealers Association again plugs the FTA (and a vote for the Conservatives.) *Pro free trade.*

That is the extent of the FTA coverage for November 11, 1988. Again, the tally was: pro free trade 21, anti free trade 4, and neutral 1. So much for objectivity and balance. Others will no doubt read the same stories and see them differently, as Norman Webster has done. Such is the nature of subjective human beings. Nevertheless, the overwhelming conclusion here is one of overt bias in favour of the FTA and the Progressive Conservative Party. As discussed, it is extremely difficult to justify many of these *Globe* decisions based on supposedly universal news judgements and news values alone.

Earlier, mention was made of the November 1st 1988 issue of *The Globe.* As indicated, this issue played up the charges by Finance Minister Michael Wilson, that Turner and Broadbent were lying to the elderly. This is the top story of the day, with a three column, bold, black headline, with two rows: "Wilson charges foes with lying to elderly." The occasion is a luncheon speech by Wilson. Below this story on the front page, with a smaller headline, is a report on the latest Globe-Environics Poll, headed: "Liberals move ahead of PCs in wake of leaders' debates." Through its positioning and emphasis, what *The Globe* is telling us is that Michael Wilson's accusations at a luncheon are more important than the results of their own poll which puts the Liberals ahead of the PCs for the first time in the election campaign.

As if that were not bad enough, there is a third relevant story just below this: "Dollar takes nosedive as Conservatives fall in opinion poll results." Hence, the good news for the Liberals is sandwiched, by *The*

Globe, between two pieces of bad news. In this manner, as we have seen elsewhere, *The Globe* carries the "other side," it gives play to the anti free trade forces in the appearance of "balance," all the while undermining that position.

This may be seen clearly from what was done to Senator Gigantes, or John Turner. It is thus, through position and emphasis, that the really not-so-subtle biases come into focus. Unquestionably, strictly from the perspective of news values, the Liberal lead deserved top billing. The argument that Gallup already had revealed this information, just doesn't stand up: Gallup's was widely regarded as a "rogue poll," (see the discussion in Chapter Seven) and the Globe-Environics study at least partially backed up Gallup's findings. As such, it warranted prominence.

It is important not to draw the wrong kind of conclusions from this non-traditional analysis. In the usual study, we look at the number of stories on each Party, and their direction or favour-ability. Since this isn't a representative sample, or census of *Globe* coverage, we would be remiss in inferring, for example, that only 2 out of every 26 or 8% of free trade and/or election stories in *The Globe* were on the NDP. Proportionately, the NDP didn't fare very well on this day, a finding which would probably stand up under extensive analysis, but possibly not to the same degree. Afterall, there is an expectation of some 'balance' at least in the amount of coverage of the three major Parties during an election. What we can conclude is that there is a distinct pattern to *Globe* coverage: pro free trade, pro Progressive Conservative. So deep-seated are these biases, relating to stories and subjects covered, manner of reporting, emphasis, positioning, *et cetera*, that it is unthinkable that the nature of this coverage would be different at any other time during the six week campaign. This, then, is our evidence, for contrast and comparison with the inevitable spate of content analysis studies, some of which are discussed in Chapter Two. It is difficult to imagine the more "Tory-minded" publication, which publisher Roy Megarry has in store.

(As an aside, even the ultra-conservative Fraser Institute found in a content analytic study that *The Globe*'s election campaign coverage of Ed Broadbent, excluding the Report on Business, was "twice as likely to be critical as favourable...")[51]

The prognosis, as I observe *The Windsor Star* drooling in anticipation of Frank Stronach's Magna International coming to Windsor, (Figure Three) is not good. *Star* and *Globe* staffers would do well to heed the words of American publisher E.W. Scripps, founder of one of the first modern newspaper chains at the turn of the century.

> You must remember that...advertisers are men of extremely sordid minds. Their lives are given up to dollar-getting. They presume that every man is equally sordid...The advertiser is the enemy. The big advertiser is the mortal foe of honest journalism. I would rather go through a dark alley with a thug than to couple up, in a business way, as a young newspaperman, with a big advertising patron. [52]

Scripps' antipathy towards advertising went so far that he created and for a while supported, an adless newspaper.

All of us have indeed lost sight of the advice of Nova Scotian journalist and politician Joseph Howe: "I conjure you to leave an unshackled press as a legacy to your children." Today, our press wears corporate shackles, hand and foot. Were Harold Innis still alive, one wonders where he would turn for the keys to unlock them; to lend reality to our colourful dream of press freedom.

***

1. Mass Media: The Uncertain Mirror, Report of the Special Senate Committee on Mass Media, Volume 1, Information Canada, Ottawa, 1970, p. 173.

2. One author who makes this mistake is Andrew Osler, "From Vincent Massey to Thomas Kent; The Evolution of a Press Policy in Canada," in Benjamin Singer (Ed) Communications in Canadian Society, Addison-Wesley, Don Mills, 1983.

3. Harold Innis, Political Economy in the Modern State, Ryerson Press, Toronto, 1946, pp. 7-9.

4. Edward Herman and Noam Chomsky, Manufacturing Consent: The Political Economy of the Mass Media, Pantheon, N.Y., 1988, p.14.

5. Innis, Political Economy, p.11.

6. See the Kent Royal Commission on Newspapers, Ministry of Supply and Services, Ottawa, 1981; Ben Bagdikian, The Media Monopoly, Beacon Press, Boston, 2nd Edition, 1987.

7. Kent Commission, p.72.

8. Innis, Political Economy, p.23.

9. The Kent Commission, pp. 9,13.

10. Herman and Chomsky, Manufacturing Consent, p.4.

11. A.J. Liebling, The Press, Pantheon, N.Y., 1981, p.15.

12. Kent Commission, pp. 9,13.

13. James Winter, "Interlocking Directorships and Economic Power," in Robert Picard, James Winter, Maxwell McCombs and Stephen Lacy, Press Concentration and Monopoly, Ablex, New Jersey, 1988, p.107.

14. Innis, Political Economy, p.31.

15. Innis, Political Economy, p.27.

16. Kent Commission, p.136.

17. Quoted in Carlin Romano, "Leadership for Beginners," Gazette Center Journal, 3:1, Winter 1989, p.138.

18. Kent Commission, p.141.

19. Kent Commission, p.172.

20. Harold Innis, The Press: A Neglected Factor in the Economic History of the 20th Century, Oxford University Press, Toronto, 1949.

21. Michael Parenti, Inventing Reality: The Politics of the Mass Media, St. Martin's Press, N.Y., 1986, p.213.

22. Dallas Smythe, Dependency Road: Communications, Capitalism, Consciousness and Canada, Ablex, N.J., 1981.

23. Senate Committee, pp. 39-40.

24. Senate Committee, p.67.

25. Roy Megarry, quoted in Bagdikian, The Media Monopoly, p.195.

26. Cited in Wallace Clement, The Canadian Corporate Elite, McLelland and Stewart, Toronto, 1975, p.288.

27. Kent Commission, p.91.

28. John Porter, The Vertical Mosaic, University of Toronto Press, Toronto, 1965, p.462.

29. Clement, The Canadian Corporate Elite.

30. John Miller, "Bee Knew What He Didn't Like," Content, November/December, 1988, p.30.

31. Kent Commission, p.28.

32. See, for example, Robert Lichter, Stanley Rothman, Linda Lichter, The Media Elite: America's New Powerbrokers, Adler & Adler, Bethesda, 1986, for an example of this kind of argument.

33. See for example, Herbert Gans, Deciding What's News, Pantheon, N.Y., 1979; Gaye Tuchman, Making News, Free Press, N.Y., 1978; David Altheide, Creating Reality, Sage, Beverly Hills, 1974.

34. Herman and Chomsky, Manufacturing Consent, p.27.

35. Knowlton Nash, "The Imperfect Necessity," Content, January/February, 1988, pp.7-11.

36. Herbert Altschull, Agents of Power, Longman, N.Y., 1984, p.146.

37. Michael Schudson, Discovering The News: A Social History of American Newspapers, Basic, N.Y., 1978, p.7.

38. Schudson, Discovering The News, p.184.

39. Herman and Chomsky, Manufacturing Consent, p.23.

40. Parenti, Inventing Reality, p.7.

41. For a discussion of the combined efforts of business generally, the media and government, see Nick Fillmore, "The Big Oink: How Business Won the Free Trade Battle," This Magazine, 22:8, March/April 1989, pp.13-20.

42. Bagdikian, The Media Monopoly, p.47.

43. Parenti, Inventing Reality, p.111.

44. Antonio Gramsci, Selections From the Prison Notebooks, International Publishers, N.Y., 1971, p.171. Cited in Parenti, Inventing Reality, p.244.

45. Patrick Martin, "Black Takes Over 'The Voice of Israel,'" The Globe and Mail, May 6, 1989, p. D3.

46. Murray Goldblatt, "Globe Tremors: Shaking and Quaking at Canada's National Newspaper, Reflects More Conservative, Business-Minded Image," Content, March/April, 1989, p.19-20.

47. Geoff Heinricks, "Whose News? Business Circles The Globe," This Magazine, Vol. 23:3, September 1989, p.17.

48. Walter Stewart, "Fulfilling a Prophecy: The Globe: Just Another Thomson Newspaper," Content, March/April, 1989, p.21-22.

49. For an overview of discourse analysis and comparison with the traditional method, cf. Tuen van Dijk, News As Discourse, Lawrence Erlbaum, N.J., 1988; Jonathan Potter and Margaret Wetherell, Discourse and Social Psychology, Sage, Beverly Hills, 1987.

50. Personal correspondence with Norman Webster, then editor-in-chief of The Globe, November 30, 1988. Webster wrote: "Instructions to our staff were clear. News coverage of the campaign was to be as fair and accurate as we could make it...On the whole, I think we acted fairly and responsibly." Mr. Webster is now with The Gazette in Montreal.

51. On Balance, II:1, January, 1989, p.2, The Fraser Institute, B.C.

52. Cited in Carlin Romano, "Leadership For Beginners," p.130.

Figure One

Media giant's chief denies concentration

HULL, Que. (CP) — Concentration and cross-media ownership will not increase with Maclean Hunter Ltd.'s $606-million-dollar purchase of Selkirk Communications Inc., Maclean Hunter president Ron Osborne said Tuesday.

But he could not guarantee, during a public hearing before the federal broadcast regulator, that the situation would never change.

Maclean Hunter already owns or will acquire from Selkirk several radio and TV stations in Calgary, Edmonton, Toronto and Ottawa. It also owns the Sun chain of newspapers which operate in those cities.

But Osborne said cross-media ownership isn't a problem because Maclean Hunter's control over the Sun newspapers is limited by an agreement with the Toronto Sun Publishing Corp.

MACLEAN HUNTER, which owns 62 per cent of the corporation, is limited to two directors on the 12-member board, Osborne told the Canadian Radio-television and Telecommunications Commission, which regulates the broadcast industry.

He said it's Maclean Hunter's policy to operate all its media companies — including magazines such as Maclean's and Chatelaine — on a hands-off basis.

Osborne would not commit his company to continuing the agreement for as long as Maclean Hunter owns broadcasting properties.

COMMISSIONER Rosalie Gower asked if there was ever a chance Maclean Hunter might want to become a full operating partner with the Toronto Sun.

"I don't like to say there's never a chance because never is a long time," Osborne responded.

If Maclean Hunter ever felt the Toronto Sun needed management direction, for example, it might step in but would never want to run the company, he added.

Maclean Hunter will also acquire Ottawa Cablevision in the takeover, but Osborne didn't believe that would increase cross-media ownership in the Ottawa market.

However, Barry Gage, president of Maclean Hunter Cable TV, said cross-media ownership will become a problem in the future as cable companies step more into providing programs other than community programs.

Maclean Hunter has decided to stay out of programming for that reason but other cable companies want very much to get into it, Gage said.

Figure Two

Gun lobby warns that ban on assault rifle imports will result in more crime

BY PAUL KORING
The Globe and Mail

OTTAWA

The Conservative government's plans to outlaw imports of "assault rifles" will result in more, not less, violent crimes involving firearms, says the president of the National Firearms Association.

David Tomlinson yesterday accused the government of failing to understand the basic realities of gun control. He said Justice Minister Douglas Lewis "was sucked in again, . . . he doesn't understand the problem and is putting Band-Aids on an unworkable system."

Mr. Lewis announced last week that the import of firearms originally designed to be fired as automatics — such as the Soviet AK-47 and the Israeli Uzi — would be banned, even if the weapons had been modified to fire as semi-automatics. Gun-control advocates welcomed the tighter rules, which are designed to stop the import of so-called "assault weapons."

But Mr. Tomlinson said the legislation "will have no effect on criminals or crime" and will only hurt responsible gun collectors and sportsmen.

"Frankly, criminals don't pay any attention to firearms control legislation," Mr. Tomlinson said. "The more firearms control you bring in, the more violent crime" occurs, he said.

Restrictions on firearms only make it more difficult for law-abiding citizens to own them, rather than reduce their avail-

GUNS — Page A2

• From Page A1

ability to criminals, he said.

Mr. Tomlinson contended that Canadians are five times more likely to be victims of a burglary while they are in their homes than Americans, because the "average Canadian" who does not own a gun "is helpless and defenceless."

Meanwhile, in the United States, where there is far less gun control, "American burglars avoid occupied homes like the plague."

The National Firearms Association is "not advocating that anybody and everybody should carry a firearm . . . we're not a far-out redneck outfit that wants everybody wandering around with a 45 (calibre pistol)." However, he said, careful screening of gun owners to ensure they are competent and fewer restrictions on the weapons themselves could reduce the crime rate in Canada.

The association has an active membership of "between 5,000 and 7,000" but is widely supported by hundreds of gun clubs across Canada, and generated more than 48,000 "hostile messages" to Mr. Lewis about his proposed changes, Mr. Tomlinson said.

He said the "arrogance, ignorance and incompetence" of government in its approach to firearms control should be replaced by a co-operative screening of owners in conjunction with gun clubs.

And he proposed that no firearms be outlawed. Asked whether that included heavy weapons, such as machine guns mounted on Jeeps, Mr. Tomlinson replied that "there are lots of people currently in Canada who own vehicle-mounted automatics."

It is not legally owned weapons that cause the problem, he said. "No legally owned fully automatic has been used for any criminal purpose (in Canada) since 1934," he said.

Meanwhile, "if criminals thought that 2 per cent of the cab drivers had a firearm and know how to use it" there would be fewer crimes against taxis, he said.

Figure Three

Weather

Low tonight 14
High Friday 25
Details A2

The Windsor Star

40 Cents

★★

THURSDAY, MAY 18, 1989

Magna and city close to a deal

By Doug Williamson
Star Staff Reporter

Magna International and the city of Windsor are apparently very close to signing a deal that could result in construction of up to 10 new auto parts plants employing 3,000 people in Windsor and Essex County in the next few years. In an interview today aboard one of his company's three corporate jets, Magna chairman Frank Stronach told *The Windsor Star* he's confident his conditions for low-priced land will be met by the city, which would also install necessary services.

Construction could start next year, he said.

"If we could get 3,000 or 5,000 acres at a reasonable cost, we'd make a commitment," he said. "If I can't get that I'll make a commitment somewhere else."

But he said he was confident Windsor would accommodate Magna's needs, and said an informal agreement was possible for today with formal arrangements following in a few months.

"Yeah, we would shake hands. We have the need," he saio. "They indicated that they will be able to get a large tract of land together. We want to see what the market is. If it's flipped we'd say screw it.

"I have some indication that unserviced land sells anywhere between $5,000 and $15,000 (per acre)," he said.

"I'm confident. It might not happen today but it will be over the next few months.

"We could start construction next year, we do have growth. When we go the whole economy goes up."

Flying from Markham in 45 minutes, Stronach was greeted at Windsor airport today by a stretch limousine containing Mayor John Millson,

See CITY, A4

Reprinted with permission of The Windsor Star

Figure Three Cont'd

We're 'number one' on Magna's list

By Doug Williamson
Star Staff Reporter

The final details of a multi-million dollar land deal with Magna International could be ironed out in the next few weeks, leading to an extensive housing and industrial development in Windsor and Essex County.

Mayor John Millson and Magna Chairman Frank Stronach said they'd be in daily contact in completing the land prices, Stronach's main concern.

Windsor is co-ordinating the deal with Magna, which wants to build up to 10 new auto parts factories over the next five years and eventually employ 3,000 people.

"It's number one on the list at this point," Stronach said Thursday, describing Windsor's chances of getting the investment.

In an interview, Stronach told *The Windsor Star* the proposed development would cost $500 million, excluding the cost of land. He said Magna wants to assemble a total of 3,000 to 5,000 acres in Windsor and Essex County, for factories and housing units including co-op housing.

The development depends on the city successfully negotiating the purchase of Twin Oaks golf club from its owner, and then arranging a boundary adjustment with Sandwich South Township which has about half the property in its current boundaries.

That parcel and the CN-owned land on Windsor's east side are the two tracts Windsor hopes Magna will initially buy. According to Millson, CN has agreed to let Windsor handle the sale, at an undisclosed price.

The Twin Oaks land — 127 hectares sitting in Windsor and Sandwich South — has an estimated price tag of $6.5 million, translating to about $15,000 an acre. Windsor would buy it and then resell it to Magna.

After touring the sites Thursday morning and hearing proposals from city and CN officials, Stronach said he is optimistic Magna will go ahead with the development, which would include 3,000 to 5,000 housing units and offer co-operative housing.

"It's not final yet," Stronach told a news conference before boarding a corporate jet and heading back to Magna headquarters in Markham. "I'm optimistic that we're getting closer and closer. I'm very confident that we should arrive at a specific ... agreement."

While Magna is looking to expand in southern Ontario and the southern United States, Windsor heads the list.

"We do hope that Windsor would be the first city outside of Toronto where we would have new development. We will make every effort. You have a number of things here which creates a natural (business) environment," Stronach said.

"You must have an environment which is conducive to business."

Millson said the city property department will present a report on

See WE'RE, A4

Weather
Low tonight 16
High Saturday 23
Details A2

The Windsor Star

FRIDAY, MAY 19, 1989

40 Cents
★★

CONCLUSION

In Chapter One, Maude Barlow said we are going through a revolution. It entails, she said, the privatization and "Thatcherization" of Canada. These observations are particularly timely as we hear and read of Tory Government plans for privatizing Via Rail's Quebec - Windsor corridor, the most travelled and potentially profitable route in the country. Likewise, the fate of Canada Post currently is in limbo. Air Canada has been sold. The CBC, as CBC Winnipeg journalist Lesley Hughes indicated, is under siege. Legislation has been passed which will axe Unemployment Insurance benefits by $1.3 billion. $1.8 billion is to be cut from the foreign aid budget. At the First Ministers' Conference in November, 1989, Mulroney warned the premiers that federal payments for medicare and universities will be cut. And we haven't even mentioned the Tories' new, regressive tax known as the "GST," or Goods and Services Tax.

But this is not a book about the new Right in Canada, so much as an analysis of media coverage and collusion with that new corporate Right. To aid us in our evaluation of the media's role, we have the previous chapter in which we review some of the academic thinking and literature. To appease critics of these views, some of whom, like Tony Westell and Brian Bannon, have been heard in these pages, we've also included an in-depth case study analysis of *The Globe and Mail.* Unlike the quantitative content analysis studies reported to date, this study cites examples of blatant biases at *The Globe.* In professor Westell's terms, this would constitute "evidence," to buttress individual casual observation on the part of many people. But there is other important, if unscientific evidence of media biases at *The Globe* and elsewhere.

Lorne Slotnick, a ten-year reporter with *The Globe,* resigned his beat as labour reporter in protest, when he was asked by management to propagandize for business. Mr. Slotnick reports that:

> at *The Globe* there was an outright effective ban on stories that made the free trade deal look bad...reporters were told and were subtly made to feel that (these) stories were not welcome...There was a definite orientation in the news columns and there was concern about this in the newsroom.

As a result, Mr. Slotnick tells us "The *Globe and Mail* was, I would say, nearly hysterical in its support for the free trade deal."

So the academic evidence of the previous chapter simply bears out the report by one of *The Globe*'s own staffers. Not all staffers feel this way. As we saw, former editor-in-chief Norman Webster stood by his appraisal of that paper's performance as "objective," shortly after the election (and shortly before he was fired!) Former managing editor Geoffrey Stevens told us in Chapter Five (after being fired!) that he's not convinced there is direct corporate interference, and didn't experience any himself. Well, these sorts of arguments have been addressed in the previous chapter and don't require repeating here.

What does bear repetition and summary here are the words of some of the journalists on these pages, in addition to Lorne Slotnick. These are the people who are on the front lines and who must not only try to see the forest for the trees, but must try to live and work with whatever it is that they see, not only in their newspapers or broadcasts, but in their bathroom mirrors. For they are part of what Senator Keith Davey called, almost twenty years ago, newsrooms as "graveyards of broken dreams." Those of us who have laboured in newsrooms, taken a communication or journalism course, or even read a newspaper or heard a newscast, can empathize with how they feel.

Frances Russell of the Winnipeg *Free Press* has been particularly eloquent in her discussion of how she could still be "naive" while having 27 years' experience. Through the debate over free trade, her eyes have been opened to the way in which journalists are "defiling our principles and debasing our calling." In short, she can now see the presence of Upton Sinclair's Brass Check.

"Deferential," and "propaganda agents for the authorities," the media have gone from being independent to being sycophants for the mega corporations. Ms. Russell argues that in a society increasingly fractured between haves and have-nots, journalists must take off their blinkers and take out their ear plugs to see and listen to the swelling ranks of the afflicted rather than the diminishing numbers of the increasingly-comfortable.

A poignant as well as thoughtful and sincere appeal, it is in a way perhaps, misdirected. Ms. Russell's audience is her fellow journalists, the same people, ironically, blamed seventy years ago by Upton Sinclair. But Herb Gray was right when he remarked that there were too few publishers at this conference. Just as sociologist John Porter noted 25 years ago that what is needed is not journalism schools, but schools for publishers.

Frances Russell would no doubt bend publishers' ears, if she had access to them, but she doesn't, any more than the rest of us have. The ones with access are their cronies: the other members of the corporate economic elite, and the business people who advertise in their newspapers.

During the conference, in an exchange which didn't make it into these pages, *Windsor Star* editor Carl Morgan explained his newspaper's editorial position in favour of free trade. He pointed out that it was a painstaking process arrived at by a small editorial group. They made their difficult decision, said Mr. Morgan, despite the fact that the public and newspaper subscribers in the Windsor area are overwhelmingly opposed to the FTA. "So," Mr. Morgan concluded, "no one can accuse us of pandering to our readers."

Precisely. And no one would. Why would any fiscally-responsible editor pander to his or her readers when they only pay for 20% of newspaper costs, compared to 80% paid for by advertisers? While the vast majority of the public in Windsor opposed the FTA, the Chamber of Commerce, Downtown Business Association, and the business community in general overwhelmingly favoured it. So, like all of the other editors and publishers on all of the other dailies across this country, except *The Toronto Star*, and *The Edmonton Journal*, Carl Morgan was pandering to his advertisers rather than his readers. 108 daily newspapers across this country favoured the FTA; two opposed it. That's a helluva coincidence.

This is the kind of imbalance in coverage which CBC Winnipeg journalist Lesley Hughes says, casts "a lot of doubt" on the concept of objectivity in the media. She goes on to say that the CBC may be sacrificed to the government/corporate agenda, which is sad because the CBC operates largely independently of commercial pressures and the corporate agenda. And yet, even the CBC has adopted the glib economic vocabulary of the new Right.

> We know what 'privatize' means, it means to sell; we know what the deficit is, we know it's bad. We know what to rationalize is, that means to fire; we know what efficiency is and that means profit. How come we don't know what an oligopoly is?...because it's not on the corporate agenda for us to learn it...

Frances Russell made a similar point when she asked,

> What do we mean by being 'balanced'? Why do we use the phraseology "labour-NDP alliance?" Why do we not also use the phraseology of "corporate-Conservative alliance?"

Ms. Hughes has answered Ms. Russell's question as well as her own: it's not on the corporate agenda. And the mass media, newspapers, television and radio, increasingly including the CBC, are the delivery system for that corporate agenda.

Lesley Hughes has expressed for all of us, our disbelief. How is it that our paternal, good government, made up of our elected neighbours, could so abuse its children? I would sum up what she is saying, in a way, as: "We at the CBC have been good, daddy, we're not leftists. Don't beat us!" In our wide-eyed childlike innocence, we don't understand the FTA, the GST, or corporate-government or corporate-media links. It's all so complicated, with economics and everything. But it has been unnecessarily complicated by figures and data and emotionalism on both sides. It's all really very simple.

When in August 1989, *Fortune* magazine announced the richest people/families in the world for 1988, petit little Canada numbered two in the top ten. One was the Reichmann brothers of Toronto; the other Ken Thomson of Thomson International, owners among other things of *The Globe and Mail*. The Reichmann brothers ranked eighth amongst the world's billionaires, with $8.4 billion in assets; Ken Thomson ranked tenth with an estimated wealth of $6.9 billion. According to *Forbes* magazine, whose list differs slightly, K.C. Irving of New Brunswick and Bermuda ranks as the third-richest nonmonarch in the world, with assets of $10 billion. In a way, this one day news event of these announcements sums up Canadian history, a history of increasing monopolization and the accumulation of wealth by a small number of families. Since Jacques Noel, nephew to Jacques Cartier, acquired a monopoly in the fur trade in the latter part of the sixteenth century, to today, when one taxicab company owns all of the cabs in Windsor Ontario, ours has been a history of monopolies. The CPR began with a monopoly, as did Bell

Canada and Rogers Cable, Canada Post, and newspapers dotting cities across the country.

In the preface to his 1914 book, *The History of Canadian Wealth*, Gustavus Myers wrote: "...it is estimated that less than fifty men control $4,000,000,000, or more than one-third of Canada's material wealth as expressed in railways, banks, factories, mines, land and other properties and resources." By 1984, *The Globe and Mail* reported that 46% of the value of the most important companies on the Toronto Stock Exchange was controlled by just nine families.

We're surrounded by monopolies or near-monopolies in every field from food distribution to banking, from gasoline to beer companies. And yet, as Lesley Hughes points out, we don't even know the meaning of "oligopoly," the prelude to monopoly. What's all around us, what permeates our culture, is not to be found in our language.

How can we come to terms with and understand this monopolization? It's not a diabolical plot, but simply the natural outcome of the dog-eat-dog competitive capitalism which is the foundation of our economy. The goal of every business in our system is to expand and to grow, to realize the vertical and horizontal integration which spell success and profits. The ultimate achievement is either a monopoly or an oligopolistic cartel, which under the smiling countenance of the toothless grin of our Anti-Combines Legislation, can squeeze consumers dry. This, and not our "smaller market" or "the price we pay for being Canadian," and in addition to our higher taxes, is the reason for our exorbitantly-priced consumer goods, relative to the U.S. If we want lower prices we should force our government to break up the cartels and legislate competition, rather than climbing into bed with the Americans. But why would they want to legislate against their friends, or themselves? Why would they be any more interested in pandering to the voters than editors like Carl Morgan would be interested in pandering to newspaper readers?

The CBC's Knowlton Nash has said that the media represent the "hinge" and the "glue" of democracy. If that's so, we are becoming unhinged and unglued.

Historically, the development of the press consisted of efforts aimed at increasing its efficiency as an advertising medium. As the late great social scientist Harold Innis noted in the 1940s, by serving advertising interests, journalism changed "from a profession to a branch of commerce."

Some may see this as a romanticized view of history, but putting aside the debate over whether things were ever otherwise, there is considerable evidence that generally, today's newspapers are a branch of commerce. In a sense, we can deduce this from the following facts:

o Concentrated ownership of our industries means a small number of companies controls virtually every area of endeavour.

o With three of the top ten billionaires in the world, (the Reichmanns, Irvings, and Thomsons) Canada is *still* run by a small family compact.

o Sociological studies of the Canadian elite have shown that it is monolithic rather than pluralistic in nature, that is, the economic elite is the political elite, which is the media elite.

o Two newspaper chains control 70 percent of English language daily circulation; three chains control 90 percent of French circulation.

o In 1988, advertisers spent $2.8 billion in newspapers, compared to $1.2 billion on television. Advertisers pay 80 percent of the cost of newspapers, with readers paying only 20 percent.

Thus, with few exceptions, newspapers are written for advertisers. The media have become mere conduits for the ideas of the powerful elite in society; part of what has been termed the "legitimation system."

One good example of this was the July 17, 1989 cover story in Maclean's magazine, labelled "Media Wars," and featuring a front page photo of media baron Conrad Black. The story read like a cheering section for industry rationalization, describing "communications empires of breathtaking international size and scope." Of "emerging media baron" Black, the magazine gushed, "With another big takeover, Black would be well on his way to becoming an international media giant."

The 1988 federal free trade election provided a litmus test for this theory of media: the Conservatives and business favoured free trade, and everyone else opposed it. How did the media perform? As indicated, only two of 110 dailies opposed the FTA editorially, *The Toronto Star,* and *The Edmonton Journal.* Coincidence? It's unlikely.

Ironically, it was *The Toronto Star* which had to (successfully) defend its election coverage before the Ontario Press Council. But intensive analysis of *The Globe and Mail* election coverage shows extensive and fundamental biases in favour of the FTA and the Conservative Party.

First of all, in *The Globe* as elsewhere, we were told that Canadian business must get lean and mean and rationalize, in order to compete in the global economy. The alternative view that a small group of Canadian monopolists had to expand into the U.S. to maintain exorbitant profit growth, was non-existent, except for *The Toronto Star.*

When *The Globe* did provide "balance," it undermined the other side by presenting them as hysterical nationalists, or by framing such information in a biased manner. An example of this latter treatment is where the newspaper ran an opinion piece opposed to the FTA, by Liberal Senator Philippe Gigantes, headlined: "Would it be so hard to rip up the deal?" But on the front page that same day they ran a lead story headlined, "Poll says Canadians want to renegotiate, not rip up trade deal." Portrayed in this manner, the prominent poll story undermined the opinion piece.

Prominence also was given by *The Globe* to the apparent connection between the value of the dollar and the polls. We were told that "Financial markets (are) clearly on the side of the free trade deal." The money markets revived with the Liberals' "sagging fortunes." Eminence was afforded to virtual blackmail or strike threats (although they weren't identified as such) by business people, over investments which would be scrapped if free trade was defeated.

When Quebec's "captains of industry," the reported "cream of Quebec's business community," gathered in a show of force to support the FTA, they were treated as if they were synonymous with the Quebec population at large. And as with most stories representing the business point of view, there was no need to present another side for balance. Balance was only necessary to counteract the so-called nationalist hysteria.

The evidence bears out the statement by *Globe* reporter Lorne Slotnick, which bears repeating. He said his paper was "nearly hysterical in its support for the free trade deal," and that "reporters were told and were subtly made to feel that stories that made the free trade deal look bad were not welcome."

The upshot of all this goes beyond a single election or trade agreement, to threaten the foundations of democracy. Democracy requires an informed electorate, but shallow, frivolous and one-sided information in the press has led to a subsequent decline in knowledge and increased susceptibility to manipulation -- over free trade and other matters.

The difference between Liberals and Conservatives is that the former tolerate public enterprise, while the latter do not. Having sold off Air Canada, the Tories are now eyeing Via Rail, slashing it with a vigour matched only by cuts applied to the CBC. Both are an anathema to Conservatives, for they represent restrictions on the private enterprise opportunities of their friends and cronies. A publicly-owned Air Canada cannot be acquired by a Power Corp. or Argus Corp., but a private one can, thus adding to the wealth of the families of Paul Desmarais or Conrad Black. This message can be easily delivered by Peter White, as he travels back and forth from his position as right hand man to Conrad Black, to that of principal secretary to Brian Mulroney.

This, then, is part of the agenda, along with cuts to social programs, reducing the deficit, and so forth. But the CBC represents a double threat: not only is it public enterprise, remaining out of the grasp of the greedy hands of Tory cronies and Tories themselves, but it is not "part of the team." It doesn't always follow the rules about kowtowing to business, and espousing what Lesley Hughes called "the language of the new Right." So, from the standpoint of Tory Government strategy, what you do is to increase the CBC's reliance on advertisers, to make it more like the other media. You do this by cutting back on government money. (This is the broadcast equivalent of making Petro Canada function just like the other big sister oil companies.) Eventually, of course, your goal is to eliminate the CBC entirely, replacing it with a chain of corporate-controlled private stations. But you have to do this slowly, to keep public outcry to a minimum.

Other "nuisances" can be accounted for as well. For example, if some Tory crony can be persuaded to buy up *The Toronto Star* and make it part of a chain of newspapers, with the accompanying sole preoccupation with profit rather than the occasional twinge of public responsibility, then both financial and ideological purposes may be served.

What the media tell us is *crucial*, for they determine how we interpret the events going on around us: our very consciousness. They decide whether we are constantly exposed to one view versus another. For example, we may be told that free trade and the accompanying rationalization and concentration of our economy is absolutely essential if Canada is to remain competitive in a world economy. If they don't expand, companies will wither and die, and jobs will die with them. As indicated above, this was the message delivered to us time and again during the course of the free trade election. Or, we may be told that the small number of corporations which control the Canadian economy must expand into American and global markets, in order to preserve their exorbitant profits and growth rate. Such expansion will be good for business and profits, but devastating for employees: it is always thus with rationalization.

Media which are blind to corporate concentration and monopolies and indeed, which are part and parcel of this problem, are incapable of presenting the latter argument. Thus, we are stuck with the former, and opposition to free trade coalesces around vague feelings of "nationalism," "sovereignty," a desire to protect Canadian culture, and a dislike for American life which is only outweighed by the love (and promise) of things which are American.

Thus, while it is important for us to understand the motive behind corporate concentration and the FTA ("efficiency" or profits), we must not ignore the delivery system: the mass media, for ultimately, they are the reason why we are undergoing a silent rather than a noisy or violent revolution.

Needless to say, all of this is very depressing. It's difficult to envision a way out of the Catch 22 situation we find ourselves in. Both government and media effectively are controlled by business interests. Many social critics spend so much of their time trying to *point out* and provide evidence for the above problems that there is little time or energy left over for drumming up alternatives. Those who do are likely to present bandaid solutions, such as those suggested by the Kent Royal Commission on Newspapers in 1981. In retrospect, of course, even those bandaids would have been preferable to nothing.

Which problem do we tackle? Since this is a book focused primarily on the media, can we not simply begin with them? Well, the answer, obviously, lies in government action, legislation, which will help to make the media more democratic institutions. But as professor Baer pointed out in Chapter Seven, we should first reform our inherently undemocratic electoral process, so we stop "electing" majority governments which have a minority of the votes cast. It's time to consider and to implement a system of proportional representation, (PR) so that a party with 46% of the popular vote will have *exactly* 46% of the vote in the House of Commons. Such a system is not without its drawbacks, as the Israelis have proved over the years. But with all of its shortcomings it is far preferable to having the majority of your voting population effectively disenfranchised. Yet, this is the sad state of our current affairs. What manner of "democracy" is this?

Evidently, providing solutions is a more complex matter than identifying the problems. We can't simply patch up the shortcomings of the media, for those problems are endemic to our socio-political-economic system. If we revise our electoral system in the suggested manner, which is a far more pressing problem than that posed by the Senate or Meech Lake, then we will have made a start. From there, we can then bring about changes in our media which will help them to better reflect the wishes of their readers, rather than their advertisers. A "print CBC" or publicly-run national daily newspaper is one suggestion which was unduly rejected by the Kent Commission. The vast majority of us living in monopoly newspaper cities *deserve* such an alternative. Government subsidies and tax breaks for establishing competing newspapers are other viable suggestions, as are taxes on newspaper and broadcasting profits, which could be funnelled to competition. These steps have been successfully undertaken in European countries such as Sweden. There is no good reason for not adopting them here in Canada, where our problems of media concentration and monopolization are much more severe.

At the risk of providing a "cookbook" list of social remedies, allow me to briefly outline a plan of action for those who are as mad as hell and would like to do something about it.

1. Educate the public. The fragmented nature of news presentations prevents us from getting the bigger picture which is the basis of this book: we must remove the earplugs and blindfolds concealing Canada's silent revolution. This book is a part of that process, as are popular movements and coalitions, with their pamphlets and flyers (and hopefully TV ads as well). Grade school, high school, and university courses are badly needed too, and it is with some relief that 25 years after the

publication of Marshall McLuhan's book *Understanding Media*, the Ontario Government finally has introduced a media literacy programme in high schools.

2. Democratize our political system. Voters must *demand* a system of proportional representation, so that we get what we ask for in our government, rather than the product of fluky quirks in our winner-take-the-riding system. In addition, as Ian Waddell and others have suggested, we must reform the Elections Act to prevent third parties such as the "National Citizens Coalition" and the "Canadian Alliance for Trade and Job Opportunities," from making a mockery of spending limits imposed upon the political parties. It's already quite clear who has the most money to spend: Corporate Canada, its pockets bulging with untaxed profits, is only too ready to further expand into the business Noam Chomsky has called, "manufacturing consent," or the creation of "necessary illusions."

3. Democratize our media. Owing to the limited number of broadcast channels *and* daily newspapers, these should be public property. Their role in a democratic society is far too important to be entrusted solely to the hands of Corporate Canada. The possibility and reality of abuse with an ideas-for-profit system is far too likely. Ideas and information are *not* just commodities like any other: if we consider nuclear energy important enough to preserve as a public resource, then our media are no less deserving. We must ignore the American bogey-man of government intervention. Flawed though our political democracy may be, we do at least get to vote for our government, albeit in an imperfect manner. Yet, who voted to allow Ken Thomson to control *The Globe and Mail* and 39 other dailies across this country?

4. Return to Canadian traditions. By this we don't mean our tradition of monopoly industries! We must rip up the FTA, restore funding to Via Rail and the CBC, and buy back Air Canada from the corporate sector. Sectors of industry should be nationalized, (including media industries) in order to provide competition and alternatives to the corporate perspective. We must find some means of preventing obscene levels of private accumulation of wealth, and better means of redistribution of that wealth.

As Maude Barlow points out, the newspaper monopoly is evidenced by the fact that while 70% of the Canadian public opposed the FTA, only two of 110 daily newspapers did so. In comparison, public corporations can focus on serving the majority rather than the advertisers. They can serve Canadians rather than looking abroad to increase their profits.

In the era of the "new and improved," suggestion number 4 will no doubt invoke howls of derision. Opponents will point to a fast-paced, changing world, as evidence that Canada too must change or be left behind. Well, we are not modern day Luddites, opposed to change. But changes should be appraised rather than blithely adopted, wholesale, and for their own sake. You don't change your Constitution over night, as the result of a quick confab on the part of a dozen or so men. You don't make a blind "leap of faith" into the precipice of free trade, because your cronies think it will make them a fast buck. Countries are not like family fortunes, to be gambled away on the stock market or at the horse races. It's one thing to take a chance on the lottery, and quite another to risk your country's sovereignty. Buying into the changes of free trade is altogether different from upgrading your computer, or changing the style of your clothes or hair.

Needless to say, this is a plan for the long term. In the short term, one can only root for and join the popular movements and coalitions which Rick Salutin describes as constituting "everyone but business." These groups have received a moral boost from the nearly universal opposition to the Tories' planned Goods and Services Tax (GST). In the medium term we can throw this Tory government out on its collective ear. We can do more than publishing an anti-free trade comic book: we can score additional victories for democracy, as we continue to fight the sound of silence, and as we bring an end to this silent revolution.

***

APPENDIX I[1]

April 19, 1989

To all concerned, in
the labour movement:

After 4-plus years of covering labour for *The Globe and Mail,* I'd like to say goodbye to many of the people who have made my job so interesting and enjoyable. *The Globe* has decided to abolish the labour beat, and I have asked to be taken off the newly constituted "workplace beat."

When the beat was renamed several weeks ago, I thought the transformation might be a mild and ultimately palatable one. But it has become apparent that *The Globe* is seeking a radical change in the way it has covered labour for more than 50 years.

In a conversation on April 14, *The Globe's* new managing editor, Tim Pritchard, told me the paper is no longer interested in covering developments in collective bargaining or the activities of organized labour. Rather, the paper's management wants coverage of the "good" things that are happening at non-union establishments, as well as stories about workplace "trends" -- apparently from a management point of view.

Aside from pointing out the obviously disturbing ideological content of such an approach, I have tried to argue with *Globe* management that these changes are journalistically foolhardy; that a paper like *The Globe* -- with more than 30 reporters covering business -- must have at least one staff member whose job it is to understand and report on collective bargaining and the politics and structure of the labour movement.

However, *The Globe* is not interested in such arguments, and I cannot make the changes that are being asked of me without feeling completely compromised as a journalist. In the past, I could live with what *The Globe* was interested in -- even though I could not do every story I thought was valid, I was happy with the stories *The Globe* did enable me to pursue, and I never encountered political interference. That is obviously no longer going to be the case.

In recent weeks, I have been labelled by *Globe* management as too "pro-labour" and have been told that I am "protecting" people -- in other words, covering up stories that I know about, because they would make my "friends" look bad. As all of you who have dealt with me know, I have never been in anyone's pocket. I have always prided myself on my independence, and I have striven, I hope successfully, for fair and accurate reporting. In my experience, that's the only thing most news sources want, and they have a right to expect it.

You may be aware that the abolition of the labour beat is only one of many changes taking place at *The Globe* since a major power play early this year by the paper's publisher, Roy Megarry, resulted in the forced departure of the paper's three top editors. Their replacements, while well-intentioned and personable, are completely beholden to Megarry.

The result will be a paper much less open to a wide range of points of view. It's not going to change overnight and it's not going to be apparent in every story in the paper, but the shift has already clearly begun. Already some of our best people have left *The Globe*, and many of the rest of us are assessing our situations.

For now, I will be staying at *The Globe*, likely as a general assignment reporter -- covering whatever they assign me to. Thanks to a good collective agreement, they cannot just turf me out.

I want everyone to know that I've had great fun covering labour for the past few years, and I wish all of you well in the future.

Lorne Slotnick

1. This letter is printed with the permission of Lorne Slotnick.

1. Page A1[1]

Dollar leaps in reaction to the polls

BY MURRAY CAMPBELL
and ANDRE PICARD
The Globe and Mail

More election news
Pages A14, A16 and A17

The Canadian dollar continued its roller-coaster ride on foreign exchange markets yesterday, driven upward by news that the Conservatives and Liberals were neck-and-neck in two new opinion polls.

The dollar gained almost three-quarters of a U.S. cent yesterday, to close at 81.90, up from 81.19 at the beginning of the trading day.

It gained throughout the day, and then put on a further spurt in the late afternoon on the strength of news that President Ronald Reagan will deliver a speech in Washington next Thursday defending free trade.

White House spokesman Marlin Fitzwater said Mr. Reagan will be careful not to intrude in the Canadian election on Nov. 21, but will defend the deal that has become a central issue in the race.

The financial markets, clearly on the side of the free-trade deal pro-

DOLLAR — Page A2

[1] All articles reprinted with permission of The Globe and Mail, and Environics Research Ltd.

Page A2

Dollar

● From Page One

posed by the Conservatives, have reacted immediately to any news that the government's re-election, and hence the deal, could be threatened.

"The volatility of the dollar is directly affected every time a poll is released. It's a whiplash market, and the polls are the driving force," said James Snook, vice-president of foreign exchange at Citibank Canada.

The money markets, which had enjoyed a relatively tranquil time after the free-trade deal was negotiated late last year, began to heat up after initial public opinion polls showed that the sagging fortunes of the Liberal Party had been revived by the performance of leader John Turner in the televised debates more than two weeks ago.

The Canadian dollar had ended trading on Oct. 24, just before the first of the two debates, at 83.42 cents (U.S.). The frenzied trading took hold on Monday of this week after the release of a Gallup poll that showed the Liberals with the support of 43 per cent of the Canadian electorate, a stunning reversal of earlier polls that had showed the party flirting with oblivion.

The dollar lost two-thirds of a U.S. cent in value in trading that day, closing at 80.94 cents.

"In terms of the Canadian dollar, almost 80 per cent of market movement is based solely on polls these days. Dealers around the world are watching the polls and reacting to them immediately," said Suzanne Iskander, vice-president of trading at Deak International Canada Ltd.

The Globe and Mail newsroom was flooded with calls from traders anxious to get an advance glimpse of the Environics Research Group Ltd. poll published yesterday. The poll showed the Liberals with the support of 37 per cent of decided voters, compared with 35 per cent for the Conservatives and 24 per cent for the New Democrats.

Money market analysts interviewed yesterday said it is possible for traders to make large sums of money with the advantage of advance information contained in public opinion polls.

"I would certainly trade all my positions if I had advance information," said Miss Iskander. "We're talking millions of dollars changing hands based on that sort of information."

Michael Bastian, vice-president of investment banking and treasury for the Royal Bank of Canada, sounded a note of caution, however, about how many fortunes are being made.

"I would suggest as many people have lost as have won. It's a zero-sum game," he said.

The volatility of the money markets is much higher during this election campaign for two reasons: the increased number of polls being published and the widespread feeling that the fate of the free-trade pact is crucial to the future of Canada.

There have been 18 media-financed public opinion polls since the campaign began on Oct. 1 and another four are expected before voting on Nov. 21. In 1984, there were 12 media polls and in 1980 there were only two.

"The more information the market gets, the more it can react to," said Roderick Fowler, manager of foreign exchange for Wood Gundy Inc. in Toronto.

"With polls with very different results coming out every day, you have a hurting effect on the market, and it's unrelenting. The view of the market can change 100 per cent with the results of one poll," he said.

John Clinkard, senior economist with the Canadian Imperial Bank of Commerce, said the fate of the free-trade deal is being watched closely by investors around the world because they believe the atmosphere for investment in Canada would not be as receptive if the deal were scuttled — as the Liberals and NDP have threatened to do if they form a government.

The commonly held belief in the investment community is that a victory by Brian Mulroney would spell low interest rates and a strong currency while a victory by either of the two opposition parties would mean a weaker dollar and higher interest rates.

Poll says Canadians want to renegotiate, not rip up trade deal

BY MICHAEL ADAMS, DONNA DASKO and JAMES MATSUI

GLOBE-ENVIRONICS POLL

A majority of Canadians opposes the Conservative government's free-trade agreement with the United States, but 44 per cent want it renegotiated rather than torn up, according to the latest poll for The Globe and Mail by Environics Research Group Ltd.

Fifty-one per cent of eligible voters polled between Nov. 3 and Nov. 8 say they are against the trade deal, up from 42 per cent at the outset of the campaign for the Nov. 21 federal election. Thirty-nine per cent are in favor — down from 44 per cent. Eleven per cent are undecided, a drop of three points since early October.

The poll results show a reversal in the popularity of the agreement since the start of the election campaign, when more people supported the pact than opposed it.

Thirty-four per cent of voters surveyed in the new poll say that free trade is the most important problem facing Canada today, nearly double the 19 per cent who said so in a Globe-Environics poll conducted at the beginning of the election campaign.

But ambivalence toward the free-trade agreement is evident when voters are asked what the government should do about the agreement.

A total of 44 per cent would like to

MOST — Page A14

ENVIRONICS TRACKING ON SUPPORT FOR FREE TRADE*

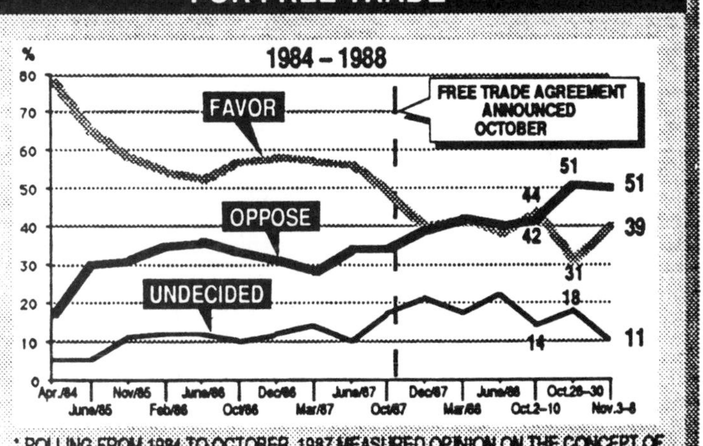

* POLLING FROM 1984 TO OCTOBER, 1987 MEASURED OPINION ON THE CONCEPT OF FREE TRADE WITH THE UNITED STATES. SINCE OCTOBER, 1987, ENVIRONICS HAS TRACKED OPINION ON THE FREE TRADE AGREEMENT ITSELF.

BERNARD BENNELL/The Globe and Mail

Most voters oppose trade deal with U.S.

Page A14

● **From Page One**

see the government renegotiate the deal, while 23 per cent would have the government cancel it. Twenty-six per cent would carry through with the current agreement, while 1 per cent would prefer another alternative and 5 per cent say they do not know.

The ambivalent attitude appears to be reinforced by the fear of the economic consequences of cancelling the deal. Thirty-nine per cent of those surveyed in the new poll think that cancellation of the agreement would be bad for the Canadian economy. Seventeen per cent feel that course would be good for the economy, and 31 per cent say it would make no difference. Fourteen per cent say it would have some other effect or do not know.

The latest poll was conducted among a representative nation-wide sample of 1,275 eligible voters.

The margin of error for a sample this size is plus or minus 2.7 percentage points in 19 out of 20 samples.

Other results of the poll, published in The Globe yesterday, show the Liberals, with 37 per cent of popular support, in a virtual tie with the Conservatives, who have 35 per cent. The New Democrats have 24 per cent and other parties have 5 per cent.

Concern about the free-trade agreement is evident right across the country, but is most salient in Toronto, where 43 per cent of those polled say it is the most important problem facing Canadians today. It is also of concern in Saskatchewan, where the poll found that 40 per cent consider it the most important problem, and Montreal, where the figure is 38 per cent.

(The regional figures are based on smaller sample sizes than the national sample and have higher margins of error.)

It was also found that the strong sentiments in favor of the deal have declined somewhat since the outset of the campaign, while strong opposition has grown. In early October, 17 per cent strongly favored the pact and 23 per cent strongly opposed it. Today, 15 per cent strongly favor the deal and 29 per cent strongly oppose it.

The polling also shows that the leaders' debates have influenced public attitudes toward free trade.

Seventeen per cent of those polled from Oct. 2 to 10 strongly favored the free-trade agreement. This dropped to 11 per cent in a Globe-Environics poll taken from Oct. 28 to 30, immediately after the leaders' debates in which Liberal Leader John Turner strongly attacked the

(Continued)

Page A14 Cont'd

poll finds

poll. Twenty-four per cent choose Mr. Broadbent, a drop of three points. Eighteen per cent choose none of the three or could not make a judgment.

Mr. Broadbent, however, remains Canadians' first choice as the most likeable leader and the most trustworthy, but Mr. Turner's rating has improved on these dimensions as well.

Forty-one per cent pick Mr. Broadbent as "most likeable," a drop of two points since early October. Twenty-eight per cent pick Mr. Mulroney, a drop of five points. Eighteen per cent pick Mr. Turner as most likeable, but this represents a six-point increase for him. Thirteen per cent choose none of the three or have no opinion.

Mr. Broadbent is the choice of 32 per cent of Canadians as the "most trustworthy" leader, but this is a drop of four points since early October. Twenty-four per cent pick Mr. Mulroney, down one point, and 19 per cent pick Mr. Turner as most trustworthy, an increase of eight points. Twenty-four per cent choose none of the leaders or have no opinion.

In strategic terms, Mr. Mulroney remains an asset for his party in Quebec, Manitoba and Alberta, and Mr. Broadbent is an asset for his party in Ontario, Saskatchewan and British Columbia. Mr. Turner's ratings have improved in all regions of the country, but he stands above the national average only in the Atlantic Provinces.

Re-interviews with respondents who were polled in early October showed that 71 per cent of those choosing Mr. Mulroney as best man for prime minister at that time still choose him today, and 70 per cent of those who chose Mr. Turner still choose him today. However, only 55 per cent of Canadians who thought Mr. Broadbent was the best choice in early October still choose him today.

Michael Adams is president of Environics Research Group Ltd. Donna Dasko and James Matsui are vice-presidents.

Page A14 Cont'd

Results are from interviews with 1,275 voters

The Globe and Mail
and Environics Research Group Ltd.

The results from today's poll for The Globe and Mail by Environics Research Group Ltd. are based on interviews with a representative nation-wide sample of 1,275 eligible voters. The interviews were conducted between Nov. 3 and 8, in English and French.

Interviewing was conducted from Environics' Toronto office using computer-assisted telephone interviewing techniques.

The margin of error for a sample of 1,275 is plus or minus 2.7 percentage points in 19 out of 20 samples.

The regional distribution of respondents and the corresponding margins of error in 19 out of 20 samples are set out in the table below.

All respondents in today's poll had originally been interviewed as part of the Globe-Environics poll conducted from Oct. 2 to 10 and published in The Globe from Oct. 12 to 15. By returning to this panel, the pollsters were able to track changes in voting intentions over the past four weeks and determine the effect of significant events during the election campaign on individual voters.

Of the 1,745 people interviewed in early October, 73 per cent were interviewed again for the new poll. The original sample was drawn using a multi-stage stratified sampling procedure in which interviews were distributed according to the population of each province and the number of individuals living in each of five community size groups. Household telephone numbers were generated by a random-digit-dialling technique.

Region	Number of respondents	Margin of error
Atlantic	123	± 8.8%
Quebec	314	± 5.5%
Ontario	460	± 4.6%
Manitoba	61	±12.5%
Saskatchewan	53	±13.5%
Alberta	120	± 8.9%
B.C.	144	± 8.2%

With respect to free trade, people were asked:

- In your opinion, what is the most important problem facing Canadians today?
- Do you strongly favor, somewhat favor, somewhat oppose or strongly oppose the free-trade agreement that has been negotiated between Canada and the United States?
- Would you like to see the federal government . . .

a) carry through with the free-trade agreement?

b) renegotiate the agreement?

c) cancel the agreement?

- Do you think the cancellation of the free-trade agreement would be good or bad for the Canadian economy, or would it make no difference?

With respect to leadership, people were asked:

- In your opinion, which of the three major party leaders would make the best prime minister of Canada?
- Of the three leaders, whose performance has improved the most during the election campaign?
- Which of the three leaders do you feel . . .

a) is the most trustworthy?

b) has the best ideas and policies?

c) is the most competent leader?

d) is the most likeable?

3. Page A6

Costs? What costs?

BY JEFFREY SIMPSON

VANCOUVER

To borrow a phrase from recent U.S. politics, a large chunk of the Liberal Party's program may be fairly described as "voodoo economics."

That was how a campaigning George Bush once depicted the economic prescriptions of his then-rival, Ronald Reagan. Mr. Bush meant — and he was not mistaken — that his rival's economic policies were a mixture of pure ignorance, blind faith and dubious assumptions.

In one sense, however, "voodoo economics" does not do justice to the Liberal economic campaign. It was always plausible that Mr. Reagan actually believed what he was saying. The same cannot be said for Liberal leader John Turner, who, as he likes to remind everyone, was once the finance minister of Canada.

As a former finance minister, Mr. Turner knows perfectly well that he is being disingenuous at best, and mendacious at worst, in refusing to say how he will finance his party's hugely expensive campaign promises.

Whether those promises amount to $26.5-billion over four years (as calculated by the C. D. Howe Institute) or $35-billion or $25-billion or $20-billion is almost beside the point. We know that when the Liberals total up the costs, their numbers will be manifestly unreliable. After all, the party moved in four days early in this campaign from not knowing how much its day-care policies would cost to estimating that cost at $4-billion, then $6-billion and finally $10-billion.

Whatever the cost, the programs must be paid for somehow. Any school child knows that, let alone a former minister of finance.

But Mr. Turner, staring blankly into the television cameras, insists he can say nothing until he "examines the books" and consults with senior government officials.

This is palpable and breathtaking nonsense, a stinging insult to the intelligence of the electorate. Unless, of course, Mr. Turner and his Liberal advisers really do take the Canadian people for chumps.

The chances are excellent that, in their profound cynicism, this is precisely how they view the Canadian people. The Liberals have calculated that Canadians do not care about the deficit and prefer the politics of the tooth fairy to even marginally honest economic talk.

Naturally enough, this calculated cynicism extends to all phases of the party's economic message.

Take the proposed national sales tax. One day, the Liberals scream that it would represent a tax grab of $12-billion to $14-billion. The next day, they explain their pledge to scrap the tax by saying such a move would have no adverse fiscal consequences. The tax would be "revenue-neutral," they explain, meaning it would not bring in additional revenue.

Clearly, the tax cannot be both a massive new burden and no new burden at the same time. Asked how the party would rearrange the sales tax, Mr. Turner stares blankly again.

Those of us who covered the 1984 campaign vividly remember Mr. Turner hounding Conservative leader Brian Mulroney to "come clean" and tell the people the cost of his promises and how the Conservatives would pay for them. Mr. Turner used to travel with a binder itemizing the Tory promises which he would hold up on public platforms as he demanded to know how the Tories could pay for all of them.

As the 1984 election turned out, such theatrics got Mr. Turner nowhere. He obviously believes that what didn't work for him in 1984 won't work for his opponents in 1988.

So Mr. Turner says simply, trust me. That's asking a lot for a leader who didn't know the price of his own child-care policies, won't estimate as yet the cost of his promises, won't hint how his party would pay for them and won't say how to reform the national sales tax.

4. Page A6

LETTERS TO THE EDITOR

block from the current school, the new facilities would mean no dislocation or inconvenience to students and their families.

From the $32-million lease arrangement, the board would end up, after all other costs, with more than $14-million to be used to update facilities in other schools.

The proposal would mean the transfer of the Toronto board's warehouse to the waterfront and the removal of traffic problems now caused by the 650 daily arrivals and departures of trucks.

My colleagues and I are astounded that Trustees Doiron and Chow and their fellow NDP members at the aldermanic level are trying to turn this opportunity into some cheap political issue to grab media attention just before the municipal elections.

David Moll
Chairman
Toronto Board of Education

A stronger Canada

In the emotion-charged context of an election campaign, it is sometimes possible to lose sight of the basics, especially for an issue such as free trade.

As an organization representing more than 60,000 business people in all parts of Ontario, the Ontario Chamber of Commerce has supported Canadian-U.S. free trade for a number of years.

We see it as an opportunity to give greater access to the huge U.S. market. Thirty per cent of Canada's gross national product and three million jobs depend on trade — two million of these jobs depend directly on trade with the United States.

We believe that sovereignty is not in question. Indeed, Canada stands to be stronger as the country succeeds in the positive environment offered by free trade.

Peter M. Brophey
President
Ontario Chamber of Commerce
Toronto

•

William French quotes Robertson Davies as writing with obvious pride, "We have created an elaborate and successful welfare state which is itself a declaration that there are things of national importance above politics and finance" (Trade Deal A Threat To Canadian Culture, Warns Veteran Writer — Oct. 18). Successful welfare state, what nonsense! We have created a wealth-destroying monster, which will, if not contained, bankrupt the country, leaving our children and grandchildren to face a mountain of debt, currently more than $300-billion and growing so rapidly that we must work half the year to pay the cost of government.

When the inevitable breakdown of our democracy becomes a reality, who then will be concerned for the Canadian culture that Mr. Davies sees as being jeopardized by the free-trade agreement?

Donald S. Harris
Toronto

Fractions survive

Paul Melly (U.K. To Keep Pint, Mile In Metric Era — Oct. 26) writes that "retaining miles will at least preserve the practice of writing fractions in an age when most children learn arithmetic using decimals." The writing of a fraction is a statement equivalent in meaning to the division of one quantity by another. A decimal is a particular kind of fraction. Unless British children are no longer taught the process of dividing numbers, they will get their share of fractions, metric era or not.

Hans Havermann
Weston, Ont.

Drugs in public housing

I am a lawyer and I am a liberal. But I disagree with Michael Valpy's contention that drug dealers and those who support them should be allowed to operate their sinister businesses in public housing (Evicting Dealers' Kin No Clear-cut Solution; MTHA Drug Policy Uses Tools Of Tyranny — Oct. 24, 25).

Why should 125,000 law-abiding citizens be harassed and intimidated in their own homes by a thousand dangerous criminals?

Remember that poverty denies our tenants any choice about where they live. They cannot just up and move to another neighborhood when criminals move in.

Mr. Valpy hasn't heard, as I have, elderly and frail tenants and exhausted and frightened single young mothers plead for help against ruthless and strung-out dealers who intimidate, mug and rob them. He would have been better informed if he had talked to some of the tenants who are fighting back. For example, Carole Scott, who organized the Say No To Drugs parade at Jane and Finch, or Margaret McDonald, the brave woman who organized Neighborhood Watch at Jane and Finch at considerable risk to her safety.

What the Ontario Housing Corp.

5.

THE GLOBE AND MAIL, FRIDAY, NOVEMBER 11, 1988 A7

Would it be so hard to rip up the deal?

BY PHILIPPE DEANE GIGANTES
Senator Gigantes is the author of Is the Free Trade Deal Really for You? published by Stoddart.

OTTAWA

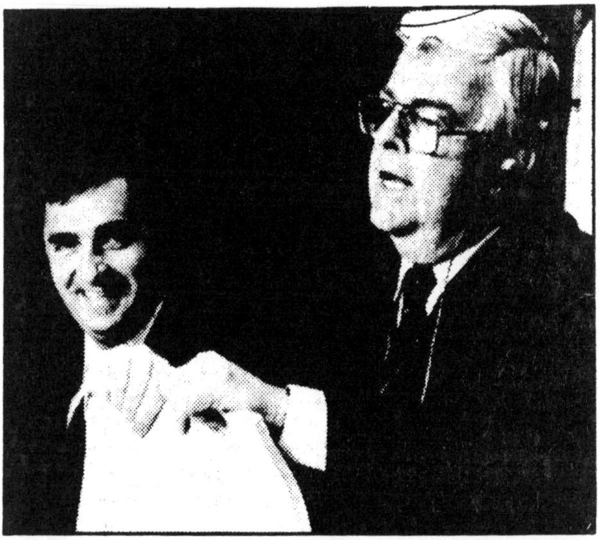

Not such a bad idea: Trade Minister John Crosbie mimics those who would have Canada tear up the free-trade pact.

THOSE WHO reject the free-trade deal are accused of doing so on emotional grounds. But it can also be rejected unemotionally, as a badly drafted, unequal contract.

A "good deal" gives its signatories an equivalent share of the important things each wants. In the trade deal with the United States we wanted additional guarantees that U.S. protectionists would not keep out our growing exports. The Americans wanted better access to our resources and freedom to operate in Canada without restrictions on their investors, financiers and service and manufacturing industries. They got what they wanted; we did not.

Prime Minister Brian Mulroney told The New York Times that the "most important vital condition" that had to be met for him to sign the deal was "that Canada must be permanently exempt from the U.S. fair-trading laws," the countervailing duty law and anti-dumping law.

Mr. Mulroney did not get "his most important vital condition." Article 1902 of free-trade agreement gives the United States the right to continue applying "its anti-dumping law and countervailing duty law" to Canadian goods; further, the United States "reserves the right to change or modify" these laws. We are now being told that, instead of Mr. Mulroney's "most important vital condition," we have a "binding" binational dispute-settlement mechanism. But it isn't binding. Article 1806.3 of the free-trade deal reads:

"If a party fails to implement in a timely fashion the findings of a binding arbitration panel . . . the other party shall have the right to suspend the application of equivalent benefits of this agreement to the non-complying party." Simply put, if the Americans do not like the verdict of an arbitration panel, they can ignore it and we can retaliate.

But 24 per cent of our gross domestic product (everything we produce) is involved in trade with the United States: one Canadian in four is affected. Only 2 per cent of the U.S. GDP is involved in trade with Canada: one American in 50 is affected. They wouldn't notice if we retaliated: we would if they did. So the arrangement is not binding and retaliation is hardly effective when it means that the mouse may kick the elephant.

(Continued)

Page A7 Cont'd

Canadians shouldn't be craven, say proponents of the trade deal, and we should look at how well the small nations have done in the European Community, another free-trade area. The EC's small nations have done well because, in the institutions that make and enforce EC rules, the eight small nations have nine votes; the four big ones have only eight.

Moreover, the big four are not always united and can be played one against the other: not at all like one Canadian mouse facing one U.S. elephant in seven years of negotiations to decide on common definitions of what are permissible subsidies. Hence the fear for our social programs and regional development grants that the Americans have repeatedly challenged as unfair subsidies.

We also agreed that, over 10 years, we would abolish all tariffs in our mutual trade with the United States. But before the free-trade agreement, the General Agreement on Tariffs and Trade was already working at eliminating those remaining tariffs. Besides, 80 per cent of goods crossing our border with the United States are already free of tariffs and, in this 80 per cent tariff-free regime, our trade with the United States has grown 2.8 times in the past 20 years, much faster than our economy, our population, our labor force or our trade with others.

We also obtained a promise in the free-trade agreement that, without discrimination, Canadians can take their money south of the border, build factories there and create jobs for Americans. Economist Richard Lipsey of the C.D. Howe Institute, a defender of the deal, says this is great. Canadians who need to earn salaries or wages here may not agree with him.

In exchange, this is what we gave up:

■ We can no longer ask that a U.S. firm do research in Canada, buy spare parts made here, use Canadian sub-contractors, export part of its production and sell some of its shares to Canadians (Article 1603).

■ Three years from now, any competent corporate lawyer will be able to sell all the parts of any Canadian corporation to Americans with no conditions, simply by breaking up the corporation into parts worth less than $150-million each. U.S. firms can buy their Canadian competitors, move the good parts (including brains) south and leave here only the warehousing operations (annex to Article 1607.3).

■ We have agreed not to "impose a higher price for exports of an energy good (to the United States) than the price charged for such energy good when consumed domestically." We must not reduce the domestic price by "any measures such as licences, fees, taxation" (Article 904b).

Canadian provincial governments derive revenues from energy sales, through royalties, taxes, licences. If they offer a lower price for energy to a firm within their territory, they are open to challenge from the firm's U.S. competitors. No more attracting U.S. investors with the lure of cheap energy if they build factories here.

■ The United States says it will challenge our right to insist that East Coast fishermen land their catch in Canada. If the United States wins that challenge, it will make no sense for Canadian fishing vessels to deliver their catch to processing plants in Canada. To cut out the cost of transporting the finished product south, landing in Boston makes much more sense.

■ What holds for fish will hold for everything else that entails transportation costs: a Canadian firm thinking of building a newer, larger plant to serve its new U.S. market will, after the trade agreement, build that plant in the middle of its large U.S. market, not in the middle of its small Canadian one. So will a U.S. manufacturer.

■ And then there is the "if nothing else works" clause the Americans put in the agreement. Article 2011 says that, if the United States considers that any Canadian "measure, whether or not such measure conflicts with the provisions of this agreement, causes nullification or impairment of any benefit reasonably expected" by the Americans, complainants can appeal to the arbitration panel which, we have seen, settles disputes by pitting the mouse against the elephant.

A commercial U.S. hospital chain can use Article 2011 to ask for the right to establish private hospitals for the rich in Canada. Those U.S. hospitals pay much higher fees to surgeons than do our medicare systems. Guess where the best surgeons will work? We could end up with superlative health care for the rich and much lesser health care for the not-so-rich.

■ Our food-processing industry will move south to use the cheaper produce of the 12-month U.S. growing season. Canadian food processers operating in the United States will serve the Canadian market from their U.S. plants. That is what Harrison McCain, of the New Brunswick food multinational, told Maclean's magazine.

Would the price of rejecting the agreement be unacceptable? No. Mr. Mulroney keeps quoting an Economic Council of Canada report that, after 11 years, we shall have 251,000 more jobs than we would otherwise have, if we sign the agreement. The same study says that, if we do not sign and the Americans turn very protectionist in consequence, the increase in the number of jobs will be cut by 22,000 and personal income will be 0.2 per cent less.

This works out to 11.4 cents less a day for each of us in 1998 — not exactly a catastrophe. The Conference Board of Canada and Informetrica (independent think-tanks) confirm that not signing the agreement would not lead to a disaster.

How can this disparity be so small? Because there are things the Americans need from us that they cannot buy for less from other sources and because our economy can adapt to and compensate for U.S. protectionism, as our shakes and shingles producers have shown.

If the Americans turn nasty, it will not be only against us but against others. Then, these others will want to buy some of the things we sell to the United States in exchange for some of what they sell there.

Besides, unlike the proponents of the trade deal, I do not believe that the Americans will want to damage us if they do not get their way. They are good neighbors, as are we, their faithful allies.

6. Page A7

One more kick at the can

THOMAS WALKOM

AJAX, Ont.

CAN JOHN ROBERTS return from the dead? The erstwhile federal Liberal cabinet minister was defeated in the general election of 1984, defeated in the nomination battle for the Toronto riding of Trinity-Spadina this spring and squeezed out of the Waterloo Liberal nomination in July. He finally contested and won the Liberal nomination in the Tory-held riding of Ontario, just east of Toronto.

It was a thanks-for-nothing win. The federal Liberal organization in Ontario riding has dwindled to almost a family affair. Gwen Mowbray is vice-president and past president of the Liberal riding association. Milton, her husband, is the association's recording secretary. He telephoned Australia to recruit Mr. Roberts, who was lecturing there. Daughter Jane (who ran the successful campaign of provincial Liberal MPP Norah Stoner in 1987) became campaign manager.

Mr. Roberts was not exactly the search committee's first choice. They had tried two local mayors and Liberal MP Aideen Nicholson before approaching the 54-year-old former environment minister.

"For a while, there was just no one who would come forward locally," explains Jane Mowbray. "It's not that there wasn't anyone suitable — there was no one." Finally, three people contested the nomination. Mr. Roberts won on the second ballot.

The Liberal candidate has reorganized his teaching schedule at Montreal's Concordia University so he can spend more time in the riding. He still lives in downtown Toronto, but occasionally spends the night at the Mowbray home. Jane Mowbray says Mr. Roberts has discovered that he rather likes the area, and is thinking of buying a country home there — whether he wins or not.

Nonetheless, it was not a sparkling campaign the Liberals were running in Ajax, Whitby and Pickering, the towns that make up the riding. Most of those who had worked for Ms Stoner, the victorious provincial Liberal, were interested in specific local issues, such as garbage dumps.

These people tended to stay away from the Roberts campaign and concentrated instead on municipal politics."The number of Liberals who would work federally did dwindle," acknowledges Jane Mowbray. Then came the debates — the famous televised leaders' debates in which Liberal leader John Turner was said to shine. For Mr. Roberts and the Mowbrays, it was a reprieve.

"Since the debates, we've even had a run on Turner posters," says Jane Mowbray, pointing to a portrait of the Liberal leader glaring from the wall.

Across the road, in his campaign office, Conservative candidate René Soetens agrees. "The Liberals were totally disorganized until the debates. Now they have workers."

Mr. Soetens, a 40-year-old municipal councillor, says the effect of the debate on this riding was classic. It caused most of the anti-free-trade vote, previously split between the New Democrats and the Liberals, to coalesce behind Mr. Turner.

But he says the debate has also hardened the resolve of his supporters. Local Conservatives, he says, are becoming more aggressive in support of free trade.

The riding of Ontario has been Tory since 1979; however, MP Scott Fennell is retiring, and this makes the current race more interesting.

Added to this is the tremendous recent growth in population, now standing at about 155,000. The old towns of Ajax, Pickering and Whitby have been surrounded by new subdivisions, making the riding a bedroom community for Toronto. About half of its residents have moved to the area since 1984; no one is sure how they will vote.

Mr. Soetens acknowledges that he could be swamped if the national trend turns strongly in favor of the Liberals. But the idea of losing to John Roberts, someone he considers a Toronto carpetbagger, peeves him. "He hardly even knocks on doors," complains Mr. Soetens. "He goes to shopping centres sometimes, but he is not really doing much work."

Turner moves to 2nd place

8. Page A14

Mulroney 1st choice as PM,

BY MICHAEL ADAMS, DONNA DASKO and JAMES MATSUI
© The Globe and Mail and Environics Research Group Ltd.

BEST PRIME MINISTER

	TOTAL	ATLANTIC	QUEBEC	ONTARIO	WEST
MULRONEY	37	42	45	30	37
BROADBENT	23	15	15	28	24
TURNER	27	37	25	28	26
NONE/DK/NA	13	6	14	15	13

Conservative Leader Brian Mulroney remains Canadians' first choice for prime minister, but Liberal Leader John Turner has moved into second place ahead of New Democratic Party Leader Edward Broadbent, according to the latest poll for The Globe and Mail by Environics Research Group Ltd.

In the poll, conducted between Nov. 3 and 8, 37 per cent of voters chose Mr. Mulroney as best man for prime minister, 27 per cent favored Mr. Turner, and 23 per cent picked Mr. Broadbent. Six per cent liked none of the three and seven per cent had no opinion.

Mr. Turner's current standing represents a 12-point jump since a Globe-Environics poll conducted in early October, and reflects his enhanced stature among Canadians following a strong performance in the televised leaders' debates on Oct. 24 and 25.

A Globe-Environics poll conducted shortly after the televised debates showed that 46 per cent of Canadians who watched the debates or followed media reports about them thought Mr. Turner won. Nineteen per cent thought Mr. Mulroney won, and 10 per cent thought Mr. Broadbent won.

The new poll indicates a six-point drop for Mr. Broadbent since early October, leaving the NDP leader at his lowest popularity in more than two years. Since October, 1986, Mr. Broadbent had consistently been the first choice for prime minister.

Mr. Mulroney's standing is down by three points since early October, but the gap between him and his two rivals remains large.

The most recent poll was conducted among 1,275 eligible voters.

The margin of error for a sample of that size is plus or minus 2.7 percentage points in 19 out of 20 samples.

As reported yesterday, the current party standings show a close race between the Liberals and Conservatives.

A Globe-Environics poll found that the Liberals hold 37 per cent of the decided electorate, unchanged from their post-debate high point. The Conservatives are backed by 35 per cent, an increase of four points, and the New Democrats have the support of 24 per cent, down two points, the poll shows. Five per cent support other parties.

On a regional basis, the poll shows Mr. Mulroney leading as preferred choice for prime minister by a wide margin in Quebec, Manitoba, and Alberta. He is closely followed by Mr. Turner in the Atlantic region, and all three leaders are neck-and-neck in Ontario, Saskatchewan and British Columbia.

The regional figures are based on smaller samples than the national one and have a higher margin of error.

The public's more favorable assessment of Mr. Turner's leadership qualities is reflected in his improved ratings in a more detailed series of leadership questions.

Sixty-four per cent of those polled think Mr. Turner is the leader whose performance has improved the most during the election campaign. Twelve per cent think Mr. Mulroney has improved the most, and 10 per cent think Mr. Broadbent has improved most. Fourteen per cent pick none or offer no opinion.

Mr. Mulroney is chosen by 38 per cent as the "most competent" of the three leaders, and this rating was unchanged since early October. However, 22 per cent now choose Mr. Turner as most competent, an incease of 11 points. Mr. Broadbent is chosen by 21 per cent, down seven points. Eighteen per cent pick none of the leaders or have no opinion.

Similarly, Mr. Mulroney remains the choice of 31 per cent of Canadians as the leader with the "best ideas and policies." But 26 per cent choose Mr. Turner as having the best policies and ideas, an increase of 11 points since the early October

Brian Mulroney

(Continued)

Page A14 Cont'd

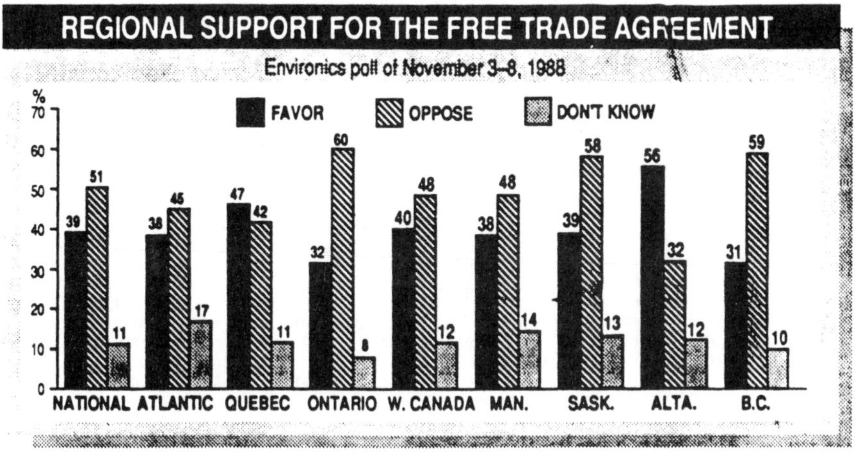

BERNARD BENNELL/The Globe and Mail

agreement.

Today, strong support for the deal is up four points to 15 per cent, suggesting that the Conservative counterattack is having an impact on voters.

Strong opposition to the agreement started at 23 per cent in early October and jumped to 32 per cent after the leaders' debates. Today, strong opposition to the pact is down slightly to 29 per cent.

Strong opponents of the agreement outnumber strong proponents in every region of the country except Alberta. Areas in which strong opposition to the pact was found to be greatest are Saskatchewan (44 per cent strongly opposed), Ontario (35 per cent) and British Columbia (34 per cent).

Areas in which support for the agreement was found to be strongest are Alberta (22 per cent strongly favor), Manitoba (20 per cent) and Quebec (17 per cent.)

The survey also provides further evidence that the campaign has changed some people's minds about the agreement. Twenty-six per cent of those who favored the pact in the Oct. 2-to-10 poll now either oppose the deal or are undecided. On the other hand, only 15 per cent who were opposed are now either in favor or undecided.

A plurality in nearly every region would like the agreement to be renegotiated. The highest levels found to prefer this alternative were in British Columbia (53 per cent), Quebec (48 per cent) and Toronto (46 per cent.)

Alberta is the only province where more than one-third of voters — 37 per cent — wants the government to carry through with the current deal. And in no province does more than 28 per cent of the electorate want the deal cancelled.

It is clear that Canadians want neither to accept the current deal as it is, nor do they wish to scrap it completely. Voters apparently want a middle course in which the pact is renegotiated, presumably in a way that concerns that have been raised about social safety programs and other issues can be clearly and specifically addressed.

Michael Adams is president of Environics Research Group Ltd. Donna Dasko and James Matsui are vice-presidents.

9. Page A14

Broadbent unwilling to make a judgment on need for Bill 101

BY CHRISTOPHER WADDELL
The Globe and Mail

QUEBEC CITY

As he is not a native Quebecker, New Democratic Party Leader Edward Broadbent said yesterday he cannot judge whether Quebec's controversial language law, Bill 101, is still required to protect the rights of the province's francophone majority.

"I can't decide as an outsider whether the bill is needed or not," Mr. Broadbent told reporters at a mid-morning news conference held aboard a vessel on the St. Lawrence River between Quebec City and Levis. He was accompanied by John-Paul Harney, NDP federal candidate in Levis and former leader of the provincial NDP.

"Neither can I make a judgment on that . . . in terms of the sociological reality . . . . It's not up to me to do it. It's up to the people of the province of Quebec," Mr. Broadbent continued.

However, earlier this year, the NDP leader was outspoken in his opposition to minority-rights legislation introduced by the Saskatchewan government.

In a hastily arranged scrum with reporters, as Mr. Broadbent's plane arrived in Toronto late yesterday afternoon, the NDP leader said his position on the various pieces of legislation regarding minority rights has been totally consistent.

"I have been a defender of the objectives of Bill 101," he said, describing them as the promotion of French language and culture in Quebec without reducing minority rights.

"I commented on Bill 101 when it was introduced," he continued, adding that he also commented on Saskatchewan's language legislation when it was introduced in April.

"But when I'm asked as I was asked this morning, do I think certain legislative action is required in a province, quite literally that is not my responsibility as a federal leader. That's up to the province," Mr. Broadbent said.

Once a province acted, he stated, then he would feel free to comment.

A decision is now pending from the Supreme Court of Canada on a challenge to the constitutionality of the provisions of Bill 101 that restrict the use of English on signs in Quebec.

Mr. Broadbent said yesterday he might have more to say on Bill 101 after the decision is released.

Yesterday's news conference was held to announce an NDP government would spend an extra $20-million a year for sewer and water-treatment facilities in part to help clean up the St. Lawrence River. That comes on top of previous campaign promises of a $250-million annual fund for municipal upgrading of sewer and water-treatment facilities and another $200-million a year for a general environmental clean-up. Of that total, $100-million will be dedicated to the St. Lawrence and Great Lakes region.

Reporters, however, were more interested in questioning Mr. Broadbent and Mr. Harney about the apparent contradictions between the views of the federal party and its Quebec wing on minority language rights, recent amendments to the Official Languages Act and the "notwithstanding" clause of the Charter of Rights and Freedoms.

"We have the only party leader who favors preserving the collective rights of Quebec through the "notwithstanding" clause," Mr. Harney proclaimed.

Earlier this week in Kingston, Mr. Broadbent maintained the policy difference was nothing more than nuances reflecting the constitutional argument of whether the Charter or Parliament should be supreme.

A group of seven NDP candidates in Quebec last weekend proclaimed that the "notwithstanding" clause, which allows provinces to override the Charter, should be available only for use by Quebec to maintain majority-language rights in the province.

"They don't see that particular nuance, frankly, as being very significant. Nor do I," Mr. Broadbent told reporters in Kingston on Tuesday, adding that he speaks for the national party.

NDP candidates in Quebec do not want to see the "notwithstanding" clause used to deny rights to the English-speaking minority in Quebec, the NDP leader said.

"But clearly it could be used from time-to-time to improve the position of the francophone majority in a number of matters that did not entail the denying of rights to the minority," he said at the time.

10. Page A14

Liberal ads get go-ahead from judge

BY PAUL KORING
The Globe and Mail

OTTAWA

A Federal Court judge has ordered Canada's three English-language television networks to broadcast Liberal Party advertisements showing excerpts from the TV debates. The ads include John Turner's summation and a dramatic moment of confrontation over free trade with Conservative Leader Brian Mulroney.

In a nine-page ruling yesterday, Mr. Justice Leonard Martin rejected the networks' arguments that they had the right to refuse the advertisements on the grounds that the Liberal Party had infringed on copyright by using footage from the debates.

"The networks are no longer in the business of censoring political advertising," said Allan Lufty, counsel for the Liberal Party.

Although the networks could appeal the decision, Mr. Lufty said CTV had already told the party the ads would run immediately.

Global, which had originally voiced no objection to the advertisements but then joined the CBC and CTV to show solidarity in the case, was not included in the terms of the injunction, with the consent of the plaintiffs.

In granting the injunction, the judge said that while the issue of copyright had not been decided and the matter should be heard at a full trial, any further delay would amount to denying the Liberals their rights.

William Green, who argued the party's case, said the advertisements could affect the outcome of the Nov. 21 election.

Mr. Lufty said the judge had "cut down" the contention of the CBC that its claim to copyright gave it the right to accept or reject a paid political advertisement based on its content.

Liberal officials were delighted by the decision. Conventional wisdom has it that Mr. Turner won the nationally televised debates; the party wanted to use excerpts from them in its advertising to remind voters both of Mr. Turner's message and his performance.

11. Page A16

Books are open to Liberals, Mulroney tells party rally

BY SUSAN DELACOURT
The Globe and Mail

TIMMINS, Ont.

Nothing is stopping Liberal Leader John Turner from looking at the country's books to assess the cost of his campaign promises, Conservative Leader Brian Mulroney says.

"Mr. Turner has all the information he needs right now to tell Canadians the truth about his amazing spending proposals," Mr. Mulroney said at a party rally yesterday in Timmins.

"All he lacks is the courage to do so."

With opinion polls showing a neck-and-neck race in the election campaign between the Liberals and the Tories, Mr. Mulroney is sharpening his attacks on the Liberal's list of promises and Mr. Turner's refusal to provide an accounting for them.

It was Mr. Mulroney's main theme on the campaign trail in Northern Ontario yesterday and the focus of a speech in Toronto at the same time by Finance Minister Michael Wilson, in which a partial list of Liberal pledges was estimated to cost about $37-billion over four years.

To emphasize the point, Mr. Wilson was summoned to give more details last night to reporters covering the tour, even though the same figures were announced in Montreal on Wednesday by Industry Minister Robert de Cotret. And, if the halls outside the meeting room in Timmins yesterday were any indication, it is also the strategy that workers on the ground are adopting to fight local Liberals.

While the crowd was filing into the Timmins meeting room, several party workers were huddled with small clusters of people, pressing the point.

"All those promises — that's the big thing," one worker said to a group of sweatshirt-clad Tory youth.

So far, Mr. Turner has said only that he would be able to tell voters how much his programs cost by election day, but not how he would pay for them.

Day after day, when reporters pose the question, Mr. Turner has said that he cannot deliver this information until he has had a closer look at the country's finances.

"Mr. Turner now seeks to hide behind the argument that he hasn't seen the books. That statement is unfounded and misleading. All Canadian budgetary provisions are public," Mr. Mulroney said.

In 1984 election, same complaint was made by PM

If Mr. Turner wants to see the books, the Tory leader said, all he has to do is examine public information.

"As a former finance minister, Mr. Turner knows that."

What Mr. Mulroney did not mention yesterday, though, was that in 1984 he, too, said he could not properly total up the impact of his promises because he needed to have a closer look at the state of the country's finances.

He said at the time that the Tories did not have what he called the computing capacity to give accurate estimates of the impact of their plans on the country's deficit. Mr. Mulroney accused the Liberals at the time of keeping secret the latest forecasts of the deficit.

In recent days, Mr. Mulroney has been trying to resume the position of attacker in this election while surging Liberal fortunes have forced him on to the defensive on free trade.

He is still going after Mr. Turner over his promise to tear up the trade deal, saying, for example, that the election is "boiling down to a contest between John the Ripper and Brian the Builder, " but he has also been lashing out more at the Liberals on other matters than he did in the first days of the campaign. In Quebec earlier this week, Mr. Mulroney portrayed the Liberals as potential destroyers of the Meech Lake constitutional accord. In Ontario, during the past couple of days, he repeatedly predicted that recession and Liberal rule would go hand in hand.

The large, highly partisan crowds at this week's campaign events have cheered wildly at his reminders of economic conditions during the last years of Liberal government in the early 1980s.

At his first event in Sault Ste. Marie yesterday, Mr. Mulroney painted a dismal picture of Canada and its status in the world after Nov. 21 if there is a Liberal victory.

Poorer regions in Canada would stay poorer for "another generation or more," he said, while eight out of 10 premiers, who support free trade, would feel betrayed by the election result.

In the meantime, he added, protectionist forces in the United States would gain a firmer hold and push Canada out of the marketplace.

Mr. Mulroney said Mr. Turner advocated a return to the failed policies of the 1970s. He added, "Canada never again wants to return to those bad economic times under the Liberals and NDP."

Mr. Mulroney pronouced himself "well pleased" with poll results showing a tight race between the Liberals and Tories.

Though recent numbers do not show the Tories as having the massive lead they had at the beginning of the campaign, they also did not show the Liberals well out in front, as the post-debate polls did two weeks ago.

Mr. Mulroney reminded reporters yesterday that he had consistently predicted a tight three-way race and that this was still the case, despite the sinking standings of the NDP.

"I don't write off anybody," he said.

12. Page A16

Wilson calls Turner liar, coward, defends national sales tax plan

BY ROBERT SHEPPARD
The Globe and Mail

MIKE BLAKE/Reuter
Michael Wilson reads from a Liberal policy book yesterday.

John Turner is a liar and a coward for trying to scare votes out of elderly Canadians, Finance Minister Michael Wilson said yesterday in a harshly personal attack against the Liberal leader.

"Wake up Canada. Wake up to the cyncial Grit election tactics," an agitated Mr. Wilson told a Conservative business club in Toronto. "They scare the voters to win an election and then they turn around and do what they said they would not do."

He asked his audience to think back to the wage- and price-control campaign in 1974, when the Liberals first opposed and then implemented the controversial program. And he recalled the 1980 election that destroyed the Joe Clark government over gasoline taxes, only to have these raised substantially higher than the government had proposed.

"Now Mr. Turner says, join his crusade. Well, if you are the leader of a crusade, you have to be a leader, you have to have courage," the Conservative minister said.

"Does it take courage to scare senior citizens about their medicare just to get a vote? Does it take courage to run up a string of spending promises early in the campaign when he was desparate for a vote at any cost, and now not to have the character to face the questions of how he will finance them?"

Mr. Wilson argued that, by contrast, the Conservatives' election promises were being planned within a framework of fiscal responsibility. But he was still somewhat vague on the effects of the government's proposed national sales tax.

Mr. Wilson took pains to play down the effect of his controversial tax proposal, saying Canadians will pay "not one penny of additional tax" as a result of these measures.

However, he did acknowledge implicitly that the proposed tax itself would generate substantial new revenue, but said this would be returned to taxpayers in the form of tax credits for low-income earners and a lowering of the tax rate for those in the middle brackets.

Some of those involved with the proposal, such as Conservative MP Donald Blenkarn and Ontario Treasurer Robert Nixon, have estimated that a national sales tax would bring in between $10-billion and $14-billion in additional revenue.

Mr. Wilson would not comment directly on these estimates, but he said the "net, bottom line" was that all additional sales tax revenue would be disbursed back to taxpayers in one form or another.

The Conservatives recently gave a general commitment to home builders that they would introduce measures to offset the tax and keep the price of houses affordable for many families. But Mr. Wilson said he could not be more specific about what this would entail.

He also noted that the wide-ranging sales tax, to be applied to a host of new and traditionally untaxed goods and services, would not be added to dental services as some opponents have charged.

But he would not rule out applying the national sales tax to resource revenue, a traditionally provincial preserve that was the subject of a Supreme Court of Canada challenge in the early 1980s when the Liberals' National Energy Program was first set up.

As part of his attempt yesterday to "be open with Canadians" about this proposal, Mr. Wilson made the commitment that the rate of a new national sales tax would be lower in every province than the existing federal and provincial taxes taken together.

13.-15. Page A16

ELECTION BRIEFS

Mazankowski offers to quit if deal a threat

EDMONTON —Donald Mazankowski says he would resign his seat in the House of Commons if the free-trade deal adversely affects Canadian social programs. Mr. Mazankowski, seeking re-election in the Vegreville riding in Alberta, made the pledge Wednesday while defending the Canadian-U.S. trade deal to a group of about 30 senior citizens at a home in Edmonton. "If there is anything in this agreement which affects your medicare or your old age pension, I'll resign my seat," he said. /CP

B.C. Women speak

VANCOUVER —Women candidates for the Progressive Conservative Party in British Columbia issued a 15-page statement Wednesday called Issues of Concern to Women, but the paper didn't mention their position on abortion. Pressed by reporters on what they would do about the issue if elected, Mary Collins, who represented North Vancouver in the last Parliament, said the women are pro-choice, even though the party on the whole has no position on the issue. "All of us recognize that this is an extremely difficult issue," Mrs. Collins said. "We all agree there needs to be greater emphasis on education . . . we believe that fundamentally women must be responsible for the decision." Five of the party's six women candidates in the province attended the news conference. /CP

Metis favor NDP

Canada's Metis and non-status Indians are afraid that the free-trade deal will damage their natural resources and jeopardize their right to negotiate land claims in the future. Charles Recollet, president of the 200,000-member Ontario Metis Aboriginal Association, warned yesterday that the next federal government can expect more civil disobedience from native people unless it acts quickly to resolve outstanding land claims and convenes a first ministers' conference on aboriginal rights. "Our people are getting restless," Mr. Recollet told a news conference in Toronto. After examining all three parties' election promises on native issues, the association prefers the New Democrats. But it refused to endorse the NDP, saying that promises are easy to make. /Staff

Grit wants new deal

EDMONTON —Alberta Liberal Leader Laurence Decore says he would ask federal party leader John Turner to renegotiate the free-trade deal if the Liberals were to form the next federal government. Mr. Decore, who has been attacked for his support of free trade by provincial Liberals, said Wednesday he would ask Turner to ensure Canadian sovereignty if the Liberals win the Nov. 21 federal election. The deal should include new clauses ensuring that "medicare would not be affected, social programs would not be affected . . . all of the things that Canadians are groping with and grappling with." /CP

16. Page A17

Tories set for effort to rebuild their lead

BY ROSS HOWARD
The Globe and Mail

OTTAWA

Conservative Party strategists have narrowed their focus to a final seven-day effort to rebuild their campaign for a majority government on Nov. 21.

The two-pronged campaign will feature advertisements that hammer Liberal Leader John Turner's credibility on free trade, while Conservative Leader Brian Mulroney seeks a higher road on the theme of economic prosperity.

The campaign effectively begins on the weekend, after voters have digested a series of opinion polls that the Tories believe will show them in a head-to-head race with the Liberals, rather than trailing badly as reported in a Gallup poll on Monday.

Yesterday's Globe-Environics poll gave the Liberals 37 per cent, the Tories 35 per cent and the New Democrats 24 per cent. The margin of error was 2.7 percentage points, 19 times out of 20, in the survey of 1,275 people.

An Angus Reid poll of 1,501 voters, also released yesterday, found the Tories with 39 per cent support, the Liberals 35 per cent and the NDP 24 per cent. The margin of error was 2.5 percentage points, 19 times out of 20.

And last night, a CBC Television News poll reported the Liberals at 38.0 per cent, the Tories at 37.6 per cent and the New Democrats at 21.1 per cent; the margin of error in the survey of 2,199 people was put at 2.2 percentage points, 19 times out of 20.

"What happens between now and the end of the week, assuming there is no big gaffe, matters less than how we are perceived going into the final week and what we say and do," said a senior member of the Tory strategy team this week.

Party morale was severely tested by the Gallup, which gave the Liberals a staggering 43 per cent, the Tories 31 per cent and the NDP 22 per cent, and helped convince Tory strategists that the intense one-issue focus was proving deadly for Mr. Mulroney.

The Conservative leader will spend the final seven days of the campaign maintaining a controlled demeanor as he recites his government's economic achievements in Canada, and emphasizes his keen sensitivity to Quebec issues within that province.

He and other Tory campaigners will insist that they are not abandoning their support for the free-trade issue, but at every opportunity will concentrate on the government's economic record and its plans for the future.

"We're off free trade, no longer stuck on it. You'll see," said one senior strategist this week.

The Liberals, however, have no intention to move their leader out of his highly successful "Crusade for Canada" opposition to the free-trade pact.

"There is no need to change. Free trade, as an issue, works for us. Look at the polls," said a senior member of the Liberal strategy team.

And at New Democratic Party headquarters, deputy campaign manager Robin Sears noted that free trade "remains the issue that ate the election. I'm sure the Tories would like to get off it, but they haven't, not yet."

Mr. Sears predicted that both opposition parties will also broaden their focus, but tie the issues into free trade's implications at every opportunity.

The emphasis on opinion polls and public perceptions, always a subject of controversy, has taken on far greater importance in the campaign as voters report they are ill-informed and confused about the overwhelmingly dominant issue of the campaign — the trade deal with Washington.

Officials in all three camps confirm that voters this week remain as fastened on the trade issue as they were immediately after the Oct. 24-25 televised debates.

Strategists for all three parties say that, despite a plethora of competing claims about the trade pact by business and social-policy groups, current and former politicians and commentators, the public remains "confused, not yet convinced" about which party is telling the truth on free trade.

17. Page A17

Trading status with U.S. not at risk, Turner says

BY HUGH WINSOR
The Globe and Mail

VANCOUVER

Liberal Leader John Turner sought yesterday to reassure a largely business audience that failing to proceed on the free-trade agreement with the United States would not harm Canada's existing trading relationship with its largest customer.

Speaking to the Vancouver Canadian Club in a province whose economy depends on exports of lumber, natural gas and other resources to the United States, Mr. Turner said the Liberals have been portrayed mistakenly as protectionist and anti-American.

"But that is simply not true. Since the last war, we have reduced tariffs from an average of 40 per cent to 4 per cent. Today, 80 per cent of everything we trade with the United States goes free of tariff. We want that to continue," he said.

The fact that Canada is the United States' closest neighbor and ally and its largest trading partner will not change when the "Mulroney trade deal" is rejected, he added.

But Mr. Turner repeated his long-standing position that Canada has always done better by negotiating with the United States through multilateral bodies like the General Agreement on Tariffs and Trade. He also promised a new emphasis on promoting trade with Pacific Rim countries which will soon make up 50 per cent of the world economy.

DON DENTON, Reuter

Candidate Sam Stevens, John Turner and wife Geills tour Atlantic furniture factory.

Included in this promise was the creation of a national trading corporation and a proposal to create a Pacific Rim Organization for Economic Co-operation and Development to emulate what has been done in Europe by the Organization for Economic Co-operation and Development.

The bulk of Mr. Turner's speech to the non-partisan crowd was devoted to spelling out the kind of foreign policies a Liberal government would puruse if he were to win the election.

That would include an immediate break in diplomatic relations with South Africa since that country has done nothing to dismantle its apartheid policy of racial segregation, "and we should no longer give validity to a regime which imposes it."

Mr. Turner said he would prefer to act in concert with Canada's allies but he would be prepared to act alone.

He also said Canada has a bigger role to play in promoting disarmament and criticized the Conservative government for continuing to allow cruise-missile testing over Canada now that this class of missile is being phased out under a U.S.-Soviet agreement to eliminate intermediate-range nuclear weapons.

Although Mr. Turner's speech was generally warmly received, people sitting at about 10 of the 70 tables in the banquet hall remained seated when the rest of the crowd gave him a standing ovation at the end.

But one of his audience, Kim Campbell, a Social Credit MLA and now the Conservative candidate in Vancouver Centre, called an impromptu press conference in the hallway next to the banquet hall to accuse Mr. Turner of giving a misleading interpretation of the free-trade agreement.

Mr. Turner was taking advantage of most people's lack of detailed knowledge about international trade law, she said. "He insults Canadians, he insults Canadian politicians, he insults the political will of Canadians when he suggests that what is involved will somehow impinge on our sovereignty. It really is unacceptable."

Mr. Turner has changed the position he used to hold on free trade, Ms Campbell said, adding "I don't really think that in his heart, he believes the position he now espouses."

Although he told his Canadian Club audience he wants to pursue more reductions in tariffs through the GATT negotiations, Mr. Turner took a different position when he visited a small family-owned furniture making plant in Surrey yesterday.

He told reporters he agreed with Atlantic Furniture president Rick Ripoli that such Canadian firms needed tariff protection from furniture imported from the United States.

18. Page A18

Queen's Park acts to ban export of water

BY CHRISTIE McLAREN
The Globe and Mail

The Ontario government has introduced legislation to ban the export of water to the United States.

"Our water resources are for the people of Ontario and the people of Canada," Natural Resources Minister Vincent Kerrio told the Legislature as he introduced an amendment to Bill 175 yesterday.

"This government recognizes water as a precious, limited, strategic resource," he said, urging speedy passage of the bill.

Bill 175, the Water Transfer Control Act, was introduced in June as one of three anti-free-trade bills drafted by Ontario's Liberal government to defy federal legislation implementing the Canadian-U.S. free-trade agreement.

The agreement — which will take effect Jan. 1 if the Progressive Conservatives win a majority in the Nov. 21 federal election and if Parliament approves it — does not specifically mention water exports.

However, Ontario believes that the pact "places the control of Canada's water supply at risk" by failing explicitly to exclude exports of Canadian water to the United States, Mr. Kerrio said.

No Ontario water is exported to the United States now.

Yesterday's amendment, introduced by Mr. Kerrio as the bill came up for second reading, was prompted by protests from the Opposition New Democrats.

When Bill 175 was introduced last June, it asserted provincial control over transfers of water from "a provincial drainage basin," despite any federal laws to the contrary.

At the time, Premier David Peterson said it would control water transfers only within Canada. He acknowledged that the federal government has jurisdiction over water exports.

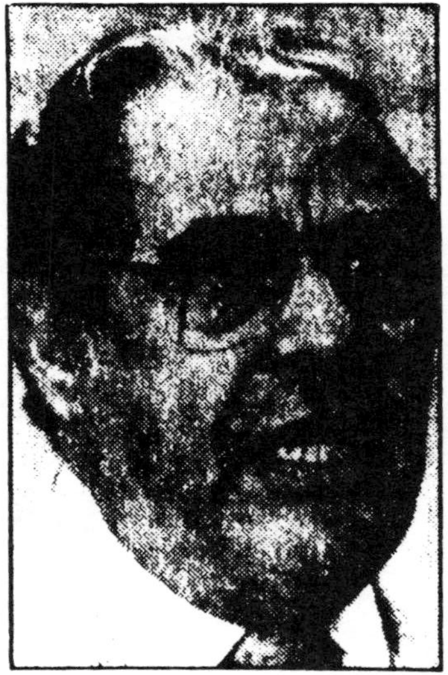

Vincent Kerrio

Last week, NDP Leader Bob Rae charged that Bill 175 would actually pave the way for water exports, since it merely gave Mr. Kerrio the authority to set prices for such sales.

With the amendment, the bill now says that despite the free-trade agreement, or the federal legislation, the Minister of Natural Resources "shall refuse to give approval to a transfer of water out of a provincial drainage basin to a place outside Canada."

Yesterday, the NDP paid Mr. Kerrio a backhand compliment for changing the proposed legislation.

It is "what he should have done last June," Algoma MPP Bud Wildman told the House.

Now, he said, "we're going to have to completely rewrite this legislation because it never did what it purported to do" in the first place.

19. Page B1

Steel industry under pressure from U.S. actions

BY KEN ROMAIN
The Globe and Mail

The Canadian steel industry is bracing for more charges of dumping by U.S. steel companies.

The dumping action is seen as a concerted effort by the U.S. steel industry to create pressure to have Canada brought under the U.S. Voluntary Restraint Arrangement covering steel imports into that country.

"I think the rail dumping case last week (against two Canadian steel companies) by the Americans is the first tip of the iceberg. We are beginning to hear stories there are all kinds of other cases waiting in the wings," said Daniel Romanko, managing director of the Canadian Steel Producers Association.

When the U.S. VRA went into effect in 1984, Canada gained an exemption from the agreement that would have placed a limit on its steel exports to the United States. The U.S steel industry at the time sought to curb surging steel imports, and wanted a breathing space in which to restructure its operations to become more cost efficient.

The agreement, which now covers 29 countries, expires Sept. 1, 1989, but the U.S. industry wants an extension for another five years and the inclusion of those steel exporting countries still outside the system.

A U.S. steel industry spokesman confirmed the industry is seeking the extension, but said its actions are not aimed exclusively at Canada.

Canada is the biggest steel supplier not covered by the U.S. Voluntary Restraint Arrangement.

"The U.S. steel industry continues to urge that Canada come into the VRA system, but I emphasize that this is not a policy aimed at Canada only. We are urging that other countries enter the system," said Sheldon Wesson of the American Iron and Steel Institute.

Canada happens to be the biggest supplier outside the system, but there are also a dozen other countries and their exports account for about two-thirds

STEEL — Page B2

Page B2 Cont'd

Steel industry under pressure over U.S. dumping action

● From Page B1

than last year, but are still higher than in the past, Mr. Wesson said.

He would not comment on whether more dumping charges would be made against Canadian steel companies, stating that he did not know on what information that was based.

Mr. Wesson said the U.S. industry has also received a commitment from president-elect George Bush that the voluntary restraint agreement would be extended beyond its September expiry date.

Mr. Romanko said he recognized that because the United States would seek to include all other countries not now in the agreement, "Canada would be caught up in that web," and more charges of dumping were likely to follow to bring pressure on the Canadian industry. However, he said he did not think the federal government would ever agree to come under the U.S. restraint program.

The U.S. International Trade Commission last week said it found there was evidence of dumping by Algoma Steel Corp. Ltd. of Sault Ste. Marie, Ont., and Sydney Steel Corp. of Sydney, N.S., in the export of steel rails to the United States. The case is now before the U.S. Department of Commerce for a ruling on the dumping allegations and whether the U.S. rail makers were harmed.

The charges also allege the Canadian steel companies gained advantages over the U.S. companies from government subsidies, thereby inviting the imposition of countervailing duties.

Mr. Romanko said it was his belief that the move toward more U.S. dumping charges against Canadian companies was being orchestrated by the U.S. steel lobby in Washington "in order that they can easily demand that Canada come under the VRA."

Mr. Romanko said it would not matter to the U.S. steel lobbyists if the dumping cases they brought forward were viable or not. "That is immaterial. The more cases they get on the books, the better it looks for them," he said.

Mr. Romanko said the Canadian steel industry would also find itself caught between a rock and a hard place if the Canada-U.S. free-trade agreement is cancelled following the Nov. 21 federal election.

"Without the FTA, we would not have the appeal process that would be available to us under the pact to deflect these kind of (dumping) actions much more easily," he said.

Both the Liberal and the New Democratic parties have rejected the free-trade deal negotiated by the Conservative government, and have said they would cancel the trade agreement if elected to office.

The agreement contains a mechanism for trade dispute settlements to be heard before a five-member panel. A bi-national panel, whose finding would be final and binding, would replace present court reviews of anti-dumping and countervailing duty orders.

Canadian steel exports to the United States account for about 3 per cent of U.S. steel consumption, and ranges between 2.2 million and 2.5 million net tons, or about 18 per cent of steel shipments from Canadian mills.

20. Page B1

Quebeckers counter-attack on free trade

BY BERTRAND MAROTTE
The Globe and Mail

MONTREAL

In an unprecedented counter-attack, Quebec's captains of industry gathered in a show of force yesterday to urge support for the free-trade agreement between Canada and the United States, and to try to correct what they consider an increasingly distorted, fear-oriented crusade against it.

"We are very disturbed by the drastic change that is occuring (in popular support for the

New arguments mustered
Page B6

deal)," Pierre Ducros, president of the province-wide Regroupement Pour le Libre-Echange, said at a news conference called to unveil a last-minute advertising campaign.

Behind him in a salon at the Ritz-Carlton Hotel sat about 100 people, including the cream of Quebec's business community. At the table with Mr. Ducros, president of DMR Group Inc., sat five others, including David Culver,

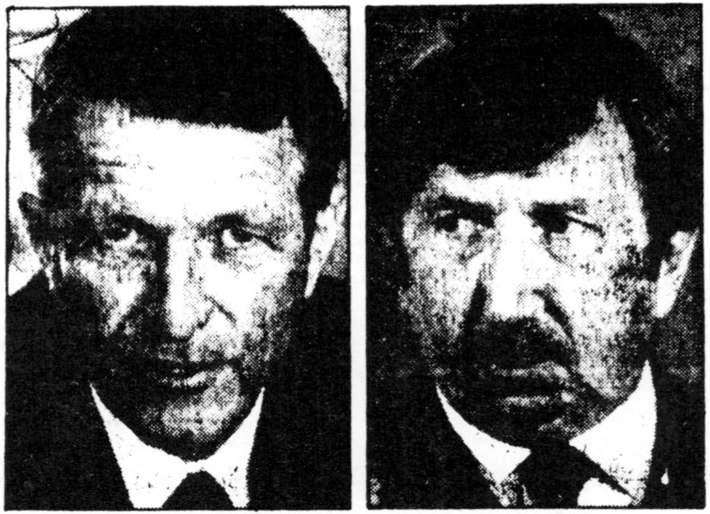

David Culver (left) and Pierre Peladeau: Business leaders "very disturbed by the drastic change" in support for free trade.

president of Alcan Aluminium Ltd.; Laurent Beaudoin, chairman of Bombardier Inc.; and Pierre Péladeau, president of Quebecor Inc.

Mr. Ducros said Quebeckers have been swayed by a "political, electoral and partisan war that has created confusion and fear."

He said his group's campaign is intended to reassure them that their social programs, pensions, jobs and pay cheques will not be in jeopardy if the proposed free-trade pact goes through.

On the contrary, Canada's social programs will be under greater threat if the deal is squelched, because economic growth will not be as strong and the means to pay for public services will be reduced, Mr. Ducros said.

In the French-language part of his statement, Mr. Culver compared free trade as an election issue with the 1980 referendum on the political separation of Quebec. Quebeckers voted then to turn their backs on the choice of remaining a "tiny enclave," he said. Now, they must turn their backs on remaining a "small Canadian market only."

Mr. Culver is also chairman of the Canadian Alliance for Trade and Job Opportunities, a national group formed by a collection of business organizations to promote free trade.

Asked by a reporter why most trade unions are against the deal, Mr. Culver replied: "I think they're against it because they tend to believe in a centralizing

QUEBECKERS — Page B4

Page B4 Cont'd

Quebeckers campaign for trade deal

● From Page B1

form of decision-making in this country, which would tell all the rest of us what we should be doing on Monday and Tuesday, and so on. And I think they realize it would be much harder under free trade to do that."

Mr. Ducros said the campaign will not necessarily come to an end on election day, Nov. 21. "If the Liberals win the election, we have to continue to work for free trade and work with them to convince them of the necessity of signing."

Liberal Party Leader John Turner has promised to scrap the deal signed by Prime Minister Brian Mulroney and U.S. President Ronald Reagan if his party takes power.

Mr. Péladeau said Canadians should work with the United States instead of "yelling at each other without saying anything."

Mr. Ducros denied that business is in a panic over what appears to be a mounting tide against free trade, but he said his group is trying to persuade all levels of society that the deal is needed if there is to be continued prosperity.

"It's a situation where we're trying to meet the other side. We worked in the past with the trade unions and we can for the future."

The corporate brass listened attentively as individuals took turns delivering testimonials to the deal, but the biggest round of applause was reserved for University of Toronto economist and tireless free-trade promoter John Crispo, who sang its praises.

"The real threat to medicare and pensions in Canada is the rising cost of them" as the population grows older, he said. To say that they are threatened by the deal is "a cruel hoax."

"There is unbelievable fear and scare-mongering that the Canadian public has been subjected to," he said.

The Quebec group, founded a little over a year ago to promote free trade, did not want to get directly involved during the election campaign, but had no choice because of the distorted debate now taking place, Mr. Ducros said.

The hastily assembled campaign was put together with "upwards of $200,000," said a spokesman, but the television ads will not be seen in the Montreal area because of cost and the scarcity of unsold air time.

The four TV ads are enthusiastic testimonials from a young woman who is a dress designer, a young man who works for a computer software company, a construction worker who says the deal means more and better jobs, and the white-bearded owner of a furniture-making company.

Breaking into the U.S. market will not be difficult, says the young man from the computer company, winking into the camera. "We're the best. We're going to grow!"

The furniture maker observes that his three children will lose out on the giant U.S. market if the deal does not go through. "Young people — let them grow!" he urges.

21. Page B2

Free-trade fears: Zap, Zap, Zap, you're frozen

PETER COOK

It is an article of faith among those who have no faith in free trade that Canada will not suffer greatly if it turns down the deal. To say any less is to be anti-democratic and a scaremonger — which has become as common an offence as jaywalking.

Because of this, what one should say is that, with luck, Canada will not suffer. But it is overwhelmingly probable that we will be luckless.

It is not, in this election, fashionable to deal with the world as it is. However, a Canada that votes down free trade and thinks there will be no consequences displays something of the same irrational phlegm as John Jacob Astor did on the deck of the Titanic. According to legend, Mr. Astor was having a drink when the iceberg struck. "I sent for ice," he quipped, "but this is ridiculous."

On free trade, Canada is surrounded by fire and ice.

The fire will come from the financial markets, which will drive the dollar down and interest rates up. The ice will come from the sub-zero relations that will develop with a U.S. administration whose top members, including its new Secretary of State-elect, personally fought for the Canadian deal and regard it as one of their major accomplishments.

As with the Titanic, it will be the ice that does the damage.

Going back to the days of Richard Nixon, when Americans imposed a 10 per cent surcharge on all foreign goods except those from Canada, this country has had a unique relationship with its neighbor on trade matters. That may be an unpopular thing to say at a time when many Canadians are wallowing in anti-Americanism. But it is true.

As some people contemplate the effects of ripping up free trade, they arrive at the odd conclusion that a lower dollar will be good for Canada.

It will mean a drop in living standards, to be sure. But it will, in theory, raise exports to the U.S. market from which we already derive a $17-billion trade surplus (versus a deficit with all other countries). In a neat, unchanging world, the argument appears to have logic. In fact, it is patently absurd.

If Canadians think that, after Ottawa throws the trade agreement back in Washington's face, the U.S. Congress is going to sit back and watch more of its domestic markets taken by "devalued, subsidized" Canadian imports, they have truly been duped by the considerable hallucinatory powers of the opposition parties.

No, the going will get much rougher in an export market that Canadians rely on and take for granted. The trade surplus is on our side. U.S. legislators, in an anti-foreign (which now means anti-Canadian) mood, are not going to sit back while we pile up bigger surpluses on the back of an artificially low dollar.

There will be more trade actions against Canada. Many more. And, under new trade legislation, a lot of actions will be won quite quickly in sectors where trade complaints have already been filed; automobiles, steel, pharmaceuticals, lumber, fish, agriculture, beer, wine, textiles. That, in turn, will force Canadian companies across a wide spectrum of the economy to revise their production and distribution strategies. Heavy investments will have to be made in the United States at the expense of investment in Canada. Meanwhile, Congress will be aiding U.S. companies to force open Canadian markets. As a result, our firms will face a loss of market share at home.

So unsettling is the process likely to be that Canadians will find themselves under vastly more pressure to revise subsidy programs and government policies without a free-trade agreement than with one.

This fact is one of many that the oppositionists have got backward. The big hit will come if the deal is undone.

That Americans are in the mood to act is borne by the ferociousness of their trade laws and by the discriminatory way that these can be used. An article in The New York Times on Wednesday speculated that, if the free-trade deal does not gain approval, there will be no actual move to penalize Canada, but the Bush administration — which has been given extra discretionary authority under the Omnibus Trade bill — will do nothing to head off future trade actions or solve disputes.

In the same article, Paul Wonnacott, a University of Maryland professor and expert on the auto pact, talks of countervail duties of 9 or 10 per cent being slapped on Japanese and South Korean cars that are made in Canada and exported to the United States under a duty remission program. That, by itself, would dry up foreign investment in the auto sector.

Daniel Patrick Moynihan, the New York Senator who has been Canada's great friend on the Senate Finance Committee, states that, if free trade fails, "trade lawyers will do well out of it because Canada's economy is much more subsidized than ours."

The plain fact is that, under the free-trade pact, Canada commits itself to a set of rules that will allow it to continue taking access to the U.S. market for granted and derive the benefits it has in the past. Without an agreement, nothing can be taken for granted.

Trade within GATT is already a negotiable instrument. Having ripped up a GATT-approved bilateral agreement negotiated in good faith, Canada's power to negotiate around U.S. trade barriers will be nil.

To say this is to engage in scaremongering. Rightly so, because it is scary.

22. Page B3

Dollar soars on rally in fortunes of Tories

BY MARIAN STINSON
The Globe and Mail

After taking a severe pummelling for the past two weeks, largely because of shifts in political polls, the dollar staged a sharp turnaround yesterday in response to an apparant rally in the fortunes of the Conservative Party.

A large corporate purchase of dollars in Japan overnight started the ball rolling, and by the end of trading in North America last night it had gained almost three-quarters of a cent, closing at 81.90 cents (U.S.).

After strengthening throughout the session, a report in late afternoon that U.S. President Ronald Reagan will deliver a speech defending free trade in Washington next Thursday added vitality to the dollar rally.

White House spokesman Marlin Fitzwater said Mr. Reagan will be careful not to interfere in the Canadian election later this month, but will defend the deal that has become a central issue in the race.

The changing view of the currency gained momentum throughout the trading day, even though the polls are pointing to a minority government. Financial markets around the world bailed out of positions in the dollar and prepared for the Remembrance Day holiday, when many large North American financial institutions are closed.

In the Far East, the dollar showed gains from its close on Tuesday, trading between 81.18 and 81.67 cents. In London, the upswing continued, with the currency ranging from 81.50 to 81.83 cents.

In North America, the trend carried the dollar to its height at the close of 81.90 cents from its low for the day of 81.45 cents.

Chicago traders, who had been negative on the currency last week when Tory support was waning, followed yesterday's trend and accumulated dollar positions. The speculative market has been whipped around by poll results and rumors, a trader said.

Money market rates between Canada and the United States widened this week, adding to the dollar's attraction. On 30-day bankers acceptances, the spread rose by about 20 basis points to 215 basis points.

The Bank of Canada has increased liquidity for the banking sector to contain upward pressure on short-term interest rates earlier in the week.

The overnight cost of money dipped by 50 basis points yesterday to 9.75 per cent.

REPORT ON BUSINESS FRIDAY, NOVEMBER 11, 1988 B3

Grain farmers to receive drought relief

BY GEOFFREY YORK
The Globe and Mail
WINNIPEG

Grain farmers who suffered from this summer's severe drought will receive $850-million from Ottawa and the provinces, the federal government announced yesterday.

The size of the drought relief plan was a surprise for many Prairie farmers because the Conservatives had raised expectations of a much larger payment.

At least one Tory MP, Jack Scowen of Saskatchewan, had predicted the drought assistance would be $1.3-billion to $1.5-billion.

However, most farm groups said they are happy with the announcement. The drought aid for the hardest-hit farmers will equal or exceed the amount requested by most farm leaders.

The opposition New Democrats and Liberals condemned the drought relief plan, calling it inadequate and too slow in arriving. The NDP had proposed a $1.4-billion drought assistance package.

The drought money was announced at four news conferences in four provinces yesterday, featuring a host of Conservative cabinet ministers, some of whom have little to do with agriculture. For example, the news conference in Winnipeg included Health Minister Jake Epp, who was ignored by reporters.

Grains Minister Charles Mayer acknowledged the relief plan was announced before Ottawa had finished its negotiations with the provinces, who will contribute some of the relief money. But, he denied the Tories rushed ahead with the announcement to help their prospects in the election campaign.

"If you're saying it's rushed, producers are saying it's too slow," Mr. Mayer told reporters.

"You don't rush a program like this. We think through the details, so there's a minimum of foul-ups. We made a commitment to help in this situation long before the election was called."

The hardest-hit farmers will receive $40 to $45 an acre, in addition to their compensation from crop insurance. Other farmers will be paid according to a formula based on average long-term yield in their district.

Mr. Mayer said Saskatchewan farmers will receive the bulk of the drought relief. About $427-million will go to Saskatchewan farmers, while $194-million will go to Manitoba, $98-million to Alberta and $77-million to Ontario.

More than half of Canada's grain farmers will be eligible for assistance, Mr. Mayer said.

He gave the example of a farmer in Morris, Man., who grows 640 acres of wheat, barley, flax and canola. If the crop was completely ruined by the drought, the farmer could expect to receive almost $30,000 in drought relief.

Most farmers carry crop insurance, so the hypothetical farmer in Morris could receive another $30,000 in insurance payments. Close to $900-million in crop insurance payments will be distributed to Canadian farmers this year.

In addition, farmers will receive a large payment from the western grain stabilization plan. That payment will be announced "very shortly," Mr. Mayer said.

Farmers will receive the drought assistance in two instalments. The first will arrive in early 1989 and the second in April or May, Mr. Mayer said.

In documents accompanying yesterday's announcement, federal officials estimated Canadian farm incomes in 1987 and 1988 are almost 50 per cent higher than the average farm income in the period from 1981 to 1984.

The increase in farm incomes came despite the severe drought this year and the low grain prices in 1986 and 1987. But, the cost to the taxpayer has been tremendous — about $3.5-billion in 1988 alone, Mr. Mayer said.

24. Page B6

Free-traders, foes in frenzied fight

BY JOHN KOHUT
The Globe and Mail

OTTAWA

Opponents and supporters of free trade unloaded new analyses of the Canada-U.S. accord yesterday in a frenzied race to sway public opinion on the major issue of the federal election.

Much of the attention focused on what acceptance or rejection of the deal would mean for Canada's multilateral trade relations, with anti-free-traders saying a more aggressive Canadian stance within the General Agreement on Tariffs and Trade is one of a number of alternatives to free trade.

But a prominent Ottawa think tank argued that Canada's trade relations with other countries would suffer if the accord were to be scuttled and the country's hand would be weakened at next month's GATT meeting in Montreal.

These arguments came as the latest poll by The Globe and Mail and Environics Research Group Ltd. showed that the Conservatives have staged a comeback in support, putting them neck-and-neck with the Liberals.

The anti-free-trade Canadian Centre for Policy Alternatives said Canadian consumers would have paid almost $93-billion more for oil and gas if the free-trade accord had been in force between 1974 and 1986 when the world economy was rocked by a series of oil price shocks.

According to a three-part analysis on free trade, edited by University of Toronto professor Mel Watkins, the free-trade accord would have prevented Canada from pegging prices at a level below that of the world market.

Mr. Watkins said the deal is "so bad that the status quo — which I rarely defend — is itself preferable."

The group's chief recommendation for improving access to foreign markets for Canadian natural resources was to adopt a more aggressive stance within GATT, professor Thomas Gunton of Simon Fraser University says in the report.

In another section of the study, Ottawa consultant Morris Miller said Canada is playing a follow-the-leader role in current GATT negotiations.

GATT has already cut average tariffs to about 4 per cent, making the chances of further tariff reductions minimal. Therefore, Canada should be working more assiduously for the removal of non-tariff barriers.

Liberal Leader John Turner has said he would work to make it tougher for countries to file unfair trading claims under GATT while fighting to improve GATT rules.

However, Murray Smith of the Institute for Research on Public Policy, an Ottawa-based think tank, argues in a four-page statement that Canada's bargaining power in GATT will be eroded if the next government rejects free trade.

GATT members are scheduled to meet in Montreal next month for a review of the current round of multilateral trade negotiations, aimed at resolving conflicts over agricultural subsidies and textiles trade and to extend GATT rules to services.

Without free trade, Canada will have to rely on GATT negotiations to create trade opportunities that will help it develop a more diversified economy.

By rejecting free trade, Ottawa will have to concentrate its attention within GATT on bilateral relations with the United States instead of working to improve trade relations the European Community, Japan and other GATT members, Mr. Smith said.

The Conservative Party repeated its argument that Canada could still charge Americans more for its energy resources. It also took a shot at the Liberal policy with regard to GATT.

Article 904 of the free-trade deal, which discusses scarcity of resources, was based on Article 20 of the GATT, which states that when resource products are in short supply, any new measures taken by a country have to be consistent with the principle that all members are entitled to an equitable share of the international supply of products, the Conservative Party said in a press release.

The release points out that it was a Liberal government that agreed to those GATT obligations 40 years ago. It was also the Liberals who entered into the agreement on an International Energy Program that obliges Canada to share its energy resources with other countries during times of shortage.

25. Page B6

Alberta may lose $14 billion in projects: IDA

BY DREW FAGAN
The Globe and Mail

CALGARY

Alberta could lose up to $14-billion in business development over the next five years if the free-trade agreement is scrapped, say officials with the Investment Dealers Association of Canada.

An economic outlook for the province released by the IDA yesterday forecasts bullish growth into the nineties, led by the natural gas and petrochemical sectors.

But estimates of an annual growth rate of 5 per cent between 1990 and 1993 are based on the assumption that the free-trade deal will become law.

Without it, IDA vice-president Ian Russell said, many large capital spending projects now planned "may go ahead on a much smaller scale or may not go ahead at all."

Defeat of the agreement, the IDA thinks, would mean the equivalent of one year of economic growth in Alberta would be lost over the next five years.

Among major development projects planned in the province are two ethylene plants and three large-scale forestry expansions.

As well, the oil and gas industry has been counting on guaranteed access to U.S. markets under free trade to buoy their own megaprojects and expansion plans.

Mr. Russell said the IDA's analysis of what defeat of free trade would mean is not based primarily on private comments from companies on how they would alter their plans.

Rather, he said, the IDA assessed "factors that lead to these projects getting off the ground."

In particular, said IDA chairman Donald Johnson, the petrochemical sector would be aided by the eradication of tariff barriers that range from 9 to 17 per cent on Canadian exports to the United States.

But he noted that the great impact of scrapping the agreement will not be immediately noticeable in investment decisions.

John Feick, president of Novacor Chemicals Ltd., emphasized in a recent interview that his company has a wait-and-see attitude toward the possible effect of defeat of free trade on Novacor's $1.5-billion ethylene plant, to be completed by 1992.

"This is all so unexpected that we haven't had time to assess our future in the absence of the agreement. We came so fully to believe that free trade was going to occur," he said.

"Generally though, to justify additional investment, we have to know that we have free access to the U.S. market and can't be hit by some frivolous countervail or dumping charge."

The IDA study notes that the Alberta economy will grow by 4 per cent this year, a rate expected to be the highest in the country.

That strong performance has been fueled, in part, by the recovery of oil prices a year ago, which contributed to stepped-up production and increased investment by the petroleum sector.

As well, the IDA noted, continued diversification of the provincial economy into petrochemicals and a rapidly developing forestry secto have played a major role in Alb ta's recovery in the past two year

But in recent months, oil pr have dropped to levels approac the lean times of 1986.

As a result, the IDA said, ta's rate of economic gro expected to slow in 1989 to b 2 and 3 per cent.

But even that may be opt

Mr. Johnson said that was based on internation ces of about $16 (U.S.) a b year. He said the consen oil analysts consulted b week was for an average about $14 — its present l

26. Page B8

Signs right for stock boom in '89, IDA says

BY DREW FAGAN
The Globe and Mail

CALGARY

Conditions are promising for new highs in stock prices next year, the Investment Dealers Association of Canada says in an analysis of international equity markets.

But the report, completed last week and released yesterday, may already be dated — at least with regard to Canadian conditions.

The study by IDA vice-president Ian Russell noted that the general upward movement in the major Canadian stock markets has been predicated on the likelihood of the free-trade agreement being implemented.

But with the sudden surge in support for the Liberal Party in the federal election, that may no longer be the case. And Canadian stock markets have reacted negatively to that possibility.

The IDA is strongly in favor of the free-trade deal, and the analysis emphasized that recent strong performances by stock exchanges in Europe can be attributed to the impending fall of trade barriers within the European Community in 1992.

In particular, the IDA contrasted the reaction to last year's stock market crash with the protectionism that followed the October, 1929, collapse.

"Governments over the past year have resisted protectionist pressures and have moved forward with major international trade arrangements," Mr. Russell said in the study.

"Evidence shows that the economies which emerge from such trade arrangements are more efficient and competitive. These policy actions assure a positive economic outlook and improving stock market performance."

The IDA concluded that last year's crash, viewed in perspective, is "more aptly termed a market correction."

That's because prices had risen to unrealistic levels by October, 1987, the analysis said, and the sudden fall was limited ultimately to price levels that better reflected the underlying value of stocks.

Since then, key market indicators on the Toronto and Montreal stock exchanges have recovered about 70 per cent of the value lost in the crash.

"In contrast, there has been no recovery at all on the regional stock exchanges." Share prices on the Vancouver and American stock exchanges "have moved steadily lower over the year."

The reduced confidence of individuals in Canadian markets has been reflected in a sharp decline of 36 per cent in the value of stock trading for the first nine months of 1988, compared with the corresponding period a year earlier.

That narrowing of the investor base also has emasculated the new issue market, with common share financings totalling $918-million for the first eight months of 1988, compared with $6.6-billion raised during the corresponding months in 1987.

On international markets, the New York Stock Exchange has outperformed the major Canadian markets, with the Standard and Poor's 500-stock index recovering 89 per cent of the losses incurred in October, 1987.

Japan has done even better. The Tokyo stock exchange had recovered to pre-crash levels by last April, a reflection of the country's strong economic performance that is setting the pace in the industrialized world this year.

European markets generally have taken longer to recover than in North America and Japan. However, the French stock market had made up for losses during the crash by mid-year.

 Page 1A Nov. 1, 1988

Campaign called cruel

Wilson charges foes with lying to elderly

BY CHRISTOPHER WADDELL
The Globe and Mail

OTTAWA

Finance Minister Michael Wilson says the Liberal and New Democratic parties are lying when they claim, particularly to senior citizens, that the proposed free-trade agreement will threaten Canada's social programs.

"Taking this lie into our senior citizens' homes is the cruellest form of campaigning that I've seen in 10 years in politics," Mr. Wilson said yesterday, adding that he had found Liberal Party brochures in senior citizens' homes claiming that the trade deal with the United States would mean an end to pensions and medicare.

"When politicians feel that they have to prey upon the fears and emotions of some of the most defenceless people in our society today, I say that is despicable," Mr. Wilson said in a luncheon speech yesterday.

"Programs which are generally available such as medicare, pensions, old age security aren't trade-distorting subsidies and are not subject to trade laws. Not even the most rabid protectionist in the United States will state otherwise," he said.

More election coverage
Pages A8, A12

In a wide-ranging attack against political opponents of the agreement in an address to a generally receptive Confederation Club meeting, Mr. Wilson outlined why he supports the deal, after opposing free trade in 1983.

As well, he challenged some of the specific campaign-trail criticisms of the agreement.

His views changed, Mr. Wilson said, after reading the report of the

WILSON — Page A2

Liberals move ahead of PCs in wake of leaders' debates

BY MICHAEL ADAMS, DONNA DASKO AND JAMES MATSUI
© The Globe and Mail and Environics Research Group Ltd.

GLOBE-ENVIRONICS POLL

The federal Liberal Party has moved into the lead over the Conservative Party, according to the latest poll done for The Globe and Mail by Environics Research Group Ltd.

A total of 1,538 eligible voters were surveyed in two waves following last week's televised debates among the three party leaders, in French on Monday night and in English on Tuesday night.

In the first wave, conducted last Tuesday and Wednesday nights, the Liberals moved into a dead heat with the Tories.

By the weekend, however, continuing momentum raised the Liberals into a six-point lead with the support of 37 per cent of decided voters, compared with 31 per cent for the Conservatives and 26 per cent for the New Democratic Party.

Six per cent would vote for other parties. These figures were reached after calculations to eliminate the 13 per cent of the total voters sampled who were undecided or refused to state a preference.

The margin of error on this wave of polling is plus or minus 3.6 percentage points in 19 out of 20 samples.

On the basis of the current party standings, the Liberals would now have enough votes to form a minority government.

Following Liberal Party Leader John Turner's strong performance in the debates, support for the party climbed to 32 per cent in interviews conducted on Oct. 25 and 26, the first wave of this poll.

It then climbed another five points to 37 per cent in polling done in the second wave, Oct. 28 to 30.

The Liberals began the campaign in early October with the support of 25 per cent of decided voters.

The Conservatives, meanwhile, went from 42 per cent support in early October to 32 per cent on Oct. 25 and 26 and 31 per cent on Oct. 28 to 30.

The New Democrats declined slightly from 29 per cent to 28 per cent to 26 per cent.

(If the two waves of the most recent poll are taken together, they would give the Liberals the support of 34 per cent of decided voters, the Tories the support of 32 per cent and the NDP the backing of 27 per cent.)

The Liberal momentum in the new poll is particularly strong in Quebec and the Atlantic Provinces. In Quebec, the Conservatives still led the Liberals in the Oct. 25 and 26 wave of polling by a margin of 40 per cent to 29 per cent, but the tables turned last weekend. The Lib-

LIBERALS — Page A12

Dollar takes nosedive as Conservatives fall in opinion poll results

BY ROBERT SHEPPARD
The Globe and Mail

The Canadian dollar followed the plummeting political fortunes of the Progressive Conservative Party yesterday, dropping by almost 1½ cents against the U.S. dollar.

In the wake of new opinion polls showing a decline in Tory fortunes, major currency traders around the world, starting with the Japanese, began selling their Canadian dollar holdings throughout the day yesterday as the money markets sensed that Conservative Leader Brian Mulroney's free-trade deal might be in danger.

Two of three opinion polls published in the past 24 hours, including one in today's Globe and Mail, have the Liberal Party leading the Tories for the first time since the election was called.

A Gallup Poll that came out yesterday morning still has the Tories ahead with 38 per cent of respondents compared to 32 for the Liberals and 27 for the New Democratic Party. The poll was released with the caveat that a one percentage point shift in popular opinion is all that is required to produce a minority government.

Details on Page B1
Why the dollar fell
Page A6

In recent weeks, with the Conservatives apparently coasting to another majority government and a wide spread in interest rates between Canada and the United States, investors were buying Canadian currency whose value increased sharply by 1¼ cents.

These gains washed away quickly yesterday as the dollar dropped back to 81.58 cents (U.S.), down 1.46 cents, even as the Bank of Canada and, at one point, the Bank of England as an ally, intervened to slow its fall.

Both Conservative Leader Brian Mulroney and Liberal Leader John Turner were taking

DOLLAR — Page A2